SAXON®MATH
Intermediate 4

Written Practice
Workbook

Stephen Hake

SAXON®

HOUGHTON MIFFLIN HARCOURT
Supplemental Publishers

www.SaxonPublishers.com
800-531-5015

Dear Student,

The single most important part of the Saxon Math program is Written Practice. Working through the Written Practice problems will refresh your memory of topics previously learned. You will deepen your understanding of concepts, you will learn to efficiently shift gears between different types of problems, and you will see how different math topics are related.

This Written Practice Workbook reprints the Written Practice for you. You should solve every problem in every Written Practice. It is best to work on the more difficult problems in class, where you can get help if you need it. Save the easier problems for later. The starred problems are a good place to start. As you work through the book the problems become more challenging. So be sure to ask for help if you do not understand a problem, because you will probably see a problem like it again.

We want you to learn math well so that you can comfortably and confidently use math to solve problems in your classes and in real life. Working through all the problems every day and asking for help when you need it are habits that will help you succeed this year and in the future!

Stephen Hake

Temple City, California

Estimado estudiante,

La parte más importante del programa de Matemáticas Saxon es la Práctica escrita. El resolver los problemas de la Práctica escrita te refrescará la memoria de temas que has aprendido previamente. Profundizarás en tu comprensión de conceptos. Aprenderás a cambiar de enfoque eficientemente entre diferentes tipos de problemas, y verás cómo diferentes temas de matemáticas se relacionan.

Este Cuaderno de trabajo de la Práctica escrita es una reimpresión de la Práctica escrita. Deberás resolver todos los problemas en cada Práctica escrita. Es mejor tratar de resolver los problemas más difíciles durante la clase, donde puedes obtener ayuda si la necesitas. Deja los problemas más fáciles para después. Es recomendable empezar con los problemas con asterisco. Conforme avanzas a través del cuaderno, los problemas se vuelven más difíciles. Asegúrate de pedir ayuda si no entiendes algún problema, porque probablemente encontrarás un problema similar otra vez.

Queremos que aprendas bien matemáticas de tal forma que puedas utilizar matemáticas para resolver problemas de una manera cómoda y con seguridad en tus clases y en la vida real.¡El resolver problemas todos los días y el pedir ayuda cuando la necesitas son hábitos que te ayudarán a tener éxito este año y en el futuro!

Stephen Hake
Temple City, California

Saxon Math Intermediate 4

Written Practice Workbook

Table of Contents

Formulate Write a number sentence for problems **1** and **2**. Then solve each problem.

*1. There were 5 students in the first row and 7 students in the second row. How many students were in the first two rows?

*2. Ling had 6 coins in her left pocket and 3 coins in her right pocket. How many coins did Ling have in both pockets?

Find each sum or missing addend:

3. $9 + 4$

4. $8 + 2$

*5.
$$\begin{array}{r} 4 \\ + n \\ \hline 9 \end{array}$$

*6.
$$\begin{array}{r} w \\ + 5 \\ \hline 8 \end{array}$$

*7.
$$\begin{array}{r} 6 \\ + p \\ \hline 8 \end{array}$$

*8.
$$\begin{array}{r} q \\ + 8 \\ \hline 8 \end{array}$$

9. $3 + 4 + 5$

10. $4 + 4 + 4$

11. $6 + r = 10$

12. $x + 5 = 6$

13.
$$\begin{array}{r} 5 \\ 5 \\ + 5 \\ \hline \end{array}$$

14.
$$\begin{array}{r} 8 \\ 0 \\ + 7 \\ \hline \end{array}$$

15.
$$\begin{array}{r} 6 \\ 5 \\ + 4 \\ \hline \end{array}$$

16.
$$\begin{array}{r} 9 \\ 9 \\ + 9 \\ \hline \end{array}$$

17.
$$\begin{array}{r} m \\ + 9 \\ \hline 10 \end{array}$$

18.
$$\begin{array}{r} 9 \\ + f \\ \hline 12 \end{array}$$

19.
$$\begin{array}{r} z \\ + 5 \\ \hline 10 \end{array}$$

20.
$$\begin{array}{r} 0 \\ + n \\ \hline 3 \end{array}$$

21. $3 + 2 + 5 + 4 + 6$

22. $2 + 2 + 2 + 2 + 2 + 2 + 2$

Represent Write a number sentence for each picture:

*23.

*24.

_____
Beginning in this lesson, we star the exercises that cover challenging or recently presented content. We encourage students to work first on the starred exercises with which they might want help, saving the easier exercises for last.

*25. (**List**) Show six ways to add 2, 3, and 4.

*26. Multiple Choice Sometimes a missing number is shown by a shape instead of a letter. Choose the correct number for $\triangle$ in the following number sentence:

$$\triangle + 3 = 10$$

    A 3   **B** 7   **C** 10   **D** 13

*27. (**Represent**) Draw a dot cube picture to show $5 + 6$.

*28. (**Connect**) Write a horizontal number sentence that has a sum of 17.

*29. (**Connect**) Write a vertical number sentence that has a sum of 15.

*30. ✏️ (**Formulate**) Write and solve an addition word problem using the numbers 10 and 8.

Saxon Math Intermediate 4

Name _____

Formulate Write a number sentence for problems **1** and **2**. Then solve each problem.

[1]***1.**
(1) Jordan's rabbit, Hoppy, ate 5 carrots in the morning and 6 carrots in the afternoon. How many carrots did Hoppy eat in all?

*2.
(1) Five friends rode their bikes from the school to the lake. They rode 7 miles and then rested. They still had 4 miles to go. How many miles was it from the school to the lake?

Find each sum or missing addend:

3. $9 + n = 13$
(1)

4. $7 + 8$
(1)

5. $\begin{array}{r} p \\ + 6 \\ \hline 13 \end{array}$
(1)

*6. $\begin{array}{r} 5 \\ 2 \\ + w \\ \hline 12 \end{array}$
(2)

7. $\begin{array}{r} 4 \\ 8 \\ + 5 \\ \hline \end{array}$
(1)

8. $\begin{array}{r} 9 \\ 3 \\ + 7 \\ \hline \end{array}$
(1)

*9. $\begin{array}{r} 8 \\ b \\ + 3 \\ \hline 16 \end{array}$
(2)

10. $\begin{array}{r} 9 \\ 7 \\ + 3 \\ \hline \end{array}$
(1)

11. $\begin{array}{r} 2 \\ 9 \\ + 6 \\ \hline \end{array}$
(1)

12. $\begin{array}{r} 3 \\ 8 \\ + 2 \\ \hline \end{array}$
(1)

13. $\begin{array}{r} 9 \\ 5 \\ + 3 \\ \hline \end{array}$
(1)

14. $\begin{array}{r} 2 \\ m \\ + 4 \\ \hline 9 \end{array}$
(2)

15. $\begin{array}{r} 5 \\ 3 \\ + q \\ \hline 9 \end{array}$
(2)

16. $\begin{array}{r} 2 \\ 3 \\ + r \\ \hline 7 \end{array}$
(2)

17. $\begin{array}{r} 5 \\ 3 \\ + t \\ \hline 10 \end{array}$
(2)

18. $\begin{array}{r} 8 \\ 4 \\ + 6 \\ \hline \end{array}$
(1)

19. $\begin{array}{r} 2 \\ x \\ + 7 \\ \hline 11 \end{array}$
(2)

20. $\begin{array}{r} 5 \\ 2 \\ + 6 \\ \hline \end{array}$
(1)

*21. $5 + 5 + 6 + 4 + x = 23$
(2)

*22. **List** Show six ways to add 4, 5, and 6.
(1)

_____
[1] The italicized numbers within parentheses underneath each problem number are called *lesson reference numbers.* These numbers refer to the lesson(s) in which the major concept of that particular problem is introduced. If additional assistance is needed, refer to the discussion, examples, or practice problems of that lesson.

Name _____

(**Represent**) Write a number sentence for each picture:

*23.
(1)

24.
(1)

25. (**Verify**) What is the name of the answer when we add?
(1)

*26. Multiple Choice Which number is ☐ in the following number
(1) sentence?

$$6 + ☐ = 10$$

A 4   **B** 6   **C** 10   **D** 16

*27. (**Represent**) Draw a picture to show $6 + 3 + 5$.
(2)

*28. (**Connect**) Write a horizontal number sentence that has a sum of 20.
(1)

29. (**Connect**) Write a vertical number sentence that has a sum of 24.
(1)

*30. ✎(**Formulate**) Write and solve an addition word problem using the
(1) numbers 7, 3, and 10.

Real-World Connection

There were 35 pictures at the art exhibit. The pictures were made using oils, pastels, or watercolors. Thirteen of the pictures were made using watercolors. An equal number of pictures were made using oils as were made using pastels. How many pictures were made using pastels? Explain how you found the answer.

4

Formulate Write a number sentence for problems **1** and **2**. Then solve each problem.

*1. Diana has 5 dollars, Sumaya has 6 dollars, and Britt has 7 dollars.
(1) Altogether, how much money do the three girls have?

*2. On Taye's favorite CD there are 9 songs. On his second-favorite CD
(1) there are 8 songs. Altogether, how many songs are on Taye's two favorite CDs?

*3. How many digits are in each number?
(3)
   a. 593   **b.** 180   **c.** 186,527,394

*4. What is the last digit of each number?
(3)
   a. 3427   **b.** 460   **c.** 437,269

Find each missing addend:

5. $5 + m + 4 = 12$
(2)

*6. $8 + 2 + w = 16$
(2)

Conclude Write the next number in each counting sequence:

*7. 10, 20, 30, ____, ...
(3)

*8. 22, 21, 20, ____, ...
(3)

*9. 40, 35, 30, 25, ____, ...
(3)

*10. 70, 80, 90, ____, ...
(3)

Generalize Write the rule and the next three numbers of each counting sequence:

*11. 6, 12, 18, ____, ____, ____, ...
(3)

12. 3, 6, 9, ____, ____, ____, ...
(3)

13. 4, 8, 12, ____, ____, ____, ...
(3)

*14. 45, 36, 27, ____, ____, ____, ...
(3)

Connect Find the missing number in each counting sequence:

*15. 8, 12, ____, 20, ...
(3)

*16. 12, 18, ____, 30, ...
(3)

17. 30, 25, _____, 15, ...
(3)

18. 6, 9, _____, 15, ...
(3)

19. How many small rectangles are shown? Count by twos.
(3)

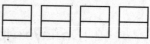

20. How many Xs are shown? Count by fours.
(3)

```
XX    XX    XX
XX    XX    XX
XX    XX    XX
XX    XX    XX
```

*21. (**Represent**) Write a number sentence for the picture below.
(1)

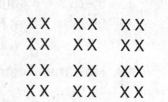

22. (1)	**23.** (1)	**24.** (1)	**25.** (1)
4	9	8	2
8	5	4	9
7	7	7	7
+ 5	+ 8	+ 2	+ 5

*26. Multiple Choice If △ = 3 and ☐ = 4, then △ + ☐ equals which of
(1) the following?

A 3   **B** 4   **C** 5   **D** 7

*27. How many different arrangements of three letters can you write using
(3) the letters a, b, and c? The different arrangements you write do not
need to form words.

*28. (**Connect**) Write a horizontal number sentence that has a sum of 9.
(1)

*29. (**Connect**) Write a vertical number sentence that has a sum of 11.
(1)

*30. (**Formulate**) Write and solve an addition word problem that has a
(1) sum of 12.

     Saxon Math Intermediate 4

Name _____

Real-World Connection

Ivan noticed that the first three house numbers on the right side of a street were 2305, 2315, and 2325.

a. What pattern do you see in this list of numbers?

b. If this pattern continues, what will the next three house numbers be?

c. The houses on the left side of the street have corresponding numbers that end in 0. What are the house numbers for the first 6 houses on the left side of the street?

d. What pattern is used for the house numbers on the left side of the street?

1. When Roho looked at the group of color tiles, he saw 3 red, 4 blue,
(1) 5 green, and 1 yellow. How many color tiles were there in all? Write the
number sentence to find the answer.

*2. **Represent** Write a number sentence for this picture:
(1)

3. How many cents are in 4 nickels? Count by fives.
(3)

5¢   5¢   5¢   5¢

Find each sum or missing addend:

4.   4
(1) $+ n$
_____
    12

5.   4
(1)   5
      $+ 3$
_____

6.   13
(1) $+ y$
_____
    19

7.   7
(1) $+ s$
_____
    14

*8. $4 + n + 5 = 12$
(2)

9. $n + 2 + 3 = 8$
(2)

Generalize Write the rule and the next three numbers of each counting sequence:

*10. 9, 12, 15, ____, ____, ____, ...
(3)

*11. 30, 24, 18, ____, ____, ____, ...
(3)

*12. 12, 16, 20, ____, ____, ____, ...
(3)

*13. 35, 28, 21, ____, ____, ____, ...
(3)

14. How many digits are in each number?
(3)
 a. 37,432   b. 5,934,286   c. 453,000

*15. What is the last digit of each number?
(3)
 a. 734   b. 347   c. 473

Saxon Math Intermediate 4

Name _____

*16. **Represent** Draw a diagram to show $342 in $100 bills, $10 bills,
(4)   and $1 bills.

17. How much money does this picture show?
(4)

Connect Find the missing number in each counting sequence:

18. 24, _____, 36, 42, …
(3)

*19. 36, 32, _____, 24, …
(3)

*20. How many ears do 10 rabbits have? Count by twos.
(3)

*21. The digit 6 is in what place in 365?
(4)

*22. **Represent** Write a number sentence for this picture:
(1)

23. Find the missing addend:
(2)

$$2 + 5 + 3 + 2 + 3 + 1 + n = 20$$

*24. **Explain** How do you find the missing addend in problem **23**?
(2)

25. Show six ways to add 6, 7, and 8.
(1)

*26. **Multiple Choice** In the number 123, which digit shows the number of
(4)   hundreds?

   A 1   **B** 2   **C** 3   **D** 4

*27. **Predict** What is the tenth number in the counting sequence below?
(3)

$$1, 2, 3, 4, 5, …$$

*28. How many different three-digit numbers can you write using the digits
(3)   2, 5, and 8? Each digit may be used only once in every number you
      write. List the numbers in counting order.

Saxon Math Intermediate 4   **9**

*29. **Connect** Write a number sentence that has addends of 6 and 7.
(1)

*30. **Formulate** Write and solve an addition word problem using the
(1) numbers 2, 3, and 5.

*Real-World
Connection*

Andres was asked to solve this riddle:

*What number am I? I have three digits. There is a 4 in the
tens place, a 7 in the ones place, and a 6 in the hundreds place.*

Andres said the answer was 467. Did Andres give the correct answer?
Use money manipulatives to explain your answer.

Saxon Math Intermediate 4

Name _____

*1. **(Formulate)** At the grocery store there were 5 people in the first line,
(1) 6 people in the second line, and 4 people in the third line. Altogether,
how many people were in the three lines? Write a number sentence to
find the answer.

Find each missing addend:

2.   2
(2)   6
    + x
    ___
    15

3.   1
(2)   y
    + 7
    ___
    14

4.   3
(2)   z
    + 5
    ___
    12

5.   1
(2)   n
    + 6
    ___
    13

6.   2
(2)   5
    + w
    ___
    10

7.   2
(1)   + a
    ___
    7

8.   r
(1)   + 5
    ___
    11

9.   3
(1)   + t
    ___
    5

*10. Tadeo was born on 8/15/93. Write Tadeo's birth date using the name of
(5)   the month and all four digits of the year.

(Conclude) Write the rule and the next three numbers of each counting sequence:

11. 12, 15, 18, ____, ____, ____, . . .
(3)

12. 16, 20, 24, ____, ____, ____, . . .
(3)

*13. 28, 35, 42, ____, ____, ____, . . .
(3)

*14. Find the missing number: 30, ____, 42, 48
(3)

*15. **(Explain)** How did you find the missing number in problem **14?**
(3)

*16. **(Represent)** Draw a diagram to show $432 in $100 bills, $10 bills,
(4)   and $1 bills.

*17. **(Represent)** Write a number sentence for the picture below.
(1)

18. The digit 8 is in what place in 845?
(4)

*19. (Represent) Use three digits to write the number that equals
(4) 2 hundreds plus 3 tens plus 5 ones.

*20. (Predict) If the pattern is continued, what will be the next circled
(3) number?

1, 2, ③, 4, 5, ⑥, 7, 8, ⑨, 10, …

21. Seven boys each have two pets. How many pets do the boys have?
(3) Count by twos.

22. (1)	**23.** (1)	**24.** (1)	**25.** (1)
5	5	9	8
8	7	7	7
4	3	6	3
7	8	5	5
4	4	4	4
+ 3	+ 2	+ 2	+ 9

*26. Multiple Choice Jenny was third in line. Jessica was seventh in line.
(5) How many people were between Jenny and Jessica?

A 3   **B** 4   **C** 5   **D** 6

27. (Predict) What is the tenth number in this counting sequence?
(3)

2, 4, 6, 8, 10, …

*28. How many different arrangements of three letters can you write using
(3) the letters r, s, and t? The different arrangements you write do not need
to form words.

*29. (Connect) Write a number sentence that has addends of 5 and 4.
(1)

*30. (Formulate) Write and solve an addition word problem using the
(1) numbers 1, 9, and 10.

    Saxon Math Intermediate 4

Name _____

Early Finishers

Real-World Connection

During the fourth month of every year, Stone Mountain Park near Atlanta, Georgia, hosts Feria Latina, one of the largest Hispanic cultural events in the state. What is the name of the month in which Feria Latina is held? If Amy and Carlos attend the festival next year on the 21st of the month, how would you write that date in month/date/year form?

Name _____

*1.
(6)
$$\begin{array}{r} 14 \\ -\ 5 \\ \hline \end{array}$$

*2.
(6)
$$\begin{array}{r} 15 \\ -\ 8 \\ \hline \end{array}$$

3.
(6)
$$\begin{array}{r} 9 \\ -\ 4 \\ \hline \end{array}$$

4.
(6)
$$\begin{array}{r} 11 \\ -\ 7 \\ \hline \end{array}$$

5.
(6)
$$\begin{array}{r} 12 \\ -\ 8 \\ \hline \end{array}$$

6.
(6)
$$\begin{array}{r} 11 \\ -\ 6 \\ \hline \end{array}$$

7.
(6)
$$\begin{array}{r} 15 \\ -\ 7 \\ \hline \end{array}$$

8.
(6)
$$\begin{array}{r} 9 \\ -\ 6 \\ \hline \end{array}$$

9.
(6)
$$\begin{array}{r} 13 \\ -\ 5 \\ \hline \end{array}$$

10.
(6)
$$\begin{array}{r} 12 \\ -\ 6 \\ \hline \end{array}$$

11.
(1)
$$\begin{array}{r} 8 \\ +\ n \\ \hline 17 \end{array}$$

12.
(1)
$$\begin{array}{r} a \\ +\ 8 \\ \hline 14 \end{array}$$

13. $3 + w = 11$
(1)

14. $1 + 4 + m = 13$
(2)

*15. **Connect** The numbers 4, 6, and 10 form a fact family. Write two
(6) addition facts and two subtraction facts using these three numbers.

Generalize Write the rule and the next three numbers of each counting sequence:

*16. 16, 18, 20, ____, ____, ____, ...
(3)

*17. 21, 28, 35, ____, ____, ____, ...
(3)

*18. 20, 24, 28, ____, ____, ____, ...
(3)

*19. How many days are in the tenth month of the year?
(5)

20. **Represent** Draw a diagram to show $326.
(4)

21. The digit 6 is in what place in 456?
(4)

Find each missing addend:

22. $2 + n + 4 = 13$
(2)

23. $a + 3 + 5 = 16$
(2)

*24. What is the name for the answer when we subtract?
(6)

*25. **List** Show six ways to add 3, 4, and 5.
(1)

14

Saxon Math Intermediate 4

Name _____

*26. **Multiple Choice** The ages of the children in Tyrese's family are 7
(1) and 9. The ages of the children in Mary's family are 3, 5, and 9. Which
number sentence shows how many children are in both families?

A 3 + 7 = 10 **B** 7 + 9 = 16

C 2 + 3 = 5 **D** 3 + 5 + 9 = 17

27. How many different three-digit numbers can you write using the
(3) digits 6, 3, and 9? Each digit may be used only once in every number
you write. List the numbers in counting order.

*28. Write a horizontal number sentence that has a sum of 23.
(1)

*29. Write a horizontal number sentence that has a difference of 9.
(6)

*30. (Formulate) Write and solve an addition word problem using the
(1) numbers 6, 5, and 11.

Formulate Write and solve equations for problems **1** and **2**.

*1. Anitra has 8 dollars. She needs 6 dollars more to buy the radio. How much does the radio cost?
(1)

*2. Peyton poured 8 ounces of water into a pitcher containing 8 ounces of lemon juice. How many ounces of liquid were in the mixture?
(1)

Find the missing addend:

3. $5 + n + 2 = 11$
(2)

4. $2 + 6 + n = 15$
(2)

Subtract. Check by adding.

*5. $\begin{array}{r} 13 \\ -\ 5 \\ \hline \end{array}$
(6)

6. $\begin{array}{r} 16 \\ -\ 8 \\ \hline \end{array}$
(6)

7. $\begin{array}{r} 13 \\ -\ 7 \\ \hline \end{array}$
(6)

8. $\begin{array}{r} 12 \\ -\ 8 \\ \hline \end{array}$
(6)

Represent Use digits to write each number:

*9. two hundred fourteen
(7)

*10. five hundred thirty-two
(7)

Represent Use words to write each number:

*11. 301
(7)

*12. 320
(7)

*13. **Represent** Use words to write the number shown by this model:
(7)

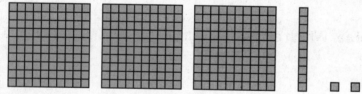

14. **Represent** Write a number sentence for this picture:
(1)

Generalize Write the rule and the next three numbers of each counting sequence:

15. 12, 18, 24, ____, ____, ____, ...
(3)

*16. 15, 18, 21, ____, ____, ____, ...
(3)

Saxon Math Intermediate 4

Name _____

Connect Find the missing number in each counting sequence:

*17. 35, 42, ____, 56, …
(3)

*18. 40, ____, 56, 64, …
(3)

19. **Connect** How much money is shown by this picture?
(4)

*20. **Connect** The numbers 7, 8, and 15 form a fact family. Write two
(6) addition facts and two subtraction facts using these three numbers.

*21. **Explain** Brad was twelfth in line. His sister was sixth in line. How
(5) many people were between Brad and his sister? Explain how you can
use the four-step problem-solving process to solve this problem.

22. Which month is five months after October?
(5)

23. Six nickels equals how many cents? Count by fives.
(3)

24. 4 + 7 + 8 + 5 + 4
(1)

25. 2 + 3 + 5 + 8 + 5
(1)

26. 5 + 8 + 6 + 4 + 3 + 7 + 2
(1)

*27. Multiple Choice Which addition equation is related to $12 - 5 = 7$?
(6)
   A $7 + 5 = 12$ **B** $12 + 5 = 17$
   C $12 + 7 = 19$ **D** $12 - 7 = 5$

*28. How many different three-digit numbers can you write using the
(3) digits 4, 1, and 6? Each digit may be used only once in every number
you write. List the numbers in order from least to greatest.

*29. Compare 126 and 162. Which number is less?
(7)

*30. The table shows the lengths of three rivers in
(7) North America.

List the rivers in order from longest to shortest.

The Lengths of Rivers (in miles)

River	Length
Alabama	729
Green	730
Kuskokwim	724

Saxon Math Intermediate 4

Name _____

Represent In problems **1** and **2,** use digits to write each number.

*1. three hundred forty-three
(7)

*2. three hundred seven
(7)

*3. Use words to write the number 592.
(7)

Find each missing addend:

4.   2
(2)   4
   $+ n$
   ‾‾‾‾
   12

5.   1
(2) r
   $+ 6$
   ‾‾‾‾
   10

6.   1
(2) t
   $+ 7$
   ‾‾‾‾
   14

7.   2
(2)   6
   $+ n$
   ‾‾‾‾
   13

*8. $25
(8) $+ \$14$
   ‾‾‾‾‾

9. $85
(8) $+ \$14$
   ‾‾‾‾‾

10. $22
(8) $+ \$ 6$
   ‾‾‾‾‾

*11. $40
(8) $+ \$38$
   ‾‾‾‾‾

*12. 13
(6) $- 9$
   ‾‾‾‾

13. 17
(6) $- 5$
   ‾‾‾‾

14. 17
(6) $- 8$
   ‾‾‾‾

15. 14
(6) $- 6$
   ‾‾‾‾

*16. **Formulate** D'Jeran has $23. Beckie has $42. Together, D'Jeran and
(1, 8) Beckie have how much money? Write an equation to solve this problem.

*17. **Represent** Use words to write the number shown by this model:
(7)

*18. Salma was born on the fifth day of August in 1994. Write her birth date
(5) in month/day/year form.

Generalize Write the rule and the next three numbers of each counting
sequence:

*19. 12, 15, 18, _____, _____, _____, . . .
(3)

*20. 28, 35, 42, _____, _____, _____, . . .
(3)

21. (1)
```
  5
  8
  7
  6
  4
+ 3
```

22. (1)
```
  9
  7
  6
  4
  8
+ 7
```

23. (1)
```
  2
  5
  7
  3
  5
+ 4
```

*24. (List) Show six ways to add 5, 6, and 7.
(1)

*25. (Connect) Write two addition facts and two subtraction facts using 7,
(6) 8, and 15.

*26. Multiple Choice If $7 + \blacklozenge = 15$, then which of the following is *not*
(6) true?

    A $\blacklozenge - 7 = 15$ **B** $15 - 7 = \blacklozenge$

    C $15 - \blacklozenge = 7$ **D** $\blacklozenge + 7 = 15$

*27. How many different three-digit numbers can you write using the digits
(3, 7) 7, 6, and 5? Each digit may be used only once in every number you
write. List the numbers in order from least to greatest.

28. Compare 630 and 603. Which is greater?
(7)

*29. The table shows the number of skyscrapers
(7) in three cities.

Write the names of the cities in order from
the least number of skyscrapers to the
greatest number of skyscrapers.

Skyscrapers

City	Number
Boston	16
Hong Kong	30
Singapore	14

*30. (Formulate) Write and solve an addition word problem that has a
(1) sum of 16.

Early Finishers
Real-World Connection

Mel works at the Cumberland Island National Seashore. He began the
day with $13 in the cash register. A family of four visiting the seashore
gives Mel $4 each for their entrance fees. What is the total amount Mel
collects from the family? How much money is in the cash register now?

Saxon Math Intermediate 4

Represent In problems **1** and **2,** use digits to write each number:

*1. six hundred thirteen
(7)

*2. nine hundred one
(7)

3. Use words to write 941.
(7)

Find each missing addend for problems **4–7.**

4.   2
(2)   4
    + f
    ____
     11

5.   5
(2)   g
    + 2
    ____
     13

6.   h
(2)   4
    + 7
    ____
     15

7.   2
(2)   7
    + n
    ____
     16

*8.   33
(9)   + 8

*9. $47
(9) + $18

*10.   27
(9)   + 69

*11. $49
(9) + $25

*12.   17
(6)   − 8

13.   12
(6) − 6

14.   9
(6)   − 7

15.   13
(6)   − 6

16. What is the name for the answer when we add?
(1)

17. What is the name for the answer when we subtract?
(6)

*18. Which month is two months after the twelfth month?
(5)

Generalize Write the rule and the next three numbers of each counting sequence:

*19. 30, 36, 42, _____, _____, _____, ...
(3)

*20. 28, 35, 42, _____, _____, _____, ...
(3)

21. Which digit is in the hundreds place in 843?
(4)

22. 28 + 6
(9)

*23. $47 + $28
(9)

24. 35 + 27
(9)

*25. **Formulate** Mio bought pants for $28 and a shirt for $17. Altogether,
(1, 9) how much did the pants and shirt cost? Write an equation for this
problem.

*26. Multiple Choice What number is shown by this
(7) model?

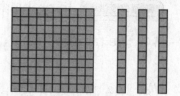

A 31   **B** 13

C 103   **D** 130

*27. How many different arrangements of three letters can you write
(3) using the letters l, m, and n? Each letter may be used only once,
and the different arrangements you write do not need to form
words.

28. Compare 89 and 98. Which is less?
(7)

*29. The table shows the maximum speed that some
(7) animals can run for a short distance.

Write the names of the animals in order from the
fastest to the slowest.

Speeds of Animals

Animal	Speed (miles per hour)
White-tailed deer	30
Mule deer	35
Reindeer	32

*30. **Formulate** Write and solve an addition word problem that has
(1) a sum of 7.

Early Finishers
Real-World Connection

Terri's basketball team has played four games this season. In the first
game, the team scored 26 points. If the team scored 14 points in the first
half, how many points did the team score in the second half?

In the first four games of the season, Terri's team scored 26, 34, 35,
and 29 points. What is the total number of points the team has scored
this season?

Saxon Math Intermediate 4

Name _____

Represent In problems **1** and **2,** use digits to write each number.

*1. five hundred forty-two
(7)

*2. six hundred nineteen
(7)

*3. The numbers 4, 7, and 11 form a fact family. Write two addition facts and
(6) two subtraction facts using those three numbers.

Represent In problems **4** and **5,** use words to write each number.

*4. 903
(7)

*5. 746
(7)

*6. Which three-digit odd number greater than 600 has the digits
(10) 4, 6, and 7?

Find each missing addend in problems **7–10.**

7.   4
(2) n
  $+ 3$
  $\overline{14}$

8. p
(2)   4
  $+ 2$
  $\overline{13}$

9.   5
(2) q
  $+ 7$
  $\overline{14}$

10. r
(2)   3
  $+ 2$
  $\overline{11}$

11. 15
(6) $- 7$

12. 14
(6) $- 7$

13. 17
(6) $- 8$

14. 11
(6) $- 6$

*15. $25
(9) $+ \$38$

16. $19
(9) $+ \$34$

*17. 42
(9) $+ 8$

18. 17
(9) $+ 49$

*19. **Generalize** Write the rule and the next three numbers of this counting sequence:
(3)

$$18, 21, 24, \underline{\quad}, \underline{\quad}, \underline{\quad}, \ldots$$

*20. **Predict** What is the eighth number in this counting sequence?
(3, 5)

$$6, 12, 18, 24, \ldots$$

*21. **Formulate** If Jabari has $6 in a piggy bank, $12 in his wallet, and $20
(1, 8) in his drawer, how much money does Jabari have in all three places?
Write an equation for this problem.

22. $2 + 3 + 5 + 7 + 8 + 4 + 5$
(1)

*23. Write today's date in month/day/year form.
(5)

*24. **Represent** Use words to write the number shown by this model:
(7)

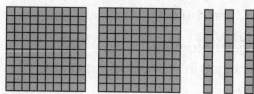

*25. What number is the largest two-digit even number?
(10)

*26. **Multiple Choice** If $\triangle + 4 = 12$, then which of these is *not* true?
(6)
    A $4 + \triangle = 12$ **B** $12 - \triangle = 4$
    C $12 + 4 = \triangle$ **D** $12 - 4 = \triangle$

*27. List in order from least to greatest all the three-digit numbers you can
(10) write using the digits 8, 3, and 0 in each number. The digit 0 may not be
used in the hundreds place.

*28. Write "odd" or "even" for each number:
(10)
    a. 73   **b.** 54   **c.** 330   **d.** 209

*29. **Connect** Write a horizontal subtraction number sentence.
(6)

*30. **Formulate** Write and solve an addition word problem. Then explain
(1) why your answer is reasonable.

Real-World Connection

Janine noticed that the top lockers at school were odd numbers and the bottom locker numbers were even. Below is a list of the first five numbers on the bottom lockers:

    300   302   304   306   308

    a. Are these numbers even or odd? How do you know?

    b. If this pattern continues, what will the next bottom locker number be?

Saxon Math Intermediate 4

Formulate Write and solve equations for problems **1** and **2.**

*1. If a winter day has 10 hours of daylight, then the day has how
(1)   many hours of darkness? (*Hint:* A whole day has 24 hours.)

*2. Tamira read 6 pages before lunch. After lunch she read some more.
(11)   If Tamira read 13 pages in all, how many pages did she read after
       lunch?

3. **Represent** Use digits to write the number six hundred forty-two.
(7)

*4. **Represent** Use digits and symbols to write this comparison:
(Inv. 1)   "Negative twelve is less than zero."

*5. Compare: $-2 \bigcirc 2$
(Inv. 1)

*6. Use the digits 5, 6, and 7 to write an even number between 560 and
(10)   650.

*7. **Represent** To what number is each arrow pointing?
(Inv. 1)

   a.

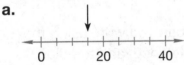

   b.

*8. **Analyze** The books were put into two stacks so that an equal
(10)   number of books was in each stack. Was the total number of
       books an odd number or an even number? Explain your thinking.

9. (2)	**10.** (2)	**11.** (2)	**12.** (2)
5	n	7	m
b	5	a	2
$+\ 7$	$+\ 3$	$+\ 4$	$+\ 8$
$\overline{18}$	$\overline{15}$	$\overline{12}$	$\overline{14}$

13. (6)	**14.** (6)	**15.** (6)	**16.** (6)
12	14	12	13
$-\ 3$	$-\ 7$	$-\ 8$	$-\ 6$

*17. 74
(9) + 18

*18. 93
(9) + 39

19. 28
(9) + 45

20. 28
(9) + 47

Conclude Write the next three numbers in each counting sequence:

*21. ..., 12, 9, 6, ___, ___, ___, ...
(Inv. 3)

22. ..., 30, 36, 42, ___, ___, ___, ...
(3)

*23. **Connect** The numbers 5, 9, and 14 form a fact family. Write two
(6) addition facts and two subtraction facts using these three numbers.

24. 4 + 3 + 5 + 8 + 7 + 6 + 2
(1)

25. **List** Show six ways to add 7, 8, and 9.
(1)

*26. **Multiple Choice** If 3 + ▲ = 7 and if ■ = 5, then ▲ + ■ equals which
(1) of the following?

   A 4   **B** 5   **C** 8   **D** 9

*27. How many different odd three-digit numbers can you write using the
(10) digits 5, 0, and 9? Each digit may be used only once, and the digit 0
may not be used in the hundreds place.

*28. Compare. Write >, <, or =.
(Inv. 1)
   a. 89 ◯ 94   **b.** 409 ◯ 177   **c.** 61 ◯ 26

*29. The land areas of three counties are
(7) shown in the table.

Write the names of the counties in
order from smallest area to largest area.

Land Area by County

County	State	Area (sq mi)
Cass	Iowa	564
Hood River	Oregon	522
Weber	Utah	576

*30. **Formulate** Write and solve an addition word problem. Then explain
(1) why your answer is reasonable.

Saxon Math Intermediate 4

Formulate Write and solve equations for problems **1–3**.

*1. Laura found nine acorns in the park. Then she found some more acorns
(11) in her backyard. If Laura found seventeen acorns in all, how many
acorns did she find in the backyard?

*2. Caterpillars change into butterflies every day at the butterfly center.
(1, 9) In one week 35 caterpillars changed into butterflies. The next week
27 more caterpillars changed into butterflies. Altogether, how many
caterpillars changed to butterflies?

*3. Demetrius used a 12-inch ruler to stir the paint in the can. When he
(11) removed the ruler, 5 inches of it were not coated with paint. How many
inches of the ruler were coated with paint?

*4. **Represent** Use words and digits to write the number
(7) shown by this model:

5. Nathan's little sister was born on the seventh day of June in 2002. Write
(5) her birth date in month/day/year form.

*6. Write a three-digit odd number less than 500 using the digits 9, 4, and
(4) 6. Which digit is in the tens place?

*7. **Connect** To what number is the arrow pointing?
(Inv. 1)

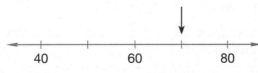

8. (2)	**9.** (2)	**10.** (2)	**11.** (2)
5	a	7	4
n	2	2	a
$+\ 6$	$+\ 5$	$+\ n$	$+\ 2$
$\overline{15}$	$\overline{15}$	$\overline{15}$	$\overline{15}$

*12. (12)	**13.** (6)	**14.** (6)	***15.** (12)
n	16	14	12
$-\ 6$	$-\ 8$	$-\ 7$	$-\ a$
$\overline{8}$			$\overline{7}$

Saxon Math Intermediate 4 **27**

*16.
(12)

$$b$$
$$- 6$$
$$\overline{6}$$

*17.
(12)

$$13$$
$$- c$$
$$\overline{8}$$

*18.
(9)

$$\$48$$
$$+ \$16$$

19.
(9)

$$\$37$$
$$+ \$14$$

Conclude Write the next three numbers in each counting sequence:

*20. ..., 28, 35, 42, ____, ____, ____, ...
(3)

*21. ..., 18, 21, 24, ____, ____, ____, ...
(3)

22. How many cents is nine nickels? Count by fives.
(3)

*23. **Explain** Write the following comparison using words and explain
(Inv. 1) why the comparison is correct.

$$-3 > -5$$

*24. Arrange these numbers from least to greatest: 0, −2, 4
(Inv. 1)

25. 7 + 3 + 8 + 5 + 4 + 3 + 2
(1)

*26. **Multiple Choice** "Five subtracted from n" can be written as which of
(6) the following?

   A $5 - n$ **B** $n - 5$ **C** $5 + n$ **D** $n + 5$

*27. How many different three-digit numbers can you write using the digits
(10) 4, 2, and 0? Each digit may be used only once, and the digit 0 may not
be used in the hundreds place.

*28. Compare. Write >, <, or =.
(Inv. 1)
   a. 310 ◯ 295   **b.** 56 ◯ 63   **c.** 104 ◯ 89

29. The table shows the typical weight of three animals.
(7)

Write the names of the animals in order from greatest
weight to the least weight.

Typical Weight of Animals

Animal	Weight (pounds)
Fox	14
Badger	17
Otter	13

   Saxon Math Intermediate 4

Name _____

30. **Formulate** Write and solve an addition word problem. Then explain
(1)
why your answer is reasonable.

Real-World Connection

Brianna earned $15 walking her neighbor's dog in the afternoons. She
used part of the money she earned to buy a CD. After buying the CD,
Brianna has $6 left. Write and solve an equation to find how much
Brianna paid for the CD.

With the money she has left, Brianna wants to purchase a book that
costs $10. Write and solve an equation to find how much Brianna
needs. Explain how you found your answer.

 29

* 1. For recess, 77 students chose to play outside and 19 students chose to
(1, 9) play in the gym. How many students were playing at recess altogether?

* 2. Five of the twelve students had no homework to take home on Friday.
(11) How many students had homework to take home?

* 3. (**Represent**) Use words to write the number 913.
(7)

* 4. (**Represent**) Use digits to write the number seven hundred
(7) forty-three.

* 5. (**Represent**) Use digits and symbols to write this comparison:
(Inv. 1) "Seventy-five is greater than negative eighty."

* 6. Compare:
(7, Inv. 1)   **a.** 413 ◯ 314   **b.** −4 ◯ 3

7. (**Connect**) The numbers 7, 9, and 16 form a fact family. Write two
(6) addition facts and two subtraction facts using these three numbers.

* 8. (**Represent**) To what number is each arrow pointing?
(Inv. 1)
   a.

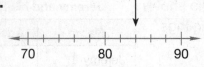

   b.

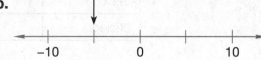

* 9. (13)	*** 10.** (13)	*** 11.** (13)	*** 12.** (13)
$475 + $332	$714 + $226	743 + 187	576 + 228

13. (2)	**14.** (2)	**15.** (2)	**16.** (2)
8 5 + k —— 17	4 n + 6 —— 15	9 a + 6 —— 17	n 3 + 7 —— 16

Saxon Math Intermediate 4

*17.   8
(12) − n
     ———
       2

18.   17
(6)   − 8
    ———

19.   13
(6)   − 7
    ———

*20.   n
(12) − 8
    ———
       7

*21.   14
(12) − n
     ———
       6

*22.   16
(12) − a
     ———
       9

23.   n
(12) − 9
    ———
       7

24. $49
(9)   + $76
    ———

*25. (Conclude) Write the next three numbers in each counting sequence:
(3,
Inv. 1)
     a. ..., 28, 35, 42, ____, ____, ____, ...

     b. ..., 15, 10, 5, ____, ____, ____, ...

*26. Multiple Choice Which number shows the sum of the sets
(7)   below?

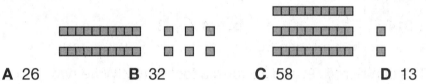

   A 26   **B** 32   **C** 58   **D** 13

*27. What temperature is 5 degrees less than 1 degree?
(Inv. 1)

*28. Brothers and sisters are siblings. The table shows
(7)   the names and ages of Jeremy and his siblings.

     Write the names in order from youngest
     to oldest.

Jeremy and his Siblings

Name	Age (in years)
Jeremy	10
Jack	8
Jackie	13

*29. (Justify) Will the sum of three even numbers be odd or even?
(10)   Explain and give several examples to support your answer.

*30. How many different three-digit numbers can you write using the digits
(10)   0, 6, and 7? Each digit may be used only once, and the digit 0 may not
     be used in the hundreds place. Label your numbers as even or odd.

Formulate Write and solve equations for problems **1** and **2**.

*1. The surf shop had forty-two surfboards. The shop received a shipment
(1) with seventeen more surfboards. How many surfboards were at the
surf shop?

*2. Machiko saw four grasshoppers in her backyard on Monday. On
(11) Tuesday she saw some more grasshoppers. She saw a total of eleven
grasshoppers on those two days. How many grasshoppers did she see
on Tuesday?

*3. Use the digits 1, 2, and 3 to write an even number less than 200. Use
(10) each digit only once.

*4. **Connect** Use the numbers 9, 7, and 2 to write two addition facts and
(6) two subtraction facts.

*5. Subtract seven hundred thirteen from eight hundred twenty-four.
(14)

*6. Compare:
(Inv. 1)
  a. 704 ◯ 407   **b.** −3 ◯ −5

7. What is the total number of days in the first two months of a common
(5) year?

*8. **Represent** To what number is the arrow pointing?
(Inv. 1)

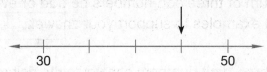

*9.	$346	***10.**	499	***11.**	$421	***12.**	$506
(13)	+ $298	(13)	+ 275	(13)	+ $389	(13)	+ $210

*13.	$438	**14.**	17	**15.**	7	**16.**	5
(14)	− $206	(12)	− a	(1)	+ b	(12)	− c
			9		14		2

Saxon Math Intermediate 4

17. 8
(1) + d
     ___
      15

*18. 15
(12) − k
      ___
       9

19. 3
(2) n
    + 2
    ___
     13

*20. 476
(14) − 252
      _____

21. 47
(14) − 16
     ____

*22. 28
(14) − 13
      ____

*23. 75
(14) + t
      ___
       87

*24. 24
(14) + e
      ___
       67

*25. (**Conclude**) Write the next three numbers in each counting sequence:
(3, Inv. 1)

    a. ... , 81, 72, 63, ____, ____, ____, ...

    b. ... , 12, 8, 4, ____, ____, ____, ...

*26. Multiple Choice If ☐ − 7 = 2, then which of these is *not* true?
(12)

    A 7 − ☐ = 2   **B** ☐ − 2 = 7

    C 2 + 7 = ☐   **D** ☐ = 7 + 2

*27. (**Verify**) When you add four even numbers, will the sum be
(10) even or odd? Explain why, and give several examples to support
your answer.

28. A piano has 36 black keys and 52 white keys. Does a piano have
(1, 7) more black keys or white keys? How many keys does a piano have
altogether?

*29. (**Verify**) Will the sum of three odd numbers be odd or even? Explain
(10) why, and give several examples to support your answer.

30. How many different three-digit numbers can you write using the digits
(10) 9, 1, and 0? Each digit may be used only once, and the digit 0 may
not be used in the hundreds place. Label the numbers you write as
even or odd.

Real-World Connection

The Helman family took a 745-mile car trip to visit relatives. The trip
took three days because they made stops to sightsee each day. On the
first day, they traveled 320 miles, and on the third day, they traveled
220 miles. How many miles did they travel on the second day? Explain
why your answer is reasonable.

Formulate Write and solve equations for problems **1 and 2**.

* 1. Jimmy found six hundred eighteen acorns under one tree. He found
(1, 13) one hundred seventeen acorns under another tree. How many acorns
did Jimmy find in all?

* 2. On the first day Rueben collected sixteen leaves. On the second day
(11, 14) Rueben collected some more leaves, giving him a total of seventy-six
leaves. How many leaves did he collect on the second day?

3. Use the digits 3, 6, and 7 to write an even number less than 400. Use
(10) each digit only once.

* 4. **Represent** Use words to write the number 605.
(7)

5. The smallest two-digit odd number is 11. What is the smallest
(10) two-digit even number?

6. Compare:
(Inv. 1)
   a. 75 ◯ 57   **b.** 5 + 7 ◯ 4 + 8

* 7. Subtract 245 from 375.
(14)

* 8. To what number is the arrow pointing?
(Inv. 1)

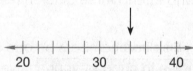

	20	30	40

* 9. $426   **10.** $278   **11.**   721   *** 12.**   409
(13) + $298   (13) + $456   (13) + 189   (13) + 198

13. d **14.**   18   *** 15.**   38   **16.** c
(1) + 7   (12) − a (14) + b (12) − 4
  12   9   59   1

17. $456   *** 18.** $54   *** 19.**   46   *** 20.**   35
(14) − $120   (15) − $27   (15) − 28   (15) − 16

    Saxon Math Intermediate 4

*21. (Analyze) What is the total number of days in the last two months of
(5) the year?

*22. (Connect) The numbers 5, 6, and 11 form a fact family. Write two
(6) addition and two subtraction facts using these three numbers.

*23. $3 + 6 + 7 + 5 + 4 + 8$
(1)

(Conclude) Write the next three numbers in each counting sequence:

24. ... , 72, 63, 54, _____,   _____,   _____, ...
(3)

*25. ... , –7, –14, –21, _____, –28_____, –35_____, ...
(Inv. 1)

*26. Multiple Choice If $\square$ = 6 and if $\square$ + $\triangle$ = 10, then $\triangle$ equals which
(1) of the following?

   A 3   **B** 4   **C** 5   **D** 6

*27. (Verify) Will the sum of an odd number and an even number be
(10) odd or even? Explain why, and give several examples to support your
answer.

28. The numbers of students who attend three different elementary schools
(7) are shown in this table:

Enrollment

School	Number of Students
Washington	370
Lincoln	312
Roosevelt	402

Write the names of the schools in order from the least number of
students to greatest.

*29. A chimpanzee weighs about 150 pounds. A gorilla weighs about
(6, 7) 450 pounds. Which animal weighs more? About how much more does
it weigh?

30. How many different three-digit numbers can you write using the digits
(10) 4, 0, and 8? Each digit may be used only once, and the digit 0 may not
be used in the hundreds place.

*Real-World
Connection*

The zookeeper keeps a chart showing how much food the giant panda
at the zoo eats each day. The chart shows that the panda ate 61 pounds
of food on Monday and 55 pounds of food on Tuesday. How much more
food did the panda eat on Monday than on Tuesday? Use base ten
blocks to solve the problem. Then check your answer using pencil and
paper.

Saxon Math Intermediate 4

Name _____

Formulate Write and solve equations for problems **1** and **2**.

*1. Twenty-three horses grazed in the pasture. The rest of the horses were
(11, 14) in the corral. If there were eighty-nine horses in all, how many horses
were in the corral?

*2. Three hundred seventy-five students were standing in the auditorium.
(1, 13) The other one hundred seven students in the auditorium were sitting
down. Altogether, how many students were in the auditorium?

3. Use the numbers 22, 33, and 55 to write two addition facts and two
(6) subtraction facts.

*4. **Represent** Write 782 in expanded form.
(16)

5. The largest three-digit odd number is 999. What is the smallest
(10) three-digit even number?

6. Compare:
(Inv. 1)
    a. 918 ◯ 819   **b.** -7 ◯ -5

7. Six weeks is how many days? Count by sevens.
(3)

*8. **Represent** To what number is the arrow pointing?
(Inv. 1)

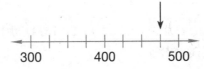

9. $\$576$	**10.** $\$243$	**11.** 186	**12.** 329
(13) $+\ \$128$	(13) $+\ \$578$	(13) $+\ 285$	(13) $+\ 186$

13. d	**14.** 17	**15.** 8	**16.** c
(14) $+\ 12$	(12) $-\ a$	(1) $+\ b$	(12) $-\ 7$
$\overline{17}$	$\overline{9}$	$\overline{14}$	$\overline{2}$

*17. 25	***18.** 42	***19.** 46	***20.** 42
(15) $-\ 19$	(15) $-\ 28$	(15) $-\ 18$	(15) $-\ 16$

*21.
(16)
$$\begin{array}{r} 68 \\ -\ d \\ \hline 34 \end{array}$$

*22.
(16)
$$\begin{array}{r} b \\ -\ 34 \\ \hline 15 \end{array}$$

*23.
(16)
$$\begin{array}{r} 62 \\ -\ h \\ \hline 21 \end{array}$$

*24.
(16)
$$\begin{array}{r} m \\ -\ 46 \\ \hline 32 \end{array}$$

*25. (**Conclude**) Write the next three numbers in each counting sequence:
(3)

　　a. …, 16, 20, 24, ____, ____, ____, …

　　b. …, 16, 12, 8, ____, ____, ____, …

*26. Multiple Choice If $n - 3 = 6$, then which of these number sentences
(12, 16) is *not* true?

　　A $6 + 3 = n$　　　　　　　　**B** $3 + 6 = n$

　　C $6 - 3 = n$　　　　　　　　**D** $n - 6 = 3$

27. Elevation is a measure of distance above sea level. The elevations of
(7) three cities are shown in the table:

Elevations of Cities

City	State	Elevation (in feet above sea level)
Augusta	ME	45
Troy	NY	35
Hilo	HI	38

　　Write the names of the cities in order from the greatest elevation to least.

*28. Draw a number line and mark the locations of the numbers 23, 26, and
(Inv. 1) 30 by placing dots on the number line.

*29. (**Explain**) Malika's age is an odd number. The sum of Malika's age
(10) and Elena's age is an even number. Is Elena's age an odd number or an
even number? Explain how you know.

*30. (**Explain**) Write an addition word problem for the equation
(11) $33 + m = 51$. Solve the problem for m and explain why your answer
is reasonable.

Real-World Connection

Trisha rolled a dot cube three times. She rolled 3, 5, and 4. Write all
the three-digit numbers Trisha can make using these digits one time in
each number. Then write the greatest and least number in expanded
form.

Saxon Math Intermediate 4

Name _____

Write and solve equations for problems **1** and **2**.

*1. Twenty-four children visited the school science fair. The remainder of
(11) the visitors were adults. There were seventy-five visitors in all. How
many visitors were adults?

*2. Four hundred seven fans sat on one side of the field at a soccer play-off
(1, 13) game. Three hundred sixty-two fans sat on the other side of the field.
Altogether, how many fans saw the game?

*3. Use the digits 9, 2, and 8 to write an even number less than 300. You
(10) may use each digit only once. Which digit is in the tens place?

*4. (Represent) Write 813 in expanded form. Then use words to write the
(7, 16) number.

5. The largest two-digit even number is 98. What is the smallest
(10) two-digit odd number?

*6. (Represent) To what number is the arrow pointing?
(Inv. 1)

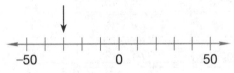

*7. 294
(17)
    312
  +   5

8. $189
(13)
  + $298

9. $378
(13)
  + $496

10. 109
(13)
  + 486

*11. 14 + 28 + 35 + 16 + 227
(17)

12. 14 − a = 7
(12)

13. 8 + b = 14
(1)

*14. c − 13 = 5
(16)

15. 11
(12)
  − d
    9

16. e
(12)
  − 5
    8

*17. 38
(15)
  − 29

*18. 57
(15)
  − 38

19. 34
(14)
  + b
   86

*20. 48
(16)
  − c
   25

21. d
(16)
  − 46
   12

22. y
(16)
  − 15
   24

Conclude Write the next three numbers in each counting sequence:

*23. ..., 48, 44, 40, ____, ____, ____, ...
(3)

*24. ..., 12, 15, 18, ____, ____, ____, ...
(3)

*25. **Connect** The numbers 6, 9, and 15 form a fact family. Write two
(6) addition and two subtraction facts using these three numbers.

*26. **Multiple Choice** Nancy is thinking of two numbers whose sum is
(1, 6) 10 and whose difference is 2. What are the two numbers?

    A 2 and 8   **B** 3 and 7

    C 6 and 4   **D** 2 and 10

27. Four friends measured their resting heart rates by counting their pulses
(7) for a minute. The results shown are in the table below:

Resting Heart Rate

Name	Beats per Minute
Miguel	72
Victoria	68
Simon	64
Megan	76

Write the names of the friends in order from the lowest resting heart rate
to the highest.

*28. Draw a number line and make dots to show the locations of the
(Inv. 1) numbers 13, 10, and 9.

*29. **Explain** Darrius's age is an even number. The sum of Darrius's age
(10) and Keb's age is an even number. Is Keb's age an odd number or an
even number? Explain how you know.

Saxon Math Intermediate 4

Name _____

*30. (Explain) Write an addition word problem for the equation
(11) $n + 10 = 25$. Solve the problem for *n,* and explain why your answer is
reasonable.

*Real-World
Connection*

Mr. Sanchez adds fresh fruit to a special display in the grocery store
several times a day. One day he added 102 oranges, 115 apples,
53 pears, 87 peaches, and 44 grapefruit to the display. How many
pieces of fruit did he add to the display that day?

Saxon Math Intermediate 4   **41**

Formulate Write and solve equations for problems **1** and **2**.

*1. Tomas ran to the fence and back in 58 seconds. If it took Tomas
(11, 14)   21 seconds to run to the fence, how many seconds did it take him
to run back from the fence?

2. Two hundred ninety-seven boys and three hundred fifteen girls attend
(1, 13)   Madison School. How many children attend Madison School?

*3. **Connect** Use the numbers 8, 17, and 9 to write two addition facts and
(6)   two subtraction facts.

*4. The tens digit is 4. The ones digit is 9. The number is between 200 and
(4)   300. What is the number?

*5. **Predict** What is the eighth number in the following counting
(3, 5)   sequence? Describe the pattern you observe.

$$4, 8, 12, 16, \ldots$$

*6. **Represent** To what number is the arrow pointing?
(Inv. 1)

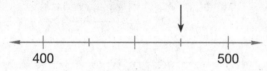

7.	$392	**8.**	$439	**9.**	774	**10.**	389
(13)	+ $278	(13)	+ $339	(13)	+ 174	(13)	+ 398

*11. 13
(17)   25
46
25
+ 29

12. 18
(16)   − a
‾‾‾‾
12

13. 8
(1)   + b
‾‾‾‾
16

14. c
(12)   − 5
‾‾‾
3

*15. 62
(15)   − 48

*16. 82
(15)   − 58

17. 28
(17)   36
57
+ 47

18. 35
(16)   − y
‾‾‾‾
14

Saxon Math Intermediate 4

Name _____

19. (14)	*20. (16)	*21. (16)	22. (14)
45 + p ――― 55	75 − l ――― 42	c − 47 ――― 31	e + 15 ――― 37

*23. (Represent) Write 498 in expanded form.
(16)

24. Compare:
(Inv. 1)

    a. 423 ◯ 432   **b.** 3 ◯ −3

*25. These thermometers show the highest Fahrenheit temperature and the
(18) lowest Celsius temperature recorded at a school last year. What were
those temperatures?

a.    **b.**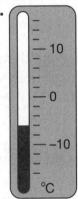

*26. Multiple Choice Which of these numbers is an odd number that
(10) is greater than 750?

    A 846   **B** 864   **C** 903   **D** 309

27. Write these numbers in order from greatest to least:
(7)

        166 48 207 81

*28. (Formulate) Lexington, Kentucky, receives an average of 46 inches of
(15) precipitation each year. Huron, South Dakota, receives an average of
25 fewer inches. Write and solve an equation to find the average amount
of precipitation Huron receives each year.

29. Write a subtraction number sentence using the numbers 15 and 10.
(12)

*30. How many odd numbers are greater than 1 and less than 20?
(10)

Real-World Connection

If the Celsius temperature is known, we can estimate the Fahrenheit temperature by doubling the Celsius temperature and adding 30.

a. Using this method, estimate the Fahrenheit temperature at which water freezes, if we know that water freezes at 0°C. Explain how you know your estimate is reasonable.

b. The average temperature in Austin, Texas, for the month of November is 20°C. Explain how you can find the estimated average Fahrenheit temperature in Austin, Texas, for that same month. Then use the method to find the estimated Fahrenheit temperature.

 Saxon Math Intermediate 4

Write and solve equations for problems **1** and **2**.

*1. (11) **Formulate** On the first day, Shaquana read fifty-one pages. She read some more pages on the second day. She read seventy-six pages in all. How many pages did she read on the second day?

*2. (11, 14) Twelve of the twenty-seven children in Room 9 are boys. How many girls are in Room 9?

*3. (6) If $a + b = 9$, then what is the other addition fact for a, b, and 9? What are the two subtraction facts for a, b, and 9?

*4. (7, 16) **Represent** Write 905 in expanded form. Then use words to write the number.

5. (Inv. 1) Use digits and symbols to write this comparison: "One hundred twenty is greater than one hundred twelve."

*6. (19) After school on Wednesday, Jana began her homework at the time shown on the clock. She finished her homework at 5:20 p.m. How much time did it take Jana to finish her homework?

*7. (18) Water freezes at 32° on the Fahrenheit scale. At what temperature on the Celsius scale does water freeze?

8. (13)
$$\begin{array}{r} \$468 \\ + \$293 \\ \hline \end{array}$$

9. (13)
$$\begin{array}{r} 468 \\ + 185 \\ \hline \end{array}$$

10. (13)
$$\begin{array}{r} \$187 \\ + \$698 \\ \hline \end{array}$$

11. (12)
$$\begin{array}{r} 14 \\ - a \\ \hline 7 \end{array}$$

12. (1)
$$\begin{array}{r} 8 \\ + b \\ \hline 16 \end{array}$$

13. (12)
$$\begin{array}{r} c \\ - 8 \\ \hline 7 \end{array}$$

14. (12)
$$\begin{array}{r} 14 \\ - d \\ \hline 9 \end{array}$$

*15. (15)
$$\begin{array}{r} 74 \\ - 58 \\ \hline \end{array}$$

*16. (15)
$$\begin{array}{r} \$44 \\ - \$28 \\ \hline \end{array}$$

*17. (15)
$$\begin{array}{r} 23 \\ - 18 \\ \hline \end{array}$$

*18. (15)
$$\begin{array}{r} \$62 \\ - \$43 \\ \hline \end{array}$$

Name _____

*19.
(17)
```
  25
  28
  46
+ 88
```

20.
(16)
```
  45
−  p
  21
```

21.
(14)
```
  13
+  b
  37
```

*22.
(16)
```
   f
− 45
  32
```

23. Four dollars equals how many quarters? Count by fours.
(3)

*24. (Connect) Write a number sentence for this picture:
(1)

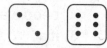

*25. ✏ (Conclude) Write the next three numbers in each counting sequence
(3, and explain the patterns you see.
Inv. 1)

a. …, 8, 16, 24, ____, ____, ____, …

b. …, 8, 6, 4, ____, ____, ____, …

*26. Multiple Choice If $9 − \triangle = 4$, then which of these is *not* true?
(7)

A $9 − 4 = \triangle$ B $\triangle − 4 = 9$

C $4 + \triangle = 9$ D $\triangle + 4 = 9$

*27. The thermometer shows the low temperature on a cold
(18) winter day in Fargo, North Dakota. What was the low
temperature that day?

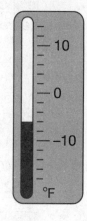

*28. (Represent) Write the expanded form of 709.
(16)

29. How many different arrangements of three letters can you
(3) write using the letters e, i, and o? The different arrangements
you write do not need to form words.

30. The numbers of goals three hockey players scored during their
(7) professional careers are shown in the table:

Career Goals Scored

Player	Number of Goals
Phil Esposito	717
Wayne Gretzky	894
Marcel Dionne	731

Write the number of goals scored from least to greatest.

Saxon Math Intermediate 4

Write and solve equations for problems **1** and **2**.

*1. **Formulate** A bakery employee baked seventy-two raisin muffins in
(11, 14) two batches. Twenty-four muffins were baked in the first batch. How
many muffins were baked in the second batch?

*2. Four hundred seventy-six people attended the Friday evening
(1, 13) performance of a school play. Three hundred ninety-seven people
attended the Saturday evening performance. Altogether, how many
people attended those performances?

3. The ones digit is 5. The tens digit is 6. The number is between 600 and
(4) 700. What is the number?

4. **Represent** Write 509 in expanded form. Then use words to write the
(7, 16) number.

*5. **Represent** Use digits and symbols to write this comparison:
(Inv. 1)
Negative twenty is less than ten.

*6. The temperature one winter day in Iron Mountain, Michigan,
(18) is shown on the thermometer. Write the temperature in
degrees Fahrenheit and in degrees Celsius.

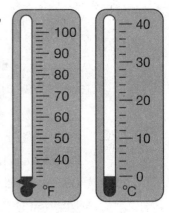

*7. **Connect** On Wednesday afternoons in September, flag
(19) football practice begins at the time shown on the clock and
ends at 5:40 p.m. How long is practice on those days?

*8. **Explain** Round each number to the nearest ten and explain how
(20) you rounded each number.

   a. 47   **b.** 74

9. $476
(13) + $285

10. $185
(13) + $499

11. 568
(13) + 397

12. 478
(13) + 196

13. 17
(12) − a
9

14. 14
(12) − b
14

15. 13
(12) − c
6

*16. $35
(15) − $28

*17. 23
(15) − 15

*18. 63
(15) − 36

*19. 74
(15) − 59

20. m
(14) + 22
45

*21. k
(16) − 15
32

*22. 47
(16) − k
34

23. 28
(17) 36
44
+ 58

24. 49
(17) 28
32
+ 55

*25. Round each amount of money to the nearest dollar:
(20)
    a. $25.67   **b.** $14.42

*26. Multiple Choice Which number sentence describes this model?
(7, 9)

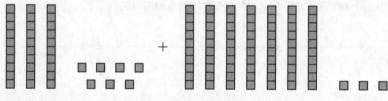

    A 307 + 703 = 1010   **B** 37 + 73 = 100
    C 37 + 73 = 110   **D** 37 + 73 = 1010

27. How many different arrangements of three letters can you write using
(3) the letters b, r, and z? Each letter may be used only once, and the
different arrangements you write do not need to form words.

*28. Round each amount of money to the nearest 25 cents:
(20)
    a. $7.28   **b.** $4.48

Saxon Math Intermediate 4

29. This table shows the land areas in square miles of four islands:
(7)

Islands of the World

Name	Location	Area (sq mi)
Micronesia	Pacific Ocean	271
Isle of Youth	Caribbean Sea	926
Isle of Man	Atlantic Ocean	227
Reunion	Indian Ocean	970

Write the names of the islands in order from greatest to least land area.

*30. **Formulate** Write and solve an addition word problem that has a
(1) sum of 18.

Write and solve equations for problems **1** and **2**.

1. Hiroshi had four hundred seventeen marbles. Harry had two hundred
(1, 13) twenty-two marbles. How many marbles did Hiroshi and Harry have
in all?

*2. Tisha put forty pennies into a pile. After Jane added all of her pennies,
(11, 14) there were seventy-two pennies in the pile. How many pennies did
Jane add to the pile?

3. The ones digit is 5. The number is greater than 640 and less than 650.
(4) What is the number?

*4. (Represent) Write seven hundred fifty-three in expanded form.
(16)

*5. (Connect) If $x + y = 10$, then what is the other addition fact for x, y,
(6) and 10? What are the two subtraction facts for x, y, and 10?

*6. These thermometers show the average daily low and high
(18) temperatures in San Juan, Puerto Rico, during the month
of January. What are those temperatures?

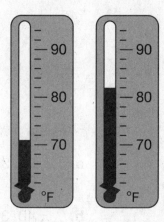

*7. (Model) Use a centimeter ruler to measure the rectangle below.
(Inv. 2)

   a. What is the length?

   b. What is the width?

   c. What is the perimeter?

Saxon Math Intermediate 4

Name _____

8. 493
(13) + 278
_____

9. $486
(13) + $378
_____

10. $524
(13) + $109
_____

*11. **Represent** Draw a triangle. Make each side 2 cm long. What is the
(Inv. 2, 21) perimeter of the triangle?

*12. **Represent** Draw a square with sides 2 inches long. What is the
(Inv. 2, 21) perimeter of the square?

13. 17
(12) − a
_____
9

14. 45
(15) − 29
_____

15. 15
(12) − b
_____
6

16. 62
(15) − 45
_____

17. 24
(14) + d
_____
45

18. 14
(16) − b
_____
2

*19. y
(16) − 36
_____
53

*20. 75
(16) − p
_____
45

21. 46
(17) 35
27
+ 39
_____

22. 14
(17) 28
77
+ 23
_____

23. 14
(17) 23
38
+ 64
_____

24. 15
(17) 24
36
+ 99
_____

*25. **Conclude** Write the next three numbers in each counting sequence:
(3, Inv. 1)

a. ..., 28, 35, 42, _____, _____, _____, ...

b. ..., 40, 30, 20, _____, _____, _____, ...

*26. **Explain** If you know the length and the width of a rectangle, how
(Inv. 2) can you find its perimeter?

*27. **Multiple Choice** Alba drew a circle with a radius of 4 cm. What was
(21) the diameter of the circle?

    A 8 in.   **B** 2 in.   **C** 8 cm   **D** 2 cm

*28. Each school morning, Christopher wakes up at the time shown on the left
(19) and leaves for school at the time shown on the right. What amount of time
does Christopher spend each morning getting ready for school?

*29. Round each number to the nearest ten. You may draw a number line.
(20)
    a. 76   **b.** 73   **c.** 75

*30. Round each amount of money to the nearest 25 cents.
(20)
    a. $6.77   **b.** $7.97

Real-World Connection

Erin and Bethany both drew circles on their paper. The radius of
Erin's circle is 14 cm. The diameter of Bethany's circle is 26 cm.
Bethany said that her circle is bigger. Was Bethany correct? Explain
your answer.

Saxon Math Intermediate 4

Write and solve equations for problems **1** and **2**.

*1. A carpenter has two boards. The sum of the lengths of the boards is
(11, 14) 96 inches. The length of one board is 48 inches. What is the length of
the other board?

2. Jafari was 49 inches tall at the beginning of summer. He grew 2 inches
(1, 9) over the summer. How tall was Jafari at the end of summer?

3. Use the digits 1, 2, and 3 to write an odd number less than 200. Each
(10) digit may be used only once.

Conclude Write the next three numbers in each counting sequence:

*4. . . . , 80, 72, 64, ____, ____, ____, . . .   ***5.** . . . , 60, 54, 48, ____, ____, ____,
(3)   (3)
. . .

*6. **Represent** Draw a square with sides 3 cm long. What is the perimeter
(Inv. 2, of the square?
21)

*7. A yard is how many feet long?
(Inv. 2)

8. What is the place value of the 9 in 891?
(4)

*9. Write 106 in expanded form. Then use words to write the number.
(7, 16)

10. Use the numbers 6, 9, and 15 to write two addition facts and two
(6) subtraction facts.

11. Use digits and symbols to write that eighteen is greater than negative
(Inv. 1) twenty.

*12. a. Round 28 to the nearest ten.   **b.** Round $5.95 to the nearest dollar.
(20)

*13. A desk is about how many meters high?
(Inv. 2)

*14. The first four odd numbers are 1, 3, 5, and 7. What is their sum?
(1)

*15. Draw a circle that has a diameter of 2 cm. What is the radius of the circle?
(21)

*16. What fraction of this rectangle is shaded?
(22)

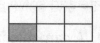

*17. The door was two meters tall. Two meters is how many centimeters?
(Inv. 2)

18. 51 − 43   **19.** 70 − 44   **20.** 37 − 9
(15)   (15)   (15)

21. $8.79 + $0.64   **22.** $5.75 + $2.75
(22)   (22)

23.   n   ***24.**   x   ***25.**   37
(14)   + 13   (16)   − 42   (16)   − p
       ―――   ―――   ―――
        17   27   14

*26. Sketch a circle. Draw two diameters to divide the circle into four
(22) equal parts. Shade one of the parts. What fraction of the circle is
      shaded?

*27. **Multiple Choice** If the equation 20 + n = 60 is true, then which of
(6)   the following equations is *not* true?

   A 60 − 20 = n   **B** 60 − n = 20
   C n − 20 = 60   **D** n + 20 = 60

*28. ✎ **Explain** One item in a supermarket is marked $1.26. Another
(22) item is marked $3.73. What is a reasonable estimate for the cost of
      both items? Explain why your estimate is reasonable.

29. This table shows the heights of four waterfalls:
(7)

Waterfalls

Name	Location	Height (ft)
Multnomah	Oregon	620
Maletsunyane	Lesotho, Africa	630
Wentworth	Australia	614
Reichenbach	Switzerland	656

Write the names of the waterfalls in order from least height to greatest
height.

*30. **Predict** What is the tenth number in this counting sequence?
(3)   4, 8, 12, 16, 20, …

54

Saxon Math Intermediate 4

Write and solve equations for problems **1** and **2**.

1. Twenty-eight children were in the first line. Forty-two children were in
(1, 9) the second line. Altogether, how many children were in both lines?

*2. Tina knew that there were 28 books in the two stacks. Tina counted
(11, 14) 12 books in the first stack. Then she figured out how many books were
in the second stack. How many books were in the second stack?

3. Use the digits 1, 2, and 3 to write an odd number greater than 300.
(10) Each digit may be used only once.

*4. **Conclude** Write the next three numbers in each counting sequence:
(3)

    a. ... , 40, 36, 32, ____, ____, ____, ...

    b. ... , 30, 27, 24, ____, ____, ____, ...

*5. **Connect** Use the numbers 15, 16, and 31 to write two addition facts
(6) and two subtraction facts.

6. Use digits and a comparison symbol to show that six hundred
(Inv. 1) thirty-eight is less than six hundred eighty-three.

*7. **a.** Round 92 to the nearest ten.
(20)

    b. Round $19.67 to the nearest dollar.

*8. **Explain** The radius of a nickel is 1 centimeter. If 10 nickels are placed
(21) in a row, how long will the row be? Describe how you found your answer.

*9. Use a centimeter ruler to measure this rectangle:
(Inv. 2)

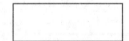

    a. What is the length?

    b. What is the width?

    c. What is the perimeter?

*10. **Multiple Choice** Which of these shapes has four right angles?
(23)

  A   **B**   **C**   **D**

*11. What fraction of this triangle is shaded?
(22)

*12. The clock shows the time that Reginald's last class of
(19) the day begins. The class ends at 2:55 p.m. How long is
Reginald's last class of the day?

*13. $83
(15) − $27

*14. 42
(15) − 27

*15. 72
(15) − 36

16. $4.28
(22) + $1.96

17. $4.36
(22) + $2.95

18. 57
(14) + k
——
88

*19. 67
(16) − b
——
16

*20. k
(16) − 22
——
22

21. 42 − 7
(15)

*22. 55 − 48
(15)

23. 31 − 20
(14)

24. 25 + 25 + 25 + 25
(17)

25. **a.** How many nickels equal one dollar?
(22)

b. One nickel is what fraction of a dollar?

c. Seven nickels are what fraction of a dollar?

*26. **Multiple Choice** If 26 + m = 63, then which of these equations is
(6) *not* true?

A m + 26 = 63   **B** m − 63 = 26

C 63 − m = 26   **D** 63 − 26 = m

*27. **Multiple Choice** Which of these figures illustrates a ray?
(23)

A ←——————→   **B** •——————•

C ←——————•   **D** ←——————→

←——————→

Saxon Math Intermediate 4

*28. (22) ✎ **Explain** A music store is having a sale. Single CDs cost $11.99 each. Double CDs cost $22.99 each. What is a reasonable estimate of the cost of 3 single CDs? Explain why your answer is reasonable.

29. (Inv. 1) Compare. Write >, <, or =.

a. 68 ◯ 71   b. 501 ◯ 267   c. 706 ◯ 709

*30. (11, 14) In the student council elections, 1300 votes were cast for the two candidates. One candidate received 935 votes. Write and solve an equation to find the number of votes the other candidate received.

*1. Rafael placed two 1-foot rulers end to end. What was the total length of
(Inv. 2) the two rulers in inches?

*2. During the one-hour television show, there were 12 minutes of
(11, 24) commercials. How many minutes of the hour were not commercials?
Write an equation.

*3. **Multiple Choice** All the students lined up in two equal rows. Which
(10) could *not* be the total number of students?

   A 36   **B** 45   **C** 60   **D** 24

*4. (Connect) Find the missing numbers in this counting sequence:
(3)

   . . . , 9, 18, ____, ____, 45, ____, . . .

*5. (Predict) Find the sixth number in this counting sequence:
(3, 5)

   7, 14, 21, . . .

6. Compare: 15 − 9 ◯ 13 − 8
(Inv. 1)

7. a. Round 77 to the nearest ten.
(20)

   b. Round $29.39 to the nearest dollar.

   c. Round $9.19 to the nearest 25 cents.

*8. (Estimate) A professional basketball player might be about how many
(Inv. 2) meters tall?

*9. Jeong and her friends attended an evening movie that
(19) began at the time shown on the clock. The movie ended
at 9:05 p.m. How long was the movie?

Saxon Math Intermediate 4

*10. (Conclude) Which street is parallel to Elm?
(23)

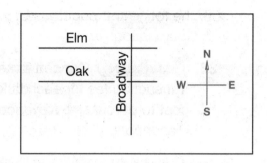

*11. a. How many dimes equal one dollar?
(22)

b. One dime is what fraction of a dollar?

c. Nine dimes are what fraction of a dollar?

*12. (Represent) Draw a rectangle that is 5 centimeters long and
(Inv. 2, 2 centimeters wide. What is the perimeter?
21)

*13. Describe each type of angle shown below:
(23)

a.   **b.**   **c.**

14. $31
(15) − $14

15. $468
(13) + $247

16. 57
(14) − 37

17. $4.97
(22) + $2.58

*18. $36 − c = 19$
(24)

19. $b + 65 = 82$
(24)

*20. $87 + d = 93$
(24)

*21. $n − 32 = 19$
(24)

22. $48 − 28$
(14)

23. $41 − 32$
(15)

24. $76 − 58$
(15)

25. $416 + 35 + 27 + 43 + 5$
(17)

*26. Multiple Choice Which point on this number line could represent −3?
(Inv. 1)

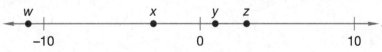

A point w   **B** point x   **C** point y   **D** point z

*27. (Explain) How is a segment different from a line?
(23)

*28. (Estimate) Concert tickets cost $18 each, not including a $4.25
(22) transaction fee for each ticket. What is a reasonable estimate of the
cost to purchase two concert tickets? Explain why your estimate is
reasonable.

29. The thermometer shows the high temperature on an
(18) April day in Nashville, Tennessee. What was the high
temperature that day?

*30. (Formulate) Write and solve an addition word problem
(1) that has a sum of 43.

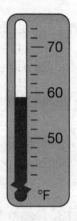

Saxon Math Intermediate 4

Formulate Write and solve equations for problems **1–3.**

*1. Barke had 75 stamps. Then he gave some stamps to Joey. Now he
(25) has 27 stamps. How many stamps did Barke give away?

*2. Rafiki had sixty-three baseball cards. He gave fourteen baseball cards
(25) to Amie. How many baseball cards does Rafiki have left?

*3. Mrs. Rushing had a package of lined cards. She used seventy-five
(25) cards in class last week. She has forty-seven cards left. How many
cards were in the package before last week?

4. There are 12 months in a whole year. How many months are in half of a
(5) year?

*5. **Connect** Find the missing numbers in each counting sequence:
(3,
Inv. 1)

    a. ..., 5, 10, ____, ____, 25, ____, ...

    b. ..., 5, 0, ____, ____, −15, ____, ...

*6. **Represent** Use digits and a comparison symbol to write that seven
(Inv. 1) hundred sixty-two is less than eight hundred twenty-six.

*7. a. Round 78 to the nearest ten.
(20)

    b. Round $7.80 to the nearest dollar.

    c. Round $7.80 to the nearest 25 cents.

*8. If the diameter of a wheel on Joshua's bike is 20 inches, then what is
(21) the radius of the wheel?

*9. The last recess of the afternoon at Taft Elementary School
(19) begins at the time shown on the clock. The recess ends
at 1:35 p.m. How long is the last recess of the afternoon?

*10. **Conclude** Which street is perpendicular
₍₂₃₎ to Elm?

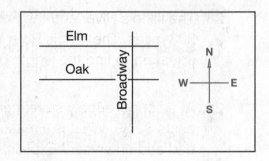

*11. What fraction of this shape is shaded?
₍₂₂₎

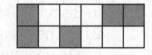

*12. Draw a square whose sides are 4 cm long. What is the perimeter of the
_(Inv. 2, 21) square?

*13. **Represent** To what number is the arrow pointing?
_(Inv. 1)

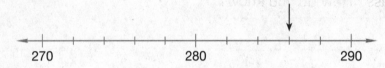

14. ₍₁₅₎	$52 − $14	**15.** ₍₁₃₎	476 + 177	**16.** ₍₁₅₎	62 − 38	**17.** ₍₂₂₎	$4.97 + $2.03

*18. ₍₂₄₎	36 − g	***19.** ₍₂₄₎	55 + b	***20.** ₍₂₄₎	d − 23	***21.** ₍₂₄₎	y + 14
	18		87		58		32

22. $42 − 37$
₍₁₅₎

23. $52 − 22$
₍₁₄₎

24. $73 − 59$
₍₁₅₎

25. $900 + 90 + 9$
₍₁₇₎

*26. Multiple Choice Which of these measurements is *not* equivalent to
_(Inv. 2) one meter?

   A 1000 mm   **B** 100 cm   **C** 1000 km   **D** 1 m

*27. **Explain** How is a ray different from a segment?
₍₂₃₎

   Saxon Math Intermediate 4

28. The Illinois River and the Potomac River have a combined length of
(11, 14) 803 miles. The Illinois River is 420 miles long. Write and solve an
equation to find the length of the Potomac River.

29. At a school supply store, pencil erasers cost 59¢ each. A drawing pad
(22) costs $3.39. What is a reasonable estimate of the total cost of a drawing
pad and an eraser? Explain why your estimate is reasonable.

30. In Bismarck, North Dakota, the average high temperature in January is
(18) 21°F. The average low temperature is −1°F. How many degrees warmer
is a temperature of 21°F than a temperature of −1°F?

*Real-World
Connection*

There were 119 third grade students, 121 fourth grade students and
135 fifth grade students in the auditorium. One hundred eighty-seven of
the students returned to class. Which number is greater, the number of
students still in the auditorium, or the number of students who returned
to class? How do you know?

Saxon Math Intermediate 4   **63**

Formulate Write and solve equations for problems **1–3.**

*1. Mandisa had 42 pebbles. She threw some into the lake. Then she had
(25) 27 pebbles left. How many pebbles did Mandisa throw into the lake?

*2. Dennis had a bag of pebbles. He put 17 pebbles on the ground. Then
(25) there were 46 pebbles left in the bag. How many pebbles were in the
bag before Dennis took some out?

*3. Salvador saw one hundred twelve stars. Eleanor looked the other way
(11, 13) and saw some more stars. If they saw three hundred seventeen stars
in all, how many did Eleanor see?

4. Use the digits 4, 5, and 6 to write an even number less than 500. Each
(4, 10) digit may be used only once. Which digit is in the tens place?

*5. **Represent** Draw a square and shade three fourths of it.
(26)

6. What is the perimeter of this triangle?
(Inv. 2)

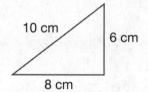

*7. **Represent** Use digits and symbols to show that negative twenty is
(Inv. 1) less than negative twelve.

8. a. Round 19 to the nearest ten.
(20)

    b. Round $10.90 to the nearest dollar.

9. One meter equals how many centimeters?
(Inv. 2)

10. This clock represents a time during a school day.
(19) Write the time.

Saxon Math Intermediate 4

Name _____

*11. **Conclude** Which street makes a right angle with Oak?
₍₂₃₎

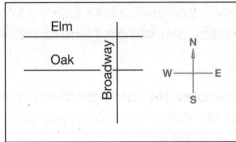

*12. What fraction of this figure is shaded?
₍₂₂₎

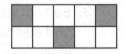

*13. The thermometer at right shows the average temperature during
₍₁₈₎ February in Galveston, Texas. What is that temperature?

*14. y
₍₂₄₎ $\underline{+\ 63}$
     81

15. $\$486$
₍₁₃₎ $\underline{+\ \$277}$

16. $\$68$
₍₁₅₎ $\underline{-\ \$39}$

17. $\$5.97$
₍₂₂₎ $\underline{+\ \$2.38}$

*18. $n + 42 = 71$
₍₂₄₎

*19. $87 - n = 65$
₍₂₄₎

*20. $27 + c = 48$
₍₂₄₎

*21. $e - 14 = 28$
₍₂₄₎

22. $42 - 29$
₍₁₅₎

23. $77 - 37$
₍₁₄₎

24. $41 - 19$
₍₁₅₎

25. $4 + 7 + 15 + 21 + 5 + 4 + 3$
₍₁₇₎

*26. Multiple Choice In which figure is $\frac{1}{2}$ *not* shaded?
₍₂₆₎

A   B   C   D

*27. **Conclude** Is the largest angle of this triangle acute, right, or
₍₂₃₎ obtuse?

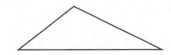

28. How many different three-digit numbers can you write using the digits
(10) 0, 7, and 3? Each digit may be used only once, and the digit 0 may
not be used in the hundreds place. Label the numbers you write as
even or odd.

*29. Estimate Is $14 a reasonable estimate for the sum of $5.45 and
(22) $8.59? Explain why or why not.

30. The numbers 8, 9, and 17 form a fact family. Write two addition facts
(6) and two subtraction facts using these three numbers.

*1. **Formulate** Just before noon Adriana saw seventy-eight people
(25) watching the game. At noon she saw only forty-two watching the
game. How many people had left the game by noon? Write an
equation and solve the problem.

*2. If each side of a square floor tile is one foot long, then
(Inv. 2, 21)   **a.** each side is how many inches long?

   b. the perimeter of the tile is how many inches?

*3. **List** Write the even numbers between 31 and 39.
(10)

Conclude Find the next three numbers in each counting sequence:

*4. ..., 12, 15, 18, ____, ____, ____, ...
(3)

*5. ..., 12, 24, 36, ____, ____, ____, ...
(3)

*6. **Represent** Write 265 in expanded form.
(16)

*7. **Represent** Use words to write –19.
(Inv. 1)

*8. **a.** Round 63 to the nearest ten.
(20)

   b. Round $6.30 to the nearest dollar.

   c. Round $6.30 to the nearest 25 cents.

9. Compare:
(Inv. 1)   **a.** 392 ◯ 329   **b.** – 15 ◯ – 20

10. To what number is the arrow pointing?
(Inv. 1)

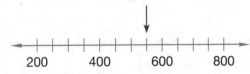

*11. Draw a square with sides 2 centimeters long. Then shade one fourth of
(21, 26)   the square.

*12. (22) ✎ **Explain** What fraction of this figure is shaded? Describe how you found your answer.

*13. (27) Aric plays percussion instruments in the school band. Band practice ends 3 hours after the time shown on the clock. What time does band practice end?

14. (15)
$$\begin{array}{r} \$67 \\ -\ \$29 \end{array}$$

15. (13)
$$\begin{array}{r} 483 \\ +\ 378 \end{array}$$

16. (15)
$$\begin{array}{r} 71 \\ -\ 39 \end{array}$$

17. (22)
$$\begin{array}{r} \$5.88 \\ +\ \$2.39 \end{array}$$

*18. (24)
$$\begin{array}{r} d \\ +\ 19 \\ \hline 36 \end{array}$$

*19. (24)
$$\begin{array}{r} 66 \\ +\ f \\ \hline 87 \end{array}$$

*20. (24)
$$\begin{array}{r} 87 \\ -\ r \\ \hline 67 \end{array}$$

*21. (24)
$$\begin{array}{r} b \\ -\ 14 \\ \hline 27 \end{array}$$

22. (14) $400 - 300$

23. (14) $663 - 363$

*24. (27) Change this addition problem to a multiplication problem:

$$9 + 9 + 9 + 9$$

*25. (22) **a.** One dollar equals how many pennies?

b. A penny is what fraction of a dollar?

c. Eleven pennies are what fraction of a dollar?

*26. (1) **Multiple Choice** If ⬜ = 3 and △ = 4, then what does ⬜ + △ + ⬜ equal?

   A 343   **B** 7   **C** 10   **D** 11

*27. (23) **Represent** Draw a dot on your paper to represent a point. Then, from that point, draw two perpendicular rays.

*28. (11, 14) **Formulate** Ronald Reagan was elected president in 1980 and again in 1984. During those elections, he won a total of 1014 electoral votes. In 1984, he won 525 electoral votes. Write and solve an equation to find the number of electoral votes Ronald Reagan won in 1980.

Saxon Math Intermediate 4

*29.  **Estimate** The cost of a new T-shirt is $15.95. Wendy would like
(22) to purchase two T-shirts. Is $40 a reasonable estimate for the cost of
her purchase? Explain why or why not.

30. Show six different ways to add 2, 4, and 6.
(1)

Early Finishers

Real-World Connection

Mr. Perez left work at 4:59 p.m. He stopped at the store for 15 minutes.
Then he drove for 24 minutes to get home.

a. What time did Mr. Perez arrive at his house?

b. How much time elapsed from the time Mr. Perez left work and the
time he arrived home?

c. Describe where the hands on the clock will be when Mr. Perez
gets home.

Formulate Write and solve equations for problems **1** and **2.**

*1. Seventy-two children attend the morning session at a preschool.
(1) Forty-two children attend the afternoon session. How many children attend those sessions altogether?

*2. Sherri needs $35 to buy a baseball glove. She has saved $18. How
(11, 24) much more does she need?

*3. **Represent** Draw a rectangle that is 4 cm long and 3 cm wide.
(Inv. 2, 21) What is the perimeter of the rectangle?

Connect Find the missing numbers in each counting sequence:

*4. ..., 12, ____, ____, 30, 36, ____, ...
(3)

*5. ..., 36, ____, ____, 24, 20, ____, ...
(3)

*6. **Connect** Change this addition problem to a multiplication problem.
(27, 28) Then find the product on the multiplication table shown in this lesson.

$$6 + 6 + 6 + 6 + 6 + 6 + 6$$

7. a. Round 28 to the nearest ten.
(20)

   b. Round $12.29 to the nearest dollar.

   c. Round $12.29 to the nearest 25 cents.

*8. **Represent** A *right triangle* has one right angle. Draw a right triangle.
(Inv. 2, 23) Draw the two perpendicular sides 3 cm long and 4 cm long.

*9. On Saturday morning, Mason went to the public library
(27) at the time shown on the clock. He arrived home
90 minutes later. What time did Mason arrive home from
the library?

Name _____

*10. What fraction of this group is shaded?
(22)

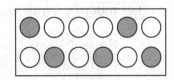

*11. (Represent) Write 417 in expanded form. Then use words to write the
(7, 16) number.

*12. a. What temperature is shown on this thermometer?
(18)

    b. If the temperature increases by ten degrees, what will the
    temperature be?

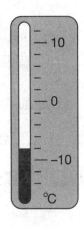

| **13.** (15) | 76 − 29 | **14.** (13) | $286 + $388 | **15.** (15) | $73 − $39 | **16.** (22) | $5.87 + $2.43 |

*17. 46 − c = 19
(24)

*18. n + 48 = 87
(24)

*19. 29 + y = 57
(24)

*20. d − 14 = 37
(24)

21. 78 − 43
(14)

22. 77 − 17
(14)

23. 53 − 19
(15)

*24. (Interpret) Use the multiplication table to find each product:
(28)
    a. 8 × 11   **b.** 7 × 10   **c.** 5 × 12

25. Compare: 1 yard ◯ 1 meter
(Inv. 1,
Inv. 2)

*26. Multiple Choice Which of the following shows 3 ones and
(4) 4 hundreds?

    A 304   **B** 403   **C** 4003   **D** 3400

*27. (Analyze) The product of 9 and 3 is 27. How many times does this
(28) product appear in this lesson's multiplication table? What property
of multiplication does this show?

*28. For a short distance, a cheetah can run at a speed of 70 miles per
(25) hour. An elk can run at a speed of 45 miles per hour. Write and solve
a subtraction equation to find the difference between the two animals'
speeds.

*29. 📝 **Estimate** During an online auction, D'Wayne bid $37 for one item
(20) and $54 for another item. If D'Wayne purchases both items at those
prices, what is a reasonable estimate of his total cost? Explain why
your estimate is reasonable.

30. **Predict** What is the tenth number in this counting sequence?
(3)

90, 80, 70, 60, 50, …

*Real-World
Connection*

Rebecca and her friend were placing pictures on pages of a scrapbook.
Rebecca put 6 pictures on five pages, and her friend put 5 pictures on
six pages. Did the girls have the same number of pictures? Explain how
you know.

Saxon Math Intermediate 4

Formulate Write and solve equations for problems **1** and **2.**

*1. Jasmine made ninety-two mums to sell at the school fundraiser. At the
(25) end of the fundraiser, twenty-four mums remained. How many mums
did Jasmine sell?

*2. Rochelle collected 42 seashells. Then Zuri collected some seashells.
(11, 24) They collected 83 seashells in all. How many seashells did Zuri
collect?

*3. Conner estimated that the radius of one of the circles on the
(Inv. 2, 21) playground was 2 yards. If Conner was correct, then

    a. the radius was how many feet?

    b. the diameter was how many feet?

Connect Find the missing numbers in each counting sequence:

4. ..., 8, ____, ____, 32, 40, ____, ...
(3)

5. ..., 14, ____, ____, 35, 42, ...
(3)

6. Use the digits 4, 5, and 6 to write a three-digit odd number less than
(10) 640. Each number may be used only once.

*7. **Represent** Use digits and a comparison symbol to write that
(Inv. 1) two hundred nine is greater than one hundred ninety.

*8. Fernando arrived home from school at the time shown
(27) on the clock. He snacked for 5 minutes, and then he
spent 35 minutes completing his homework. What time
did Fernando complete his homework?

*9. **Represent** Draw a rectangle 3 cm long and 1 cm wide. Then shade
(21, 26) two thirds of it.

*10. Find each product:
(28, 29)
    a. 2×8 **b.** 5×7 **c.** 2×7 **d.** 5×8

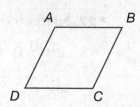
*11. **Conclude** In this figure, what type of angle is angle *A*?
(23) Explain how you know.

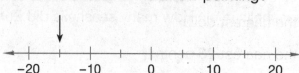

*12. **Connect** To what number is the arrow pointing?
(Inv. 1)

13. At what temperature does water freeze
(18)
    a. on the Fahrenheit scale?

    b. on the Celsius scale?

14. (15)	**15.** (13)	**16.** (15)	**17.** (22)
$83 − $19	$286 + $387	72 − 38	$5.87 + $2.79

*18. (24)	***19.** (24)	***20.** (24)	***21.** (24)
19 + *q* 46	88 − *n* 37	88 − *m* 47	*g* + 14 47

22. 870 − 470   **23.** 525 − 521
(14)   (14)

*24. **Connect** Change this addition problem to a multiplication problem.
(27, 28) Then find the product on the multiplication table.

$$8 + 8 + 8$$

25. 1 + 9 + 2 + 8 + 3 + 7 + 4 + 6 + 5 + 10
(1)

*26. Multiple Choice Which of these does *not* equal 24?
(28)
    A 3×8 **B** 4×6 **C** 2×12 **D** 8×4

Saxon Math Intermediate 4

Name _____

*27. Name the property of multiplication shown by each of these examples:
(28)

  a. $0 \times 50 = 0$

  b. $9 \times 6 = 6 \times 9$

  c. $1 \times 75 = 75$

28. a. Round $3.49 to the nearest dollar.
(20)

  b. Round $3.49 to the nearest 25 cents.

*29. (**Connect**) Write a multiplication equation that has a product of 18.
(28)

*30. Suppose $x + y = z$. Write one more addition and two subtraction
(24) equations using x, y, and z.

Formulate Write and solve equations for problems **1** and **2**.

*1. The room was full of students when the bell rang. Then forty-seven
(25) students left the room. Twenty-two students remained. How many
students were there when the bell rang? Use the subtraction formula
to write an equation and solve the problem.

*2. On Friday, 56 fourth grade students wore black shoes to school.
(11, 24) There are 73 fourth grade students in all. How many fourth grade
students did not wear black shoes to school on Friday?

*3. **Multiple Choice** A nickel is worth 5¢. Gilbert has an even number of
(10) nickels in his pocket. Which of the following could *not* be the value of
his nickels?

    A 45¢   **B** 70¢   **C** 20¢   **D** 40¢

*4. Jillian's social studies class ends 15 minutes later than
(27) the time shown on the clock. What time does Jillian's
class end?

*5. **Predict** What is the sixth number in this counting sequence?
(3)

               6, 12, 18, …

*6. **Represent** To what number is the arrow pointing?
(Inv. 1)

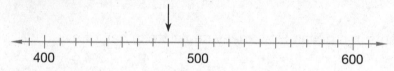

*7. **Model** Use a compass to draw a circle with a radius of 1 inch. Then
(21, 26) shade one fourth of the circle.

8. **Represent** Write 843 in expanded form. Then use words to write the
(7, 16) number.

*9. Multiply:
(28, 29)
    a. 6 × 8   **b.** 4 × 2   **c.** 4 × 5   **d.** 6 × 10

    Saxon Math Intermediate 4

*10. (Connect) Write two addition facts and two subtraction facts using the
(6) numbers 10, 20, and 30.

*11. (Model) Use a centimeter ruler to measure the rectangle below.
(Inv. 2)

    a. How long is the rectangle?

    b. How wide is the rectangle?

    c. What is the perimeter of the rectangle?

*12. (Conclude) What type of angle is each angle of a rectangle?
(23)

*13. (30)	**14.** (22)	**15.** (24)	***16.** (30)
746	$3.86	61	$4.86
− 295	+ $2.78	− 48	− $2.75

17. $51 + m = 70$
(24)

18. $86 − a = 43$
(24)

19. $25 + y = 36$
(24)

20. $q − 24 = 37$
(24)

21. (Explain) How can you round 89 to the nearest ten? Explain.
(20)

22. 25¢ + 25¢ + 25¢ + 25¢
(17)

23. There are 100 cents in a dollar. How many cents are in half of a
(22) dollar?

*24. (Represent) Change this addition problem to a multiplication problem.
(27, 28) Then find the product on the multiplication table.

$$7 + 7 + 7 + 7 + 7 + 7 + 7$$

25. $4 + 3 + 8 + 4 + 2 + 5 + 7$
(1)

*26. Multiple Choice Which of these sets of numbers is not an
(6)   addition/subtraction fact family?

   A 1, 2, 3   **B** 2, 3, 5   **C** 2, 4, 6   **D** 3, 4, 5

*27. Find each product on the multiplication table:
(28)   **a.** 10 × 10   **b.** 11 × 11   **c.** 12 × 12

*28. (Formulate) Write a subtraction word problem using the numbers
(2)   8, 10, and 18.

29. (Justify) Is $500 a reasonable estimate for the difference
(30) $749 − $259? Explain why or why not.

30. Suppose $a + b = c$. Write one more addition and two subtraction
(24)   equations using a, b, and c.

Real-World Connection

Paolo had $12.70. Then his mother paid him $3.25 for mopping. He
bought a paperback book that costs $4.99.

   a. Use compatible numbers to estimate how much money Paolo
   has now.

   b. Then find the actual amount of money Paolo has now.

   c. Was your estimate reasonable? Explain why or why not.

Saxon Math Intermediate 4

Formulate Write and solve equations for problems **1–3.**

*1. There were 43 parrots in the flock. Some flew away. Then there were
(25)   27 parrots in the flock. How many parrots flew away?

*2. One hundred fifty is how much greater than twenty-three?
(31)

*3. Twenty-three apples is how many fewer than seventy-five apples?
(31)

*4. On Saturday morning, Brady awoke at the time
(27)   shown on the clock. Three hours later, he left home
       to go to softball practice. What time did Brady leave
       home?

*5. **Represent** Write 412 in expanded form. Then use words to write the
(7, 16) number.

6. What fraction of this figure is shaded?
(22)

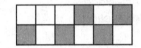

*7. The rectangle shown at right is 4 cm long and 2 cm
(Inv. 2, wide.
Inv. 3)

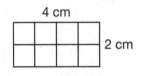

4 cm

2 cm

   a. What is the perimeter?

   b. What is the area?

8. Multiply:
(28, 29)

   a. 2 × 5   **b.** 5 × 7   **c.** 2 × 7   **d.** 4 × 11

*9. **Connect** Write two addition facts and two subtraction facts using the
(6)   numbers 20, 30, and 50.

10. At 8 p.m. the temperature was 3°C. By 8 a.m. the next morning, the
(18)   temperature had fallen 8 degrees. What was the temperature at
       8 a.m.?

Saxon Math Intermediate 4 **79**

*11. The number represented by point *A* is how much less than the number
(31) represented by point *B*?

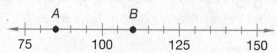

A   B
←—|—|—•—|—|—|—•—|—|—|—|—|—|—|—|—→
   75   100   125   150

12. Multiply:
(28, 29)

    a. 5×8 **b.** 2×8 **c.** 5×9

13. a. How many quarters equal one dollar?
(22)

    b. A quarter is what fraction of a dollar?

    c. Three quarters are what fraction of a dollar?

*14. (**Represent**) Use digits and symbols to write this comparison:
(Inv. 1)
    Three hundred nine is less than three hundred ninety.

*15. Three hundred nine is how much less than 390?
(31)

*16. $4.22   ***17.**   909   ***18.** $422   ***19.**   703
(30)   − $2.95   (30)   − 27   (30)   − $144   (30)   − 471

20. $4.86   **21.**   370   **22.**   22   **23.**   76
(22)   + $2.95   (30)   − 209   (24)   + *n*   (24)   − *c*
                                               37   28

*24. (**Connect**) What multiplication fact is illustrated by this
(Inv. 3) square?

*25. Find each square root:
(Inv. 3)

    a. $\sqrt{9}$ **b.** $\sqrt{25}$

*26. Multiple Choice Which of these does *not* equal 9?
(Inv. 3)
    A 3 squared   **B** $\sqrt{81}$

    C $\sqrt{18}$ **D** $\sqrt{25} + \sqrt{16}$

     Saxon Math Intermediate 4

27. Multiply:
(28,
Inv. 3)
    a. 1×1 **b.** 5×5 **c.** 8×8 **d.** 9×9

28. Compare. Write $>$, $<$, or $=$.
(Inv. 1)
    a. 510 ◯ 501   **b.** 722 ◯ 976   **c.** 234 ◯ 238

*29. **Estimate** The land area of Aztec Ruins National Monument in New
(13, 22) Mexico is 318 acres. The land area of Casa Grande Ruins National
Monument in Arizona is 473 acres. What is a reasonable estimate of
the total acreage of these two national monuments? Explain why your
estimate is reasonable.

*30. **Classify** Name each figure:
(23)

a.

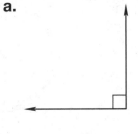

b.

c.

d.

Tricia outlined two rectangles on her paper. Rectangle *A* measured
4 cm by 6 cm, and rectangle *B* measured 5 cm by 5 cm. Use 1-cm
Real-World grid paper or a centimeter ruler to draw both rectangles. Then find the
Connection area of each rectangle. Which rectangle has the larger area? Use the
larger − smaller = difference formula.

*1. **(Formulate)** There are two hundred fifteen pages in the book. Kande
(25) has read eighty-six pages. How many more pages are left to read?
Write and solve an equation.

2. Use the digits 7, 8, and 9 to make an even number greater than 800.
(10) Use each digit only once.

3. **(Compare)** Use digits and a comparison symbol to show that four
(Inv. 1) hundred eighty-five is less than six hundred ninety.

*4. **(Conclude)** This is a sequence of square numbers. What are the
(3, next three numbers in the sequence? How do you know?
Inv. 3)

$$1, 4, 9, 16, \underline{\quad}, \underline{\quad}, \underline{\quad}, \ldots$$

5. One evening Jermaine finished washing the dishes at the
(19) time shown on the clock. What time did Jermaine finish
washing the dishes?

*6. **(Represent)** Write 729 in expanded form and use words to write the number.
(7, 16)

*7. **(Connect)** Change this addition problem to a multiplication problem.
(27, 28) Then find the product on the multiplication table.

$$6 + 6 + 6 + 6 + 6 + 6 + 6$$

8. Is the value of three nickels and two dimes an even number of cents or
(10) an odd number of cents?

9. a. Round 66 to the nearest ten.
(20)

b. Round $6.60 to the nearest dollar.

c. Round $6.60 to the nearest 25 cents.

10. a. Use a metric ruler to measure the length of each side of
(Inv. 2) this square in centimeters.

b. What is the perimeter of the square?

Saxon Math Intermediate 4

Name _____

*11. **Analyze** Which two uppercase letters are formed with only
(23)   two perpendicular line segments?

12. If $62 - w = 48$, then what is the value of w?
(24)

13. What fraction of this rectangle is shaded?
(22)

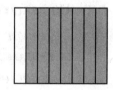

*14. **Represent** Draw an array of Xs to show the multiplication 5×5.
(Inv. 3)

*15. **Represent** The number represented by point B is how much greater
(31)   than the number represented by point A?

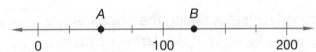

Multiply:

*16. **a.** 9×6 **b.** 9×8 **c.** 9×4 **d.** 9×10
(32)

*17. **a.** 6×6 **b.** 4×4 **c.** 7×7 **d.** 10×10
(Inv. 3)

*18. **a.** 2×11 **b.** 8×11 **c.** 5×11 **d.** 3×11
(32)

*19. **Represent** **a.** What multiplication fact is illustrated
(Inv. 3)   by this square?

   b. Find $\sqrt{25}$.

*20. $\sqrt{81}$ ***21.** $3.60 - $1.37   ***22.** $413 - 380$
(Inv. 3)   (30)   (30)

*23. $875 - 218$ **24.** Compare: $24 + 36 \bigcirc 12 + 48$
(30)   (Inv. 1)

*25. What number equals 8 squared?
(Inv. 3)

*26. Multiple Choice Jacob saw an array of freshly baked rolls on a pan.
(25, Inv. 3) There were four rows of rolls with four rolls in each row. How many rolls will be left on the pan if he eats one roll?

A 3 **B** 7 **C** 12 **D** 15

*27. Which property of multiplication does this story illustrate?
(28, Inv. 3)
> *Twenty-four desks were arranged in 4 rows with 6 desks in each row. Then they were moved into 6 rows with 4 desks in each row.*

*28. (Formulate) In 2000, a professional baseball pitcher struck out
(13) 347 batters and another professional pitcher struck out 284 batters. Write and solve an equation to find the total number of batters the two pitchers struck out.

*29. (Estimate) The average depth of the East China Sea is 620 feet. The
(30) average depth of the Yellow Sea is 121 feet. Estimate the difference between the two average depths. Explain why your estimate is reasonable.

*30. (Predict) Write the sixth term of each pattern:
(32) **a.** 11, 22, 33, 44, 55, … **b.** 12, 24, 36, 48, 60, …

Saxon Math Intermediate 4

*1. Marcos is reading a book with 211 pages. K'Neesha is reading a
book with 272 pages. How many more pages will K'Neesha read than
Marcos? Write and solve an equation.
(31)

*2. **Represent** Write the number 3425 in expanded form. Then use words
(16, 33) to write the number.

*3. **Represent** Draw two parallel lines. Then draw a perpendicular line that
(23) makes right angles where it intersects the parallel lines.

*4. The square root of 49 is how much less than four squared?
(Inv. 3, 31)

*5. **Represent** On 1-cm grid paper, draw a 6 cm by 2 cm rectangle.
(Inv. 2, Inv. 3)

    a. What is the perimeter of the rectangle?

    b. What is the area of the rectangle?

*6. Place commas in 250000. Then use words to write the number.
(33)

*7. **Conclude** What are the next four numbers in this counting sequence?
(3)

        . . . , 230, 240, 250, 260, ____, ____, ____, ____, . . .

*8. Which digit in 123,456 is in the ten-thousands place?
(33)

9. Compare: $9 \times 4 \bigcirc \sqrt{36}$
(Inv. 1, Inv. 3)

*10. After school yesterday, Luis began playing outside at the
(27) time shown on the clock. He played for 2 hours 25 minutes.
What time did Luis finish playing outside?

*11. **Represent** To what number is the arrow pointing?
(Inv. 1)

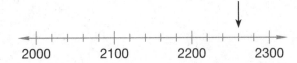

Name _____

Multiply:

*12. **a.** 5×8 **b.** 4×4 **c.** 8×8 **d.** 12×12
(29, Inv. 3)

*13. **a.** 9×3 **b.** 9×4 **c.** 9×5 **d.** 9×10
(29, 32)

*14. (Connect) Write two addition facts and two subtraction facts using the
(6) numbers 40, 60, and 100.

15. (Connect) Change this addition problem to a multiplication problem:
(27)

$$20 + 20 + 20 + 20 + 20$$

*16. $7.37
(30) $− $2.68

*17.   921
(30) $−$ 58

18.   464
(13) $+$ 247

*19.   329
(24, 30) $+$ z
   547

20. $4.88
(22) $+$ $2.69

*21.   555
(24) $−$ c
   222

22. Judy's birth date is 5/27/98. In which month was she born?
(5)

23. (Represent) Draw a circle with a radius of 1 inch. What is the diameter
(21) of the circle? Explain how you know.

24.   4
(17)   8
   12
   16
   14
   28
   + 37

25.   5
(17)   8
   7
   14
   6
   21
   + 15

*26. Compare: 25,000 ◯ 250,000
(33)

This page may not be reproduced without permission of Harcourt Achieve Inc.

Saxon Math Intermediate 4

*27. Multiple Choice Look at the sequence below. Which of the following
(Inv. 3)
numbers is *not* in the sequence?

$$1, 4, 9, 16, 25, 36, \ldots$$

A 64   **B** 49

C 80   **D** 100

*28. (**Formulate**) The state of Kentucky had 189 public libraries in 2006. The
(13)
state of Maryland had 176 public libraries. Write and solve an equation
to find the number of public libraries Kentucky and Maryland had
altogether.

*29. Eight feet is how many inches? Count by 12s.
(Inv. 2,
32)

*30. Nine centimeters is how many millimeters? Count by 10s.
(Inv. 2,
32)

Formulate Write and solve equations for problems **1** and **2.**

*1. Four hundred sixty-five is how much greater than twenty-four?
(31)

*2. Marcie had four hundred twenty marbles. Kareem had one hundred
(31) twenty-three marbles. How many fewer marbles did Kareem have?

*3. **Represent** On 1-cm grid paper, draw a square that is 4 cm on
(Inv. 2, each side.
Inv. 3)

   a. What is the perimeter of the square?

   b. What is the area of the square?

*4. **Represent** Write the number 25,463 in expanded form.
(16, 33)

5. **Represent** Draw a circle that has a diameter of 4 centimeters.
(21) What is the radius of the circle?

6. Jharma arrived home from school at the time shown on the
(27) clock and finished her homework 1 hour 35 minutes later.
What time did Jharma finish her homework?

7. **Explain** What fraction of the circles is shaded? Describe
(22) how you found your answer.

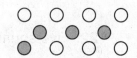

8. **Connect** Change this addition problem to a multiplication problem.
(27, 29) Then find the product.

$$12 + 12 + 12 + 12 + 12$$

*9. **Estimate** Round 76 to the nearest ten. Round 59 to the nearest ten.
(20) Then add the rounded numbers.

10. Compare:
(Inv. 1,
34)   **a.** 3 ◯ −4   **b.** two million ◯ 200,000

Saxon Math Intermediate 4

*11. The number represented by point *A* is how much less than the number
(31) represented by point *B*?

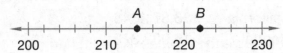

```
              A        B
   +--+--+--+--+--+--+--+--+--+--+--+-->
  200        210       220       230
```

Multiply:

12. **a.** 5 × 7   **b.** 6 × 6   **c.** 9 × 9   **d.** 10 × 10
(29,
Inv. 3)

13. **a.** 3 × 9   **b.** 9 × 7   **c.** 8 × 9   **d.** 9 × 1
(29, 32)

14. **a.** 11 × 11   **b.** 6 × 12   **c.** 8 × 11   **d.** 10 × 12
(32)

*15. **a.** (Represent) Use words to write 3,500,000.
(34, 33)

  b. (Represent) Use digits to write seven hundred fifty thousand.

*16.   535   ***17.**   908   ***18.** $471
(30)   − 268   (30)   − 43   (30)   − $346

*19. $c + 329 = 715$ **20.** $c - 127 = 398$
(24, 30)   (24)

21. If the radius of a circle is 12 inches, then the diameter of the circle is
(Inv. 2,
21) how many feet?

*22. Five squared is how much more than 5 + 5?
(Inv. 3,
31)

*23. (Connect) Select two odd numbers and one even number that form
(6, 10) an addition/subtraction fact family. Then use the numbers to write two
  addition facts and two subtraction facts.

*24. $\sqrt{9} + \sqrt{16}$
(Inv. 3)

25. (Represent) Draw a triangle that has one obtuse angle.
(23)

*26. **Multiple Choice** Which digit in 3,756,289 is in the thousands
(34) place?

  A 3   **B** 7   **C** 5   **D** 6

*27. In the year 2000, the four most populous U.S. states and their
(34) populations were:

California	33,871,648
Florida	15,982,378
New York	18,976,457
Texas	20,851,820

These states are listed in alphabetical order. List the names of the states
in order of population, beginning with the greatest population.

*28. (**Predict**) What is the twelfth term in this counting sequence?
(3, 32)

11, 22, 33, 44, …

*29. (**Predict**) What is the eighth term in this counting sequence?
(3, 32)

12, 24, 36, 48, …

*30. (**Estimate**) M'Lisa would like to purchase about 100 balloons for
(20, 22) her birthday party. One bag of 25 balloons costs $2.49. What is a
reasonable estimate of M'Lisa's cost to purchase about 100 balloons?
Explain why your estimate is reasonable.

Write and solve equations for problems **1–3.**

*1. Thirty-seven nations sent athletes to the 1968 Winter Olympics in
(31) Grenoble, France. Thirty years later, seventy-two nations sent athletes
to the 1998 Winter Olympics in Nagano, Japan. How many more
nations sent athletes in 1998 than in 1968?

*2. ✏️ **Explain** Every morning Mario runs around the block. The block is
(Inv. 2) 300 yards long and 100 yards wide. How many yards does Mario run
when he runs around the block? Did you find the perimeter or area of
the block? Explain your answer.

3. Ninety-seven oranges were in the first bunch, fifty-seven oranges were in
(1, 17) the second bunch, and forty-eight oranges were in the third bunch. How
many oranges were in all three bunches?

*4. What mixed number is pictured in this figure?
(35)

5. Armena had four dollars and sixty-five cents. Use a dollar sign and a
(35) decimal point to write this amount.

6. The thermometer shows the high temperature for
(18) one winter day in Fairlawn, Ohio. What was the high
temperature that day?

7. Multiple Choice Which of these angles does *not* look like a right
(23) angle?

   A   **B**   **C**   **D**

*8. The square root of 81 is how much less than seven squared?
(Inv. 3,
31)

*9. On Saturday night, ShayZee fell asleep at the time shown
(27) on the clock. Two hours twenty minutes later, ShayZee
woke up. What time did ShayZee wake up?

*10. **Represent** Use words to write $2\frac{3}{10}$.
(35)

*11. Find the numbers represented by point *A* and point *B*. Then find the
(31) difference.

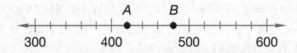

300   400   500   600

*12. **Represent** Use words to write $1.43.
(35)

Multiply:

13. **a.** 6×9 **b.** 4×9 **c.** 3×9 **d.** 10×9
(32)

14. **a.** 6×6 **b.** 7×7 **c.** 8×8 **d.** 11×11
(Inv. 3)

15. $\sqrt{25} - \sqrt{16}$
(Inv. 3)

*16. **Represent** Draw a rectangle that is 3 cm long and 3 cm wide. Divide
(21, 26) the rectangle into thirds and shade   of it.

*17. $6.05
(30) $- 2.53

*18.   489
(24, 30) $+ \quad z$
           766

19. $5.32
(22) $+ 3.44

*20.   *c*
(24, 30) $+ 294$
           870

*21.   423
(30) $- 245$

22.   670
(24, 30) $- \quad z$
           352

*23. **Represent** Use digits to write two hundred fifty million.
(34)

Saxon Math Intermediate 4

*24. (Conclude) What are the next three numbers in this counting sequence?
(3)

..., 3400, 3500, 3600, 3700, ____, ____, ____, ...

25. **a.** Round 77 to the nearest ten.
(20)

b. Round $6.82 to the nearest dollar.

*26. **Multiple Choice** If $7 + \square = 10$, then which of the following numbers
(1, 6) equals $7 - \square$?

A 3   **B** 4   **C** 7   **D** 10

*27. Compare:
(33, 35)

    a. thirty thousand ◯ 13,000

    b. 74¢ ◯ $0.74

*28. Write these numbers in order from greatest to least:
(33, 34)

    125 thousand   125 million   12,500,000

*29. (Predict) Write the twelfth term of each pattern below:
(32)

    a. 11, 22, 33, 44, ...

    b. 12, 24, 36, 48, ...

*30. Name a real-world example of
(23)

    a. parallel lines.

    b. perpendicular lines.

Real-World Connection

The school choir is having a car wash to raise money to buy new songbooks. Each car wash will cost 350¢.

    a. Write this money amount using a dollar sign and a decimal point.

    b. Draw and shade circles to represent $3\frac{1}{2}$ as a mixed number.

    c. Use words to write $3\frac{50}{100}$.

Formulate Write and solve equations for problems **1–3**.

*1. Quinh is 49 inches tall. His dad is 70 inches tall. Quinh is how many
(31) inches shorter than his dad?

*2. Smith went into the store with $36.49. He bought a book and left
(25) the store with $11.80. How much money did Smith spend in the
store?

*3. Beth answered eleven of the twenty-five questions at school. She
(24) answered the rest of the questions as homework. How many questions
did Beth answer as homework?

*4. Write the number of shaded rectangles shown as a mixed
(35) number.

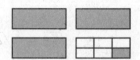

*5. **Verify** Which letter below appears to have no right angles?
(23)

T   H   E   N

*6. **Represent** Use words to write 2,700,000.
(34)

*7. **Represent** Use digits to write eighty-two thousand, five hundred.
(33)

8. Each day, classes at Kennedy Elementary School end
(27) 4 hours 20 minutes later than the time shown on the clock.
What time do classes end each day?

9. **Connect** Change this addition problem to a multiplication problem:
(27)

$$4 + 4 + 4 + 4 + 4 + 4 + 4 + 4$$

10. a. Round 176 to the nearest ten.
(20)

b. Round $17.60 to the nearest dollar.

*11. **Represent** The number represented by point X is how much less than
(31) the number represented by point Y?

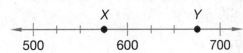

Multiply:

12. **a.** 2×8 **b.** 5×6 **c.** 4×5 **d.** 5×8
(29)

13. **a.** 3×3 **b.** 5×5 **c.** 9×9 **d.** 10×10
(Inv. 3)

14. **a.** 9×7 **b.** 9×4 **c.** 9×8 **d.** 9×12
(32)

15. $\sqrt{36} + \sqrt{49}$
(Inv. 3)

*16. $\$7.32$ **17.** $\$4.89$ ***18.** 464
(30) $- \$3.45$ (22) $+ \$2.57$ (30) $- 238$

19. 548 ***20.** 487 ***21.** 250
(13) $+ 999$ (24, 30) $+ \quad z$ (24, 30) $- \quad c$
                         721 122

22. $c - 338 = 238$ **23.** $87 - b = 54$
(24)   (24)

*24. Which digit in 8,367,254 is in the ten-thousands place?
(34)

*25. **Multiple Choice** Which of the money amounts below does *not* equal
(36) one half of a dollar?

     A 2 quarters   **B** 0.50¢   **C** $0.50   **D** 50¢

*26. **Multiple Choice** If a rectangle is 5 in. long and 4 in. wide, then its
(Inv. 3) area is _____.

     A 9 in.   **B** 18 in.   **C** 20 sq. in.   **D** 18 sq. in.

27. Compare:
(Inv. 1, 36)
     a. $-12 \bigcirc -21$ **b.** $\frac{1}{4}$ of a dollar $\bigcirc$ $0.25

28. **(Predict)** Write the tenth term of each pattern below:
(32)

    a. 12, 24, 36, 48, 60, …

    b. 11, 22, 33, 44, 55, …

*29. Look at these bills:
(36)

List all of the different ways to pair two bills.

30. **(Estimate)** The state of Louisiana has 397 miles of coastline. The state
(20) of Oregon has 296 miles of coastline. What is a reasonable estimate of
the combined length of those coastlines? Explain why your estimate is
reasonable.

Early Finishers
Real-World Connection

Maria had a quarter, a dime, and a nickel in her pocket. How much
money did Maria have in her pocket?

    a. Write the amount as a fraction of a dollar.

    b. Write the value of the coins using a dollar sign and a decimal
point.

    c. Compare the amount to $\frac{1}{2}$ of a dollar.

Saxon Math Intermediate 4

Formulate Write and solve equations for problems **1** and **2**.

*1. The Pearl River in Mississippi is 411 miles long. The San Juan River
(31) in Colorado is 360 miles long. How many miles longer is the Pearl
River?

*2. If the length of the Sabine River in Texas were 50 miles longer, it would
(11, 24) be the same length as the Wisconsin River. The Wisconsin River is
430 miles long. How long is the Sabine River?

*3. **Represent** Use digits to write four hundred seventy-five thousand,
(33) three hundred forty-two. Then circle the digit in the ten-thousands
place.

4. **Explain** Leah wants to put square floor tiles that measure one foot
(Inv. 3) on each side in a room that is 9 feet long and 9 feet wide. How many
floor tiles will Leah need? Is your answer reasonable? Explain why.

*5. **Represent** To what mixed number is the arrow pointing?
(37)

*6. **Represent** Draw a rectangle whose length is 5 cm and whose width
(Inv. 2, 21) is 3 cm. What is the perimeter of the rectangle?

*7. What mixed number is shown by the shaded rectangles?
(35)

*8. **Represent** Use words to write $12\frac{3}{10}$.
(35)

*9. **Represent** Write 7026 in expanded form. Then use words to write the
(16, 33) number.

10. On the morning of an important game, Gail woke up at the
(27) time shown on the clock. She wanted to wake up 2 hours
35 minutes later. What time did Gail want to wake up?

*11. a. Three quarters are what fraction of a dollar?
(36)

    b. Write the value of three quarters using a dollar sign and a decimal point.

12. (**Connect**) What multiplication fact is illustrated by this rectangle?
(Inv. 3)

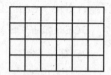

Multiply for problems **13–15.**

13. a. 9×6 **b.** 9×5 **c.** 9×0
(29, 32)

14. a. 10×10 **b.** 7×7 **c.** 8×8
(Inv. 3)

15. a. 5×7 **b.** 6×5 **c.** 2×8
(29)

16. $\sqrt{81} + \sqrt{49}$ ***17.** $6.63 - 3.55$
(Inv. 3)   (30)

18. $4.99 + 2.88$ **19.** $a - 247 = 321$
(22)   (24)

*20. $z + 296 = 531$ ***21.** $523 - z = 145$
(24, 30)   (24, 30)

22. $28 + 46 + 48 + 64 + 32 + 344$
(17)

*23. a. (**Conclude**) What are the next three numbers in this counting sequence?
(3)

        …, 450, 460, 470, 480, ____, ____, ____, …

    b. (**Generalize**) What is one rule for this sequence?

24. If the diameter of a circle is one foot, then the radius of the circle is how many inches?
(Inv. 2, 21)

*25. Compare:
(33, 36)

    a. $\frac{1}{4}$ of a dollar $\bigcirc$ $\frac{1}{2}$ of a dollar

    b. 101,010 $\bigcirc$ 110,000

Saxon Math Intermediate 4

Name _____

*26. **Multiple Choice** One yard does *not* equal which of the following?
(Inv. 2)

A 36 in.	**B** 3 ft
C 1 m	**D** 2 ft + 12 in.

*27. In the year 2000, the four least populous U.S. states and their
(33) populations were as follows:

Alaska	626,932
North Dakota	642,200
Vermont	608,827
Wyoming	493,782

List these states in order of population size, beginning with the smallest population.

*28. *Justify* An adult cheetah weighs about 130 pounds. An adult
(13) mountain lion weighs about 170 pounds. A student estimates that a mountain lion weighs about twice as much as a cheetah. Is the estimate reasonable? Explain why or why not.

29. For a very short distance, a world-class sprinter can run at a speed of
(20) about 23 miles per hour. Round that speed to the nearest ten miles per hour.

*30. In Barrow, Alaska, the average maximum temperature in July is 47°F. The
(18) average minimum temperature is 34°F. How many degrees cooler is a temperature of 34°F compared to a temperature of 47°F?

Saxon Math Intermediate 4 **99**

1. **(Formulate)** There were two hundred twenty boats on the river. There
(31) were four hundred five boats in the harbor. How many more boats were
in the harbor? Write and solve an equation.

*2. **(Represent)** Five hundred seventy-five thousand, five hundred forty-
(33) two people lived in the city. Use digits to write that number of people.

*3. **(Represent)** Write 2503 in expanded form. Then use words to write the
(16, 33) number.

*4. **(Model)** On 1-cm grid paper, draw a rectangle 6 cm long and 4 cm
(Inv. 2, Inv. 3) wide.

    a. What is the perimeter of the rectangle?

    b. What is the area of the rectangle?

*5. **(Represent)** To what mixed number is the arrow pointing?
(37)

6. **(Conclude)** Which street is parallel to Broad
(23) Street?

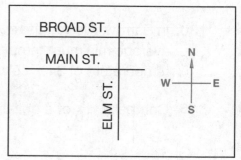

*7. What mixed number is shown by the shaded circles?
(35)

8. **a.** Round 624 to the nearest ten.
(20)

    b. Round $6.24 to the nearest dollar.

    c. Round $6.24 to the nearest 25 cents.

Saxon Math Intermediate 4

Name _____

9. On a school day, Alberto finishes eating breakfast
(19) every morning at the time shown on the clock. He
starts eating lunch at 12:30 p.m. How long after Alberto
finishes eating breakfast does he start eating lunch?

*10. a. (**Connect**) Fifty cents is what fraction of a dollar?
(36)

b. Write the value of fifty cents using a dollar sign and a decimal point.

11. (**Represent**) Use words to write $2\frac{11}{100}$.
(35)

*12. (**Connect**) This square illustrates six squared. What
(Inv. 3) multiplication fact is illustrated by the square?

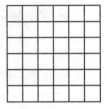

Multiply:

*13. a. 3×4 **b.** 3×6 **c.** 3×8
(38)

*14. a. 4×6 **b.** 4×7 **c.** 4×8
(38)

*15. a. 6×7 **b.** 6×8 **c.** 7×8
(38)

*16. Compare: $\frac{1}{10}$ of a dollar $\bigcirc$ $\frac{1}{2}$ of a dollar
(36)

17. $7.23
(30) $- \$2.54$

18. $5.42
(22) $+ \$2.69$

19. 943
(30) $- 276$

20. $z - 581 = 222$
(24)

21. $c + 843 = 960$
(24)

22. If the radius of a circle is 100 cm, then the diameter of the circle is how
(Inv. 2, 21) many meters?

23. $28 + 36 + 78 + \sqrt{49}$
(17, Inv. 3)

*24. $\sqrt{144} - \sqrt{121}$
(Inv. 3, 32)

Saxon Math Intermediate 4   © Harcourt Achieve Inc. and Stephen Hake. All rights reserved.   **101**

*25. **Multiple Choice** Which of the following is *not* $\frac{1}{10}$ of a dollar?
(36)

    A dime   **B** 0.10¢   **C** $0.10   **D** 10¢

*26. **Multiple Choice** Which digit in 457,326,180 is in the hundred-
(34) thousands place?

    A 1   **B** 6   **C** 4   **D** 3

27. (**Conclude**) Name and describe each angle below.
(23)

    a.   **b.**   **c.**

*28. Consider the sequence 12, 24, 36, 48, ….
(3)

    a. (**Generalize**) Write a rule that describes how to find the
    next term of the sequence.

    b. (**Predict**) What is the eleventh term of the sequence?

29. (**Estimate**) Mrs. Rojas would like to purchase a CD that costs
(20) $14.99 and a DVD that costs $18.95 for the school library. What is a
reasonable estimate of the amount of money she will spend? Explain
why your estimate is reasonable.

*30. The table below shows the cost of tickets to a game. Use the table to
(38) help find the cost of tickets for a family of six.

Number of Tickets	1	2	3	4
Cost	$11	$22	$33	$44

Real-World Connection

Yolanda planted eleven flowers in each of 12 rows. How many flowers
did she plant? Draw a table and complete it to show the number of
flowers in 12 rows.

Saxon Math Intermediate 4

1. **Explain** Trinity is twelve years old. Trinity's mother is thirty-five years
(31) old. Trinity's mother is how many years older than Trinity? Describe this
type of word problem.

* **2.** Four hundred sixty-eight thousand, five hundred two boxes were in the
(33) warehouse. Use digits to write that number of boxes.

* **3.** **Represent** Write the number 3905 in expanded form. Then use words
(16, 33) to write the number.

4. **Verify** J'Maresh collected two hundred forty-three aluminum cans
(10, 13) while volunteering at the recycling center. Leilani collected three
hundred sixty-four aluminum cans. Was the total number of cans
collected an even number or an odd number?

* **5.** **Represent** Use words to write $100\frac{1}{100}$.
(35)

6. **Represent** Use digits and symbols to show that negative nineteen is
(Inv. 1) greater than negative ninety.

* **7.** **Connect** Use a dollar sign and a decimal point to write the value of
(35) two dollars, one quarter, two dimes, and three nickels.

8. The clock shows the time that Brayden arrived at school.
(27) School begins at 8:15 a.m. Was Brayden early or late for
school? How many minutes early or late was he?

9. **Connect** **a.** Nine dimes are what fraction of a dollar?
(36)

b. Write the value of nine dimes using a dollar sign and a
decimal point.

10. Haruto lives about 1 kilometer from school. One kilometer is how many
(Inv. 2) meters?

* **11.** How many of these circles are shaded?
(35)

*12. (Estimate) Use a ruler to find the length of this screw to the nearest quarter inch:
(39)

Multiply:

*13. a. 4×3 **b.** 8×3 **c.** 8×4 **d.** 4×12
(38)

*14. a. 6×3 **b.** 6×4 **c.** 7×6 **d.** 6×12
(38)

*15. a. 7×3 **b.** 7×4 **c.** 8×6 **d.** 8×12
(38)

16. $\sqrt{64} - \sqrt{36}$
(Inv. 3)

17. $\begin{array}{r} \$4.86 \\ + \$2.47 \\ \hline \end{array}$ **18.** $\begin{array}{r} \$4.86 \\ - \$2.47 \\ \hline \end{array}$ **19.** $\begin{array}{r} 293 \\ + 678 \\ \hline \end{array}$
(22)   (30)   (13)

20. $\begin{array}{r} 893 \\ - 678 \\ \hline \end{array}$ **21.** $\begin{array}{r} 463 \\ - y \\ \hline 411 \end{array}$ **22.** $\begin{array}{r} 463 \\ + q \\ \hline 527 \end{array}$
(30)   (24)   (24)

23. This rectangle illustrates eight squared. What multiplication fact is illustrated by the rectangle?
(Inv. 3)

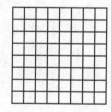

*24. (Conclude) Write the next three numbers in this counting sequence:
(3)

… , 470, 480, 490, 500, ____, ____, ____, …

25. (Represent) Draw a triangle that has three acute angles.
(23)

*26. Multiple Choice Which of these does *not* equal $9 + 9$?
(27, 38)

    A 2×9 **B** 9×2

    C 3×6 **D** nine squared

Saxon Math Intermediate 4

*27. A realtor was writing an advertisement about houses for sale in town.
(33, 34) The prices of five houses are listed below. Show how the realtor would
arrange the prices in order from most expensive to least expensive.

$385,900

$189,000

$1,280,000

$476,000

$299,000

28. ✏️ Justify Lake Huron is 206 miles long. Lake Superior is 350 miles
(14, 20) long. Anastacia estimates that Lake Superior is about 140 miles longer
than Lake Huron. Is Anastacia's estimate reasonable? Explain why or
why not.

*29. Analyze Kyle wants to form rectangles using straws. He has two
(Inv. 2, 39) straws 6 inches long, two straws 4 inches long, and two straws 2 inches
long. Using four straws attached at the ends, how many different
rectangles can Kyle form? What are the perimeters of the rectangles?

*30. The table shows a relationship between feet and inches. Use the table
(38) below to determine the number of inches in 20 feet.

Number of Feet	1	2	3	4
Number of Inches	12	24	36	48

Formulate Write and solve equations for problems **1–3.**

*1. A group of fish is called a *school.* There are twenty-five fish in the small
(31) school. There are one hundred twelve fish in the big school. How many fewer fish are in the small school?

2. A piece of ribbon that measured 1 yard was cut into two pieces. If one
(24) piece was 12 inches long, how many inches long was the other piece?

3. Mrs. Green took forty-seven digital pictures in Hawaii. Her husband
(1, 17) took sixty-two digital pictures in Hawaii. Her son took seventy-five digital pictures. In all, how many digital pictures did the Greens take?

*4. **Represent** Write the number 7,500,000 in expanded form. Then use
(16, 33) words to write the number.

5. Which digit in 27,384,509 is in the thousands place?
(34)

*6. **Connect** Use a dollar sign and a decimal point to write the value of
(35) three dollars, two quarters, one dime, and two nickels. Then write that amount of money using words.

*7. A gallon of milk is how many quarts of milk?
(40)

*8. How many squares are shaded?
(35)

*9. **Estimate** Use a ruler to find the length of the line segment below to
(39) the nearest quarter inch.

_____

*10. **Connect** Printed on the label of the milk container were these words
(40) and numbers:

1 gal (3.78 L)

Use this information to compare the following:

1 gallon ◯ 3 liters

Saxon Math Intermediate 4

Name _____

11. Destiny began reading a book last night at the time shown
on the clock. She read until midnight. How much time did
Destiny spend reading last night?
(27)

*12. **a.** **Multiple Choice** What type of angle is formed by the hands of the
(23)   clock shown in problem **11?**

   A acute   **B** right   **C** obtuse   **D** straight

   b. ✏️ **Justify** How do you know that your answer to part **a** is correct?

*13. Compare:
(Inv. 1,
36)   **a.** $-29 \bigcirc -32$ **b.** $0.75 \bigcirc \frac{3}{4}$ of a dollar

14. **Represent** Draw a circle with a diameter of 2 centimeters. What is the
(21)   radius of the circle?

Multiply:

15. **a.** 6×6 **b.** 7×7 **c.** 8×8 **d.** 12×12
(Inv. 3)

16. **a.** 7×9 **b.** 6×9 **c.** 9×9 **d.** 9×12
(32)

17. **a.** 7×8 **b.** 6×7 **c.** 8×4 **d.** 12×7
(38)

18. $4.98 + 7.65 **19.** $m - $6.70 = 3.30
(22)   (24)

20. $416 - z = 179$ **21.** $536 + z = 721$
(24)   (24)

22. $\sqrt{1} + \sqrt{4} + \sqrt{9}$
(Inv. 3)

*23. **Represent** Draw an array of Xs to show 7×3.
(Inv. 3)

24. **Represent** Use words to write $10\frac{1}{10}$.
(35)

*25. **a.** **Connect** Two quarters are what fraction of a dollar?
(36)

   b. Write the value of two quarters using a dollar sign and a decimal point.

*26. Multiple Choice A rectangle has an area of 24 square inches. Which
(Inv. 3)   of these areas could be the length and width of the rectangle?

    A 6 in. by 6 in.   **B** 12 in. by 12 in.

    C 8 in. by 4 in.   **D** 8 in. by 3 in.

*27. (**Represent**) Tarik measured the width of his notebook paper and said
(39)   that the paper was $8\frac{2}{4}$ inches wide. What is another way to write $8\frac{2}{4}$?

*28. (**Justify**) A gardener plans to build a fence around his 24-by-12-foot
(Inv. 2)   rectangular vegetable garden. Fencing for the garden can be purchased
in 50-foot, 75-foot, or 100-foot rolls. Which roll of fencing should the
gardener buy? Explain why.

*29. (**Estimate**) At a gardening center, one pair of gardening gloves
(22)   costs $12.00, not including a sales tax of 66¢. What is a reasonable
estimate of the cost of two pairs of gloves? Explain why your estimate
is reasonable.

*30. (**Analyze**) How many different three-digit numbers can you write using
(10)   the digits 6, 2, and 0? Each digit may be used only once, and the digit 0
may not be used in the hundreds place. Label the numbers you write as
even or odd.

Saxon Math Intermediate 4

*1. (Inv. 4) **Represent** The large square represents 1.
Write the shaded part of the square

    a. as a fraction.   **b.** as a decimal number.

    c. using words.

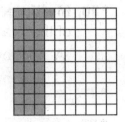

2. (35) Takeshi had a dime, a quarter, and a penny. Write this amount using a dollar sign and a decimal point.

*3. (40) Donna opened a 1-gallon container of milk and poured 1 quart of milk into a pitcher. How many quarts of milk were left in the 1-gallon container?

*4. (3) **Generalize** Describe the rule for this sequence and find the next three numbers:

    ..., 4200, 4300, 4400, ____, ____, ____, ...

*5. (Inv. 4) **Connect** Use digits and a comparison symbol to show that the decimal number five tenths equals the fraction one half.

6. (27) Anando fell asleep last night at the time shown on the clock. His alarm clock was set to ring eight hours later. What time was Anando's alarm clock set to ring?

*7. (41) Find the missing factor: $5w = 45$

*8. (Inv. 4) **Represent** The following was marked on the label of a juice container:

        2 qt (1.89 L)

Use words to write 1.89 L.

9. (35) What mixed number is illustrated by these shaded triangles?

Name _____

10. Which letter below has no right angles?
(23)

F   E   Z   L

*11. (Connect) Rewrite this addition problem as a multiplication problem:
(27)

$$\$1.25 + \$1.25 + \$1.25 + \$1.25$$

12. (Estimate) How long is the line segment to the nearest quarter inch?
(39)

13. A meter equals how many centimeters?
(Inv. 2)

14. a. Five dimes are what fraction of a dollar?
(36)

    b. Write the value of five dimes using a dollar sign and a decimal point.

*15. Compare:
(Inv. 4)

    a. $0.5 \bigcirc 0.50$ **b.** $\dfrac{1}{2} \bigcirc \dfrac{1}{4}$

16. a. 3×8 **b.** 3×7 **c.** 3×6 **d.** 3×12
(38)

17. a. 4×8 **b.** 4×7 **c.** 4×6 **d.** 4×12
(38)

*18.
(41)
$$\begin{array}{r} m \\ \times\ 8 \\ \hline 64 \end{array}$$

*19.
(41)
$$\begin{array}{r} 9 \\ \times\ n \\ \hline 54 \end{array}$$

20.
(24)
$$\begin{array}{r} z \\ +\ 179 \\ \hline 96 \end{array}$$

*21.
(41)
$$\begin{array}{r} \$3.00 \\ -\ \$1.84 \\ \hline \end{array}$$

*22.
(41)
$$\begin{array}{r} \$500 \\ -\ \$167 \\ \hline \end{array}$$

23.
(24)
$$\begin{array}{r} w \\ -\ 297 \\ \hline 486 \end{array}$$

24. (Conclude) What are the next four numbers in this counting sequence?
(Inv. 1)

$$\ldots, 28, 21, 14, \underline{\quad}, \underline{\quad}, \underline{\quad}, \underline{\quad}, \ldots$$

*25. (Represent) Use digits to write one million, fifty thousand.
(34)

Name _____

*26. Multiple Choice If the area of a square is 36 square inches, then how
(Inv. 3) long is each side of the square?

    A 6 in.   **B** 9 in.   **C** 12 in.   **D** 18 in.

*27. The distance from Riley's house to school is 1.4 miles. Write 1.4
(Inv. 4) with words.

28. Nieve quickly started and stopped a stopwatch four times. Write
(Inv. 4) these times in order from fastest to slowest:

        0.27 second, 0.21 second, 0.24 second, 0.20 second

(**Formulate**) Write and solve equations for problems **29** and **30.**

*29. (**Justify**) The Washington Monument is 153 feet taller than the
(13) City Center building in Nashville, Tennessee, which is 402 feet tall.
How tall is the Washington Monument? Explain why your answer is
reasonable.

*30. (**Explain**) The Panther waterfall in Alberta is 600 feet tall. The Fall
(25, 41) Creek waterfall in Tennessee is 256 feet tall. How many feet taller is the
Panther waterfall? Explain how you found your answer.

*1. **Represent** On 1-cm grid paper, draw a square with sides 5 cm long.
(Inv. 2, Inv. 3)

    a. What is the perimeter of the square?

    b. What is the area of the square?

Formulate Write and solve equations for problems **2** and **3**.

2. Wilbur had sixty-seven grapes. Then he ate some grapes. He had
(25) thirty-eight grapes left. How many grapes did Wilbur eat?

3. The distance from Whery to Radical is 42 km. The distance
(11, 14) from Whery to Appletown through Radical is 126 km. How
far is it from Radical to Appletown?

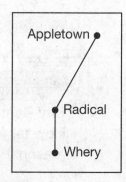

*4. Raziya arrived home from school at the time shown on the
(27) clock and began her homework half an hour later. What time
did Raziya begin her homework?

*5. **Generalize** Write a rule for this sequence and find the next three
(3, Inv. 3) numbers:

        1, 4, 9, 16, 25, 36, 49, ____, ____, ____, . . .

*6. **a.** Round 673 to the nearest hundred.
(20, 42)

    b. Round 673 to the nearest ten.

7. How many squares are shaded?
(35)

Saxon Math Intermediate 4

Name _____

*8. **a.** (Estimate) Find the length of this screw to the nearest quarter inch.
(Inv. 2, 39)

b. Find the length of this screw to the nearest centimeter.

9. (Connect) Rewrite this addition problem as a multiplication problem:
(27)

$$\$2.50 + \$2.50 + \$2.50$$

*10. (Conclude) Are the line segments in a plus sign parallel or perpendicular?
(23)

11. (Represent) To what number is the arrow pointing?
(Inv. 1)

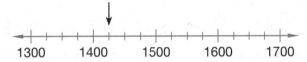

*12. (Analyze) Use the digits 4, 7, and 8 to write an odd number greater
(10) than 500. Each digit may be used only once.

*13. 6×80 ***14.** 7×700 ***15.** 9×80 ***16.** 7×600
(42)   (42)   (42)   (42)

17. z ***18.** $\$4.06$ ***19.** w
(24) $\underline{+\ 338}$ (41) $\underline{-\ \$2.28}$ (41) $\underline{\times\ 6}$
         507 42

20. $n - 422 = 305$ **21.** $55 + 555 + 378$
(24)   (17)

*22. **a.** Use words to write 5280.
(33)

b. Which digit in 5280 is in the tens place?

23. **a.** Ten nickels are what fraction of a dollar?
(36)

b. Write the value of ten nickels using a dollar sign and a decimal point.

*24. Compare:
(Inv. 4)
a. $0.5 \bigcirc \dfrac{1}{2}$ **b.** $\dfrac{1}{4} \bigcirc \dfrac{1}{10}$

25. What is the sum of three squared and four squared?
(Inv. 3)

*26. **Multiple Choice** Which of these numbers does *not*
(Inv. 4) describe the shaded part of this rectangle?

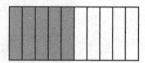

   A $\frac{5}{10}$ **B** $\frac{1}{2}$ **C** 5.0   **D** 0.5

*27. The decimal number 0.25 equals $\frac{1}{4}$. Write 0.25 with words.
(Inv. 4)

*28. Anisa used a stopwatch to time herself as she ran three 50-meter
(Inv. 4) dashes. Here are her times in seconds:

           9.12, 8.43, 8.57

Arrange Anisa's times in order from fastest (least time) to slowest
(greatest time).

*29. Joleen has six pieces of wood that she wants to fit together to make a
(Inv. 3, 39) picture frame. Two pieces are 8 inches long, two are 6 inches long, and
two are 4 inches long. Using four of the six pieces, how many different
rectangular frames could Joleen make? What would be the areas of the
rectangles formed?

*30. ✏️ **Estimate** Each of 4 school buses can carry 52 passengers. What is
(42) a reasonable estimate of the total number of passengers the four buses
can carry? Explain why your estimate is reasonable.

Real-World Connection

The zoo's insect house has 35 glass cases. An average of 17 crickets
live in 22 of the cases and an average of 15 grasshoppers live in 13
of the cases. What is a reasonable estimate of the total number of
insects that live in the glass cases at the zoo? Explain why your answer
is reasonable.

Saxon Math Intermediate 4

Formulate Write and solve equations for problems **1–3.**

*1. One hundred pennies are separated into two piles. In one pile there are
(24,41) thirty-five pennies. How many pennies are in the other pile?

*2. **Estimate** Juan opened a 1-gallon bottle that held about 3.78 liters of
(25, 43) milk. He poured about 1.50 liters of milk into a pitcher. About how many
liters of milk were left in the bottle?

*3. San Francisco is 400 miles north of Los Angeles. Santa Barbara is
(11, 41) 110 miles north of Los Angeles. Stephen drove from Los Angeles to
Santa Barbara. How many miles does he still have to drive to reach
San Francisco?

*4. Draw a rectangle that is 3 cm long and 3 cm wide.
(Inv. 2,
Inv. 3)

    a. What is the perimeter of the rectangle?

    b. What is the area of the rectangle?

*5. a. Round 572 to the nearest hundred.
(20, 42)

    b. Round 572 to the nearest ten.

*6. **Represent** Write the shaded part of this square
(Inv. 4)

    a. as a fraction.

    b. as a decimal number.

    c. using words.

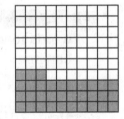

7. **Conclude** Are the rails of a railroad track parallel or perpendicular?
(23)

*8. **Represent** Draw a square to show 3 × 3. Then shade two ninths of
(26,
Inv. 3) the square.

9. The clock shows the time Santo arrived at school. He woke
(19) up that morning at 6:05 a.m. How long after waking up did
Santo arrive at school?

10. (*Represent*) To what number is the arrow pointing?
(Inv. 1)

*11. 2.45 + 4.50
(43)

*12. $3.25 − $2.47
(43)

*13. $2.15 + $3 + 7¢
(43)

*14. 3.75 − 2.50
(43)

15.   507
(24)   −   *n*
       ――――――
          456

16.   *n*
(24)   − 207
        ――――――
           423

*17. $5.00
(41)   − $3.79
        ――――――

*18. 6 × 80
(42)

*19. 4 × 300
(42)

20. 7 × 90
(42)

*21. 8*n* = 32
(41)

22. $\sqrt{100}$
(Inv. 3)

23. (*Represent*) Draw a line segment that is 2 inches long. Then measure
(Inv. 2) the line segment with a centimeter ruler. Two inches is about how many
centimeters?

24. (*Represent*) The population of the city was about 1,080,000. Use
(34) words to write that number.

*25. Multiple Choice Which of these metric units would probably be used
(Inv. 2) to describe the height of a tree?

    A millimeters

    B centimeters

    C meters

    D kilometers

*26. Multiple Choice Emily has a 2-liter bottle full of water and an empty
(40) half-gallon carton. She knows 1 liter is a little more than 1 quart. If she
pours water from the bottle into the carton, what will happen?

    A The bottle will be empty before the carton is full.

    B The carton will be full before the bottle is empty.

    C When the carton is full, the bottle will be empty.

    D The carton will be empty, and the bottle will be full.

Saxon Math Intermediate 4

Name _____

27. Here is a list of selling prices for five houses. Arrange the prices in order
(33) from highest selling price to lowest selling price.

$179,500

$248,000

$219,900

$315,000

$232,000

*28. Multiple Choice Which group of decimal numbers is arranged in
(43) order from least to greatest?

A 0.23, 0.21, 0.25

B 0.25, 0.23, 0.21

C 0.21, 0.23, 0.25

D 0.21, 0.25, 0.23

*29. An uncooked spaghetti noodle fell on the floor and broke into several
(39) pieces. Three of the pieces were $1\frac{1}{2}$ inches long, 2 inches long, and
$2\frac{1}{4}$ inches long. If two of the three pieces are lined up end to end, what
are all the possible combined lengths?

*30. **Explain** At an elementary school track meet, Ra'Shawn ran a
(43) 100-meter dash in 16.5 seconds. Sabrina ran 0.4 seconds faster.
What was Sabrina's time for the race? Explain why your answer is
reasonable.

*1. **(Represent)** The 1-gallon container of milk held 3.78 L of milk. Use
(Inv. 4) words to write 3.78 L.

2. **(Represent)** Silviano compared two numbers. The first number was
(33) forty-two thousand, three hundred seventy-six. The second number
was forty-two thousand, eleven. Use digits and a comparison symbol
to show the comparison.

*3. **(Explain)** The ticket cost $3.25. Mr. Chen paid for the ticket with a
(41, 43) $5 bill. How much change did he receive? Is your answer reasonable?
Why or why not?

4. Nine squared is how much more than the square root of nine?
(Inv. 3, 31)

*5. Find the missing factor: $8m = 48$
(41)

*6. **(Connect)** Eight fluid ounces of water is one cup of water. How many
(40) fluid ounces of water is a pint of water?

7. How many circles are shaded?
(35)

*8. **(Estimate)** Use an inch ruler to find the diameter of
(21, 39) this circle to the nearest quarter inch.

*9. Compare:
(Inv. 1, 42)
   a. $-5 \bigcirc -2$ **b.** $4 \times 60 \bigcirc 3 \times 80$

*10. $4.03   **11.** $4.33   **12.** $5.22   ***13.** $7.08
(41) $-$ $1.68   (43) $+$ $5.28   (43) $-$ $2.46   (41) $-$ $0.59

*14.   21   **15.**   40   ***16.**   73   ***17.**   51
(44) $\times$ 6   (42) $\times$ 7   (44) $\times$ 2   (44) $\times$ 6

Saxon Math Intermediate 4

18. $2 + 47¢ + 21¢
(43)

19. 8.7 − 1.2
(43)

20. 62 − n = 14
(24)

21. n − 472 = 276
(24)

22. Write this addition problem as a multiplication problem:
(27)

2.1 + 2.1 + 2.1 + 2.1 + 2.1 + 2.1

*23. a. (Connect) Which digit in 1760 is in the hundreds place?
(33, 42)

b. Use words to write 1760.

c. Round 1760 to the nearest hundred.

*24. Round 738 and 183 to the nearest hundred. Then add the rounded
(42) numbers.

*25. (Connect) Add the decimal number one and fifty hundredths to three
(Inv. 4, 43) and twenty-five hundredths. What is the sum?

*26. Multiple Choice If the area of this rectangle is
(Inv. 3, 41) 6 sq. cm, then the length of the rectangle is which of
the following?

   A 3 cm   **B** 4 cm

   C 10 cm   **D** 12 cm

2 cm

*27. a. Is $5.75 closer to $5 or to $6?
(20, Inv. 4)

b. Is 5.75 closer to 5 or to 6?

28. (Explain) How can you pay $1.23 using the fewest number of bills
(38) and coins?

(Formulate) Write and solve equations for problems **29** and **30.**

*29. The price of the notebook was $6.59. When sales tax was added, the
(11, 41) total was $7.05. How much was the sales tax?

*30. The Sutlej River in Asia is 900 miles long. The Po River in Europe is
(25, 41) 405 miles long. How many miles longer is the Sutlej River?

Real-World Connection

The school choir is ordering new choir shirts and blouses. There are 15 girls and 11 boys in the choir. The girls' blouses cost $9 each. The boys' shirts cost $8 each. What will be the total cost for the choir shirts and blouses?

Saxon Math Intermediate 4

*1. (Connect) Use the numbers 0.5, 0.6, and 1.1 to write two addition facts
(6, 43) and two subtraction facts.

2. A whole hour is 60 minutes. How many minutes is half of an hour?
(19)

3. (Explain) The space shuttle orbited 155 miles above the earth. The
(31) weather balloon floated 15 miles above the earth. The space shuttle
was how much higher than the weather balloon? Explain why your
answer is reasonable.

*4. (Justify) How much change should you get back if you give the
(41, 43) clerk $5.00 for a box of cereal that costs $3.85? How can you check
your answer?

*5. (Represent) Write 12.5 using words.
(Inv. 4)

6. (Represent) Use digits and symbols to show that negative sixteen is
(Inv. 1) less than negative six.

7. The clock shows the time Joe left for work this morning. He
(27) ate breakfast 35 minutes before that time. What time did
Joe eat breakfast?

8. (Represent) Write 4060 in expanded form. Then use words to write
(16, 33) the number.

9. How many circles are shaded?
(35)

10. Compare:
(34,36)
 a. 2 quarters ◯ half dollar

 b. 2,100,000 ◯ one million, two hundred thousand

11. Find the missing factor: $6w = 42$
(41)

*12. a. **Estimate** Use an inch ruler to measure this line segment to the
(Inv. 2)   nearest inch.

b. **Estimate** Use a centimeter ruler to measure this line segment to
the nearest centimeter.

_____

13. Compare: 12 − (6 − 3) ◯ (12 − 6) − 3
(45)

*14. ✏ **Explain** Look at problem **13** and your answer to the problem. Does
(45)   the Associative Property apply to subtraction? Why or why not?

*15.(43)	4.07 − 2.26	***16.**(41)	$5.02 − $2.47	**17.**(43)	$5.83 − $2.97	**18.**(43)	$3.92 + $5.14

*19.(44)	42 × 3	***20.**(44)	83 × 2	**21.**(42)	40 × 4	***22.**(44)	41 × 6

23. $2.75 + 50¢ + $3
(43)

*24. 3.50 + 1.75
(43)

*25. **Model** Draw a rectangle that is 2 in. by 1 in.
(Inv. 2,
Inv. 3)

a. The perimeter of the rectangle is how many inches?

b. The area of the rectangle is how many square inches?

*26. **Multiple Choice** Which of the following segments is *not* a
(21, 45)   radius of the circle?

A $\overline{RS}$
C $\overline{MT}$

B $\overline{RM}$
D $\overline{MS}$

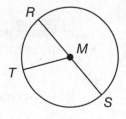

27. **Formulate** Estrella finished the first problem in 34 seconds. She
(31)   finished the second problem in 28 seconds. The first problem took how
much longer to finish than the second problem? Write an equation to
solve the problem.

Saxon Math Intermediate 4

Name _____

*28. Describe the order of operations in each expression. Then find the
(45) number each expression equals.

    a. $12 - (4 - 2)$

    b. $(12 - 4) - 2$

29. In Dodge City, Kansas, the average maximum temperature in July is 93°F.
(18) The average minimum temperature is 67°F. How many degrees warmer is
a temperature of 93°F than a temperature of 67°F?

*30. **Estimate** The population density of Connecticut is 702.9 people
(25, 42) per square mile. The population density of Kentucky is 101.7 people
per square mile. Round to the nearest hundred to estimate how many
more people per square mile live in Connecticut than live in Kentucky.

    123

Formulate Write and solve equations for problems **1** and **2**.

*1. Four hundred ninety-five oil drums were on the first train. Seven hundred
(11, 30) sixty-two oil drums were on the first two trains combined. How many
oil drums were on the second train?

*2. Workers on a Montana ranch baled 82 bales of hay on the first day.
(1, 17) They baled 92 bales of hay on the second day and 78 bales of hay
on the third day. How many bales of hay did the workers bale in all
three days?

*3. The decimal number three and seventy-eight hundredths is how much
(Inv. 4, 43) more than two and twelve hundredths?

*4. a. Round 786 to the nearest hundred.
(20, 42)

b. Round 786 to the nearest ten.

*5. **Represent** Draw and shade rectangles to show the number $2\frac{1}{3}$.
(35)

*6. **Conclude** The first five odd numbers are 1, 3, 5, 7, and 9.
(1,
Inv. 3)

a. What is their sum?

b. What is the square root of their sum?

7. The clock shows a morning time. What time was it
(27) 12 hours before that time?

*8. **Conclude** What type of angle is formed by the hands
(23) of this clock?

*9. **Estimate** **a.** Use an inch ruler to find the length of this
(23, 39) rectangle to the nearest quarter inch.

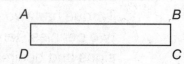

b. Which segment is parallel to $\overline{AB}$?

10. **Estimate** Kita took two dozen BIG steps. About how many meters
(Inv. 2) did she walk?

Saxon Math Intermediate 4

*11. (37) **Connect** To what mixed number is the arrow pointing?

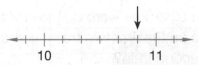

10   11

*12. (45) $64 + (9 \times 40)$

*13. (43) $\$6.25 + 39¢ + \$3$

*14. (41)
$$\begin{array}{r} \$4.02 \\ - \$2.47 \\ \hline \end{array}$$

*15. (41)
$$\begin{array}{r} \$5.00 \\ - \$2.48 \\ \hline \end{array}$$

*16. (24, 43)
$$\begin{array}{r} n \\ + 2.5 \\ \hline 3.7 \end{array}$$

*17. (16, 43)
$$\begin{array}{r} 4.3 \\ - \quad c \\ \hline 3.2 \end{array}$$

*18. (44)
$$\begin{array}{r} 42 \\ \times \quad 3 \\ \hline \end{array}$$

*19. (44)
$$\begin{array}{r} 81 \\ \times \quad 5 \\ \hline \end{array}$$

*20. (46) $6\overline{)30}$

*21. (46) $7\overline{)21}$

*22. (46) $8\overline{)56}$

*23. (46) $9\overline{)81}$

*24. (46) $7\overline{)28}$

*25. (46) $3\overline{)15}$

*26. (Inv. 2, Inv. 3) **Model** Draw a rectangle 3 in. long and 1 in. wide.

   a. What is its perimeter?

   b. What is its area?

*27. (21) **Multiple Choice** Rosario noticed that the distance from the pole in the center of the tetherball circle to the painted circle was about six feet. What was the approximate radius of the tetherball circle?

   A 12 ft   **B** 4 yd   **C** 3 ft   **D** 2 yd

*28. (4, 22) Tyrique, Dominic, and Tamasha checked their pockets for change. Tyrique had two dimes and a penny. Dominic had three nickels and two pennies. Tamasha had a nickel, a dime, and a penny. Using dollar signs and decimal points list the three amounts in order from least to greatest.

29. (3, 32) **Predict** What is the twelfth term of the sequence below?

12, 24, 36, 48, 60, …

30. (3) Generalize Write a rule that describes the relationship of the data in the table.

Number of Teachers	1	2	3	4	5
Number of Students	7	14	21	28	35

Early Finishers
Real-World Connection

Cecilia's book had 58 pages. She read for 6 hours and had 4 pages left.

a. About how many pages did Cecilia read each hour? Write a division problem to solve the problem.

b. What number will go in the division box? Explain why.

Saxon Math Intermediate 4

*1. **(Formulate)** Brand A costs two dollars and forty-three cents. Brand B
(31, 41) costs five dollars and seven cents. Brand B costs how much more than
Brand A? Write an equation and solve this problem.

*2. **(Connect)** The numbers 3, 4, and 12 form a multiplication and division
(47) fact family.

$$3 \times 4 = 12 \qquad 12 \div 4 = 3$$
$$4 \times 3 = 12 \qquad 12 \div 3 = 4$$

Write four multiplication/division facts using the numbers 4, 5, and 20.

*3. What is the sum of the decimal numbers two and three tenths and eight
(Inv. 4, and nine tenths?
43)

*4. **(Conclude)** Use the digits 1, 5, 6, and 8 to write an even number
(10) greater than 8420. Each digit may be used only once.

5. a. Compare: $1\frac{1}{2}$ ◯ 1.75
(7,
Inv. 4) **b.** Use words to write the greater of the two numbers you compared in
part **a.**

6. **(Analyze)** Carlos will use square floor tiles that measure one foot on
(Inv. 3) each side to cover a hallway that is eight feet long and four feet wide.
How many floor tiles will Carlos need?

7. **(Represent)** To what number is the arrow pointing?
(Inv. 1)

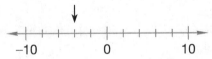

8. a. Five dimes are what fraction of a dollar?
(36)
b. Write the value of five dimes using a dollar sign and a decimal
point.

*9. The length of segment *PQ* is 2 cm. The length of segment *PR* is 11 cm.
(11) How long is segment *QR*?

Name _____

*10. **Conclude** Which segment in this triangle appears to be
(23, 45) perpendicular to segment *AC*?

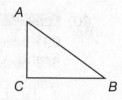

11. Round 3296 to the nearest hundred.
(42)

12. Use words to write 15,000,000.
(33)

*13. $95 - (7 \times \sqrt{64})$ **14.** $2.53 + 45¢ + $3
(Inv. 3,   (43)
45)

*15. n **16.**   40   ***17.**   51
(24, 43) $\dfrac{-\ 5.1}{2.3}$ (44) $\dfrac{\times\ 3}{}$ (44) $\dfrac{\times\ 5}{}$

*18. $28 \div 7$ ***19.** $81 \div 9$ ***20.** $35 \div 7$ ***21.** $16 \div 4$
(47)   (47)   (47)   (47)

*22. $\dfrac{28}{4}$ ***23.** $\dfrac{42}{7}$ ***24.** $\dfrac{48}{8}$ ***25.** $\dfrac{0}{5}$
(47)   (47)   (47)   (47)

*26. **Multiple Choice** Which of these does *not* show 24 divided by 4?
(47)

   A $24\overline{)4}$ **B** $\dfrac{24}{4}$ **C** $24 \div 4$ **D** $4\overline{)24}$

27. **a.** Is $12.90 closer to $12 or to $13?
(20)

   b. Is 12.9 closer to 12 or to 13?

*28. Describe the order of operations in these expressions, and find the
(45) number each expression equals.

   a. $12 \div (6 \div 2)$

   b. $(12 \div 6) \div 2$

   c. **Conclude** Does the Associative Property apply to division?
   Explain.

29. In the year 2003, each visitor to the country of Mexico spent an average
(11, 13) of $540. Each visitor to the country of Canada spent an average of
$557. How many more dollars did each visitor to Canada spend in
2003?

Saxon Math Intermediate 4

Name _____

*30. **(Estimate)** One of the largest hammerhead sharks ever caught weighed
(25, 42) 991 pounds. One of the largest porbeagle sharks ever caught weighed
507 pounds. Round to the nearest hundred pounds to estimate the
weight difference of those two sharks.

*Real-World
Connection*

The band played for 18 minutes during halftime at the football game.
Each song was 3 minutes long. How many songs did the band play
during halftime?

a. Write a division equation that could be used to find the answer.

b. Write a multiplication equation that could be used to find 18 ÷ 3.

c. Explain how multiplication and division are related.

Formulate Write and solve equations for problems **1** and **2**.

*1. There were four hundred seventy-two birds in the first flock. There were
(31) one hundred forty-seven birds in the second flock. How many fewer
birds were in the second flock?

*2. Raina hiked forty-two miles. Then she hiked seventy-five more miles.
(1, 17) How many miles did she hike in all?

*3. **Connect** Write four multiplication/division facts using the numbers 3,
(47) 5, and 15.

*4. Use the digits 1, 3, 6, and 8 to write an odd number between 8000 and
(10) 8350. Each digit may be used only once.

*5. **Represent** Write 306,020 in expanded form. Then use words to write
(16, 33) the number.

*6. **Represent** Draw and shade circles to show the number $2\frac{1}{8}$.
(35)

7. One mile is how many feet?
(Inv. 2)

8. What is the perimeter of this pentagon?
(Inv. 2)

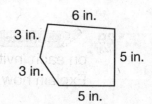

9. A board that had a length of 1 meter was cut into two pieces. If one piece
(11,
Inv. 2) of the board was 54 cm long, how long was the other piece?

*10. Find the length of segment *BC*.
(39)

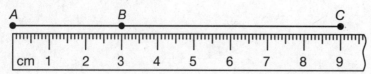

*11. 100 + (4 × 50)
(45)

12. $3.25 + 37¢ + $3
(43)

13. $\sqrt{4} \times \sqrt{9}$
(Inv. 3)

Saxon Math Intermediate 4

Name _____

*14. 33
(48) × 6

*15. 24
(48) × 5

*16. 90
(48) × 6

*17. $42
(48) × 7

18. $5.06
(41) − $2.28

*19. 1.45
(43) + 2.70

*20. 3.25
(43) − 1.50

21. 14
(17) 28
45
36
92
+ 47

*22. 28 ÷ 7
(47)

23. 5)‾35
(46)

24. 6)‾54
(46)

*25. 63/7
(47)

*26. Multiple Choice A rectangle has an area of 12 sq. in. Which of these
(Inv. 3) could *not* be the length and width of the rectangle?

   A 4 in. by 3 in. **B** 6 in. by 2 in.

   C 12 in. by 1 in. **D** 4 in. by 2 in.

*27. (Justify) Which property of multiplication is shown here?
(45)

   5 × (2 × 7) = (5 × 2) × 7

*28. Use digits and three different division symbols to show "twenty-four
(47) divided by three."

*29. (Estimate) D'Ron mailed nine invitations and placed a 39¢ stamp
(48) on each invitation. Estimate the total postage cost for the 9 invitations.
Explain how you estimated the total.

*30. (Model) Draw a number line and show the locations of 2, 3, 1.5, and $2\frac{1}{4}$.
(Inv. 1)

Formulate Write and solve equations for problems **1** and **2**.

*1. There were 8 boys in each row. There were 4 rows. How many boys
(49) were in all 4 rows?

*2. There were 7 girls in each row. There were 9 rows. How many girls were
(49) in all 9 rows?

3. A llama weighs about 375 pounds. A coyote weighs about 75 pounds.
(31) A llama weighs about how many pounds more than a coyote?

*4. **Connect** Write four multiplication/division facts using 5, 6, and 30.
(47)

*5. **Represent** Draw and shade circles to show the number $2\frac{3}{4}$.
(35)

*6. To what mixed number and decimal number is the arrow pointing?
(37)

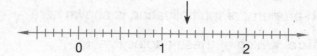

7. Tika is a college student. She began her homework last
(27) night at the time shown on the clock. She finished two
and one half hours later. What time did Tika finish her
homework?

*8. **Represent** Draw a rectangle that is 4 cm by 2 cm. Shade $\frac{7}{8}$ of it.
(21, 26)

9. **Represent** Use digits to write three million, seven hundred fifty thousand.
(33, 34) Which digit is in the hundred-thousands place?

*10. **Connect** Use the decimal numbers 1.4, 0.7, and 2.1 to write two
(6) addition facts and two subtraction facts.

*11. $56 \div 7$　　　　　***12.** $64 \div 8$　　　　　***13.** $\frac{45}{9}$
(47)　　　　　　　　　　(47)　　　　　　　　　　(47)

*14. The length of segment *RT* is 9 cm. The length of segment *ST* is 5 cm.
(6) What is the length of segment *RS*?

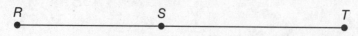

Saxon Math Intermediate 4

Name _____

15. $\$3.07$
(41) $-\ \$2.28$

16. 4.78
(43) $-\ 3.90$

*17. $(4 + 3) \times \sqrt{64}$
(Inv. 3, 45)

18. 7.07
(24, 43) $-\ \ n$
         $\overline{4.85}$

19. c
(16, 43) $-\ 2.3$
         $\overline{4.8}$

*20. $403 - (5 \times 80)$
(45)

21. $6n = 30$
(41)

22. $(587 - 238) + 415$
(45)

*23. 45
(48) $\times\ \ 6$

*24. 23
(48) $\times\ \ 7$

*25. $\$34$
(48) $\times\ \ \ 8$

*26. Multiple Choice The radius of a circle is 3 ft. Which of the following
(Inv. 2, 21) is *not* the diameter of the circle?

    A 36 in.   **B** 6 ft   **C** 2 yd   **D** 72 in.

*27. Multiple Choice Which of these angles is acute?
(23)

    A   **B**

    C   **D**

*28. Solve:
(47)

    a. $\dfrac{5}{5}$ **b.** $9 \div 1$ **c.** $6\overline{)0}$

29. 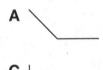 **Estimate** One human hand has 27 bones. One human foot has
(49) 26 bones. About how many bones are in two hands plus two feet? Explain
why your estimate is reasonable.

*30. **Estimate** The land area of Booker T. Washington National
(11, 17) Monument in Virginia is 239 acres. The land area of Cabrillo National
Monument in California is 160 acres. What is a reasonable estimate of
the total acreage of these two national monuments? Explain why your
estimate is reasonable.

Formulate Write and solve equations for problems **1–3.**

*1. Each of the 3 boats carried 12 people. In all, how many people were in
(49) the 3 boats?

*2. The book cost $6.98. The tax was 42¢. What was the total price?
(22, 35)

*3. Claire read six hundred twenty minutes for an afterschool reading
(31) program. Ashanti read four hundred seventeen minutes. Claire read
how many more minutes than Ashanti?

*4. **Connect** Use the numbers 4, 12, and 48 to write two multiplication
(47) facts and two division facts.

5. Justin ran the perimeter of the block. How far did Justin run? The
(Inv. 2) measurements of the block are shown on the figure below.

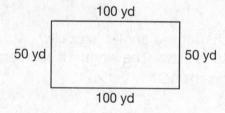

*6. Justin ran around the block in 58.7 seconds. Write "58.7" with words.
(Inv. 4)

7. **Represent** Use digits to write twelve million, seven hundred fifty
(33, 34) thousand. Which digit is in the hundred-thousands place?

*8. **Estimate** Round 783 and 217 to the nearest hundred. Then subtract
(42) the smaller rounded number from the larger rounded number.

9. The time shown on the clock is an evening time. Alyssa's
(19) school day begins 9 hours 30 minutes later than that time.
What time does Alyssa's school day begin?

10. **Connect** Write this addition problem as a multiplication problem:
(27)

$3.75 + $3.75 + $3.75 + $3.75

Saxon Math Intermediate 4

*11. $(4 \times 50) - \sqrt{36}$
(Inv. 3, 45)

*12. $3.6 + 4.35 + 4.2$
(50)

13. $\$4.63 + \$2 + 47¢ + 65¢$
(43)

*14. $\begin{array}{r} 43 \\ \times\ 6 \\ \hline \end{array}$
(48)

*15. $\begin{array}{r} 54 \\ \times\ 8 \\ \hline \end{array}$
(48)

*16. $\begin{array}{r} 37 \\ \times\ 3 \\ \hline \end{array}$
(48)

*17. $\begin{array}{r} \$40 \\ \times\ 4 \\ \hline \end{array}$
(48)

18. $4.7 + 5.5 + 8.4 + 6.3 + 2.4 + 2.7$
(43)

19. $\$5.00 - \$4.29$
(41)

*20. $7.03 - 4.2$
(50)

*21. $\begin{array}{r} n \\ -\ 27.9 \\ \hline 48.4 \end{array}$
(12, 24)

*22. $\begin{array}{r} 46.2 \\ +\ \ c \\ \hline 52.9 \end{array}$
(24, 43)

*23. $\dfrac{24}{3}$
(47)

24. $\dfrac{36}{9}$
(47)

25. The length of segment *AB* is 5 cm. The length of segment *BC* is 4 cm.
(1, 45)   What is the length of segment *AC*?

*26. (Represent) Draw and shade circles to show the number $3\frac{3}{8}$.
(35)

27. Compare: 1 minute $\bigcirc$ 58.7 seconds
(Inv. 4, 50)

*28. Multiple Choice Which of the following is more than one second but
(19, Inv. 4)   less than two seconds?

   A 0.15 sec

   B 1.5 sec

   C 2.1 sec

   D 2.15 sec

*29. Write these numbers in order from least to greatest:
(33)

   250,000   47,000   9000   3,100,000   600

30. These thermometers show the average daily minimum and maximum
(18) temperatures in New York City's Central Park during the month of July.
What is the difference in degrees between the two temperatures?

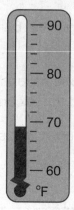 

Saxon Math Intermediate 4

Formulate Write and solve equations for problems **1–3.**

*1. In the P.E. class there were four teams. Each team had eight players.
(49) How many players were on all four teams?

*2. There were 7 pennies in each stack. There were 6 stacks of pennies.
(49) How many pennies were there in all?

*3. Lalo ran the first lap in 63.4 seconds and the second lap in 65.3 seconds.
(31, 43) Lalo ran the first lap how much faster than the second lap?

*4. **Connect** Write four multiplication/division facts using the numbers
(47) 6, 7, and 42.

5. Compare: $1 + 3 + 5 + 7 + 9$ ◯ five squared
(7, Inv. 3)

6. a. Round 367 to the nearest hundred.
(20, 42)

b. Round 367 to the nearest ten.

*7. **Represent** Draw a circle and shade 50% of it.
(Inv. 5)

8. **Classify** Name each type of angle shown below:
(23)

a. **b.** **c.**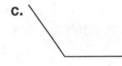

*9. A rectangle is shown at right:
(Inv. 2, Inv. 3) **a.** What is its length?

4 ft

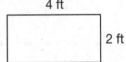

2 ft

b. What is its width?

c. What is its perimeter?

d. What is its area?

10. **Represent** The amount of liquid in a container is 2.75 quarts. Use
(Inv. 4) words to write that amount.

*11. **Estimate** The land area of Grand Portage National Monument in
(30, 42) Minnesota is 710 acres. The land area of Oregon Caves National
Monument in Arizona is 488 acres. Estimate the difference of those
areas by first rounding each area to the nearest hundred acres.

*12. Describe the order of operations in this expression and find the number
(50) it equals.

$$15.24 + (19.6 - 1.1)$$

*13.   63,285
(51)   + 97,642

14. $5.00
(41)   − $4.81

15. n
(24, 43)   + 39.8
     61.4

*16.   85
(48)   × 5

17.   37
(48)   × 7

18.   40
(42)   × 8

19. f
(41)   × 8
    72

20.   47.8
(24, 43) − c
   20.3

*21.   462,586
(51)   + 39,728

22. z
(16, 43)   − 4.78
     2.63

Divide. Check each answer by multiplying.

*23. $2\overline{)18}$
(51)

*24. $7\overline{)21}$
(51)

*25. $\dfrac{56}{8}$
(51)

26. The length of $\overline{AB}$ is 7 cm. The length of $\overline{AC}$ is 12 cm. How long is $\overline{BC}$?
(45)

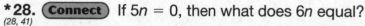

A   B   C

*27. If half the students are boys, then what percent of the students are
(Inv. 5) girls?

*28. **Connect** If $5n = 0$, then what does $6n$ equal?
(28, 41)

*29. **Multiple Choice** Which of the following does *not* name
(Inv. 4, the shaded portion of the large square?
Inv. 5)

  A $\dfrac{11}{100}$ **B** 0.11   **C** 11%   **D** 11

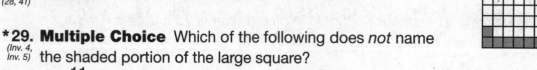

    Saxon Math Intermediate 4

Write and solve equations for problems **1–5.**

*1. There were 8 buses. Each bus could seat 60 students. How many
(49) students could ride in all the buses?

*2. Each van could carry 9 students. There were 63 students. How many
(52) vans were needed to carry all of the students?

*3. The coach separated 28 players into 4 equal teams. How many
(52) players were on each team?

4. There are 10 swimmers in the race. Only 3 can be awarded medals.
(25) How many swimmers will not win a medal?

5. Hermelinda finished first in the 100-meter freestyle race with a time of
(31, 43) 57.18 seconds. Tanya finished second in 58.26 seconds. Hermelinda
finished the race how many seconds sooner than Tanya?

6. (Connect) Write four multiplication/division facts using the numbers
(47) 7, 8, and 56.

7. Compare: $1 + 2 + 3 + 4 \bigcirc \sqrt{100}$
(Inv. 1,
Inv. 3)

*8. (Conclude) What are the next three numbers in this sequence?
(3)

..., 6000, 7000, 8000, ____, ____, ____, ...

*9. There were two hundred sixty-seven apples in the first bin. There were
(31) four hundred sixty-five apples in the second bin. How many fewer
apples were in the first bin?

*10. $8.49 + 7.3 + 6.15$ **11.** $6n = 42$
(50)   (41)

*12.   47,586   **13.** $5.00   **14.** n
(51)   + 23,491   (41)   − $3.26   (24, 43)   + 25.8
                                                                _____
                                                                  60.4

*15.   49   **16.**   84   **17.**   70
(48)   × 6   (48)   × 5   (42)   × 8

Saxon Math Intermediate 4   **139**

18. 35
(48) × 9

19. 400
(24, 41) − n
256

*20. $40.00
(52) − $24.68

21. **a.** Round 639 to the nearest hundred.
(20, 42)

   b. Round 639 to the nearest ten.

*22. **Conclude** Which side of this triangle appears to be
(23, 45) perpendicular to $\overline{PR}$?

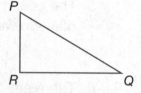

23. Compare: 49% ◯ $\frac{1}{2}$
(Inv. 5)

*24. Divide. Check each answer by multiplying.
(51)
   a. 3)̄27   **b.** 7)̄28   **c.** 8)̄72

*25. This figure has four sides, but it is not a rectangle.
(Inv. 2) What is the perimeter of this figure?

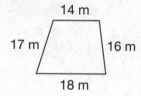

26. **Estimate** **a.** Is $24.10 closer to $24 or to $25?
(20,
Inv. 4)
   b. Is 24.1 closer to 24 or to 25?

*27. **Multiple Choice** If △ = □, which of these is *not* necessarily
(1, 41) true?

   A △ + 2 = □ + 2   **B** 2 × △ = 2 × □
   C △ − 2 = □ − 2   **D** 2 × △ = □ + 2

*28. **a.** What fraction of the large square is shaded?
(Inv. 4,
Inv. 5)
   b. The shaded part of the large square represents what
      decimal number?

   c. What percent of the large square is shaded?

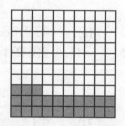

Saxon Math Intermediate 4

*29. **Explain** The answer to 33 ÷ 8 is not a whole number. What whole
(52)   number represents a reasonable estimate of the answer? Explain why
       you chose that number.

*30. Look at these coins. List all of the different amounts you could make
(22, 43) using exactly two coins. Arrange the amounts in order from least to
        greatest and write each amount with a dollar sign.

Formulate Write and solve equations for problems **1** and **2**.

*1. Evita had 56 beads that she was putting into bags. She wanted to put
(52) them into equal groups of 8 beads. How many bags will she need?

*2. There were 42 children waiting for a ride. There were 7 cars available. If
(52) the same number of children rode in each car, then how many would be
in each car?

*3. **Connect** Write four multiplication/division facts using the numbers 4,
(47) 7, and 28.

4. Which months have exactly 30 days?
(5)

*5. Consider this sequence:
(3)

$$\ldots, 16{,}000, 17{,}000, 18{,}000, 19{,}000, \ldots$$

a. **Generalize** Write a rule that describes how to find the next
term of the sequence.

b. **Predict** What is the next term of the sequence?

6. a. Round 4728 to the nearest hundred.
(20, 42)

b. Round 4728 to the nearest ten.

7. Write the time "a quarter after four in the afternoon" in digital form.
(19)

*8. **Model** One side of a square is 4 feet long. You may use tiles to solve.
(Inv. 2)

a. What is the perimeter of the square?

b. What is the area?

9. How many circles are shaded?
(35)

*10. **Explain** Describe the order of operations in this expression and
(Inv. 3, find the number it equals.
45)

$$\sqrt{64} + (42 \div 6)$$

Name _____

11. $6.35 + $12.49 + 42¢
(43)

*12. $100.00 − $59.88
(43, 52)

*13. 51,438
(52) − 47,495

14. 60
(42, 48) × 9

15. 57
(48) × 4

*16. ⟨Represent⟩ Draw dots and make groups to show 22 ÷ 5. Write the
(53) answer next to your drawing.

Divide for problems **17–19.** Write each answer with a remainder.

*17. 25 ÷ 4
(53)

*18. $6\overline{)39}$
(53)

*19. $7\overline{)30}$
(53)

20. 46
(48) × 8

21. 38
(48) × 7

22. z
(24, 43) − 16.5
_____
40.2

*23. 6.75 + 4.5 + 12.5
(50)

*24. ⟨Represent⟩ Use digits to write seven million, two hundred sixty
(34) thousand.

25. A half-gallon container holds about 1.89 L of fluid. Use words to
(40) write 1.89 L.

*26. Multiple Choice Shakir said, "I am thinking of two numbers. Their
(28) product is 6." The two numbers Shakir was thinking of could *not* be _____.

    A 1 and 6   **B** 2 and 3   **C** 3 and 2   **D** 6 and 0

*27. a. A quarter is what percent of a dollar?
(40,
Inv. 5)
    b. A quart is what percent of a gallon?

*28. a. What fraction of the large square is shaded?
(Inv. 4,
Inv. 5)
    b. The shaded part of the large square represents what
    decimal number?

    c. What percent of the large square is shaded?

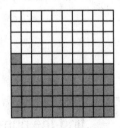

*29. (53) ✏️ **Estimate** Brandon purchased 1 liter of juice, which is about 67.6 fluid ounces. Estimate the number of cups of juice that Brandon purchased. Explain your thinking.

*30. (25, 30) ✏️ **Explain** The 900 North Michigan Avenue Building in Chicago is 871 feet tall. The 181 West Madison Street Building is 680 feet tall. How many feet taller is the 900 North Michigan Avenue Building? Explain how you found your answer.

Real-World Connection

Ellen needs at least 25 feet of ribbon to make bows. The ribbon she uses is sold only in yards. How many yards should she buy? Explain how compatible numbers can be used to solve the problem.

Saxon Math Intermediate 4

*1. In Mr. Jensen's math class, 24 students are seated in 4 rows of desks.
(52) The same number of students are in each row. Write and solve a
division equation to find the number of students in each row.

*2. An art teacher works with 42 different students each day. During the
(44) school year, each student will complete 9 art projects. Write and solve a
multiplication equation to find the total number of projects the students
will complete.

*3. Write and solve a subtraction equation to find the number of years from
(54) 1921 to 1938.

*4. Multiple Choice How many years is 5 decades?
(54)
    A 5 years   **B** 50 years   **C** 500 years   **D** 5000 years

*5. According to this calendar, what day of the week was
(54) December 25, 1957?

| DECEMBER 1957 |||||||
S	M	T	W	T	F	S
1	2	3	4	5	6	7
8	9	10	11	12	13	14
15	16	17	18	19	20	21
22	23	24	25	26	27	28
29	30	31				

*6. Round 5236 to the nearest thousand. Round 6929 to the nearest
(54) thousand. Then add the rounded numbers.

7. One side of a rectangle is 10 miles long. Another side is 20 miles long.
(Inv. 2,
21)
    a. Draw the rectangle and write the lengths of the sides.

    b. What is the perimeter of the rectangle?

    c. What is the area of the rectangle?

*8. a. What fraction of this circle is shaded?
(22,
Inv. 5)
    b. What percent of this circle is shaded?

*9. (**Represent**) To what number is the arrow pointing? Write the number
(Inv. 1) two different ways.

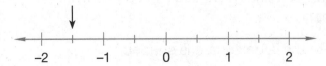

*10. **Analyze** When T'Von emptied his bank, he found 17 pennies,
(35)   4 nickels, 5 dimes, and 2 quarters. What was the value of the coins in
his bank?

*11. 794,150   **12.** $51,786   **13.** 87.6
(51)   +   9,863   (51)   + $36,357   (17, 50)   4.0
                                                31.7
                                                 5.5
*14. $20.00   ***15.** 41,315   1.1
(52)   − $18.47   (52)   − 29,418   + 0.5

16. 46   **17.** 54   **18.** 39   **19.** 40
(48)   × 7   (48)   × 8   (48)   × 9   (42)   × 9

*20. 3.68 + 2.4 + 15.2   **21.** $4y = 32$
(50)   (41)

*22. $43 \div 7$ ***23.** $9\overline{)64}$
(53)   (53)

*24. **Represent** One inch equals 2.54 cm. Use words to write 2.54 cm.
(Inv. 4)

*25. **Explain** The answer to 52 ÷ 9 is not a whole number. What whole
(52)   number represents a reasonable estimate of the answer? Explain why
you chose that number.

26. a. Which line segment is the diameter of the circle?
(21, 45)

b. **Explain** Name two intersecting line segments.
Explain your answer.

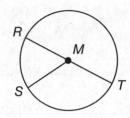

27. a. Is $136.80 closer to $136 or to $137?
(20)

b. Is 136.8 closer to 136 or to 137?

*28. a. What fraction of the large square is shaded?
(Inv. 4,
 Inv. 5)
b. The shaded part of the large square represents what
decimal number?

c. What percent of the large square is shaded?

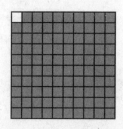

    Saxon Math Intermediate 4

*29. **Generalize** Write a rule that describes the relationship of the data
(32, 38) in the table.

Number of $1 Bills	10	20	30	40	50
Number of $10 Bills	1	2	3	4	5

*30. Show all of the different ways these bills can be arranged in a row.
(36)

Early Finishers

Real-World Connection

Five friends played a video game. Aureli scored 7305 points, Brett scored 3595 points, Sarah scored 2039 points, Jamin scored 9861 points, and Danielle scored 1256 points.

a. Who had the highest score?

b. Use words to write the highest score.

c. Round each score to the nearest thousand.

Formulate Write and solve an equation for problems **1–3.**

1. Raimi bought a toy for $1.85 and sold it for 75¢ more. For what price
(1, 43)   did he sell the toy?

*2. Two thousand people entered the contest. Only seven will win prizes.
(25, 52)   How many entrants will not win prizes?

*3. A recent census in Arkansas showed that 11,003 people live in Scott
(31, 52)   County and 8484 people live in Newton County. How many more
people live in Scott County than in Newton County?

*4. Sixty percent of the students in the class were boys. Were there more
(Inv. 5)   girls or more boys in the class?

5. Draw a rectangle that is 4 cm long and 3 cm wide.
(Inv. 2,
Inv. 3)

    a. What is the perimeter of the rectangle?

    b. What is the area of the rectangle?

*6. **Analyze** Fidelia found the third multiple of 4. Then she subtracted two
(55)   from this number. What was her answer?

*7. Two factors of 15 are 1 and 15 because 1 × 15 = 15. Find two more
(55)   factors of 15.

8. Brenda arrived home from school 30 minutes before the
(27)   time shown on the clock. What time did Brenda arrive home
from school?

*9. George Washington became the first U.S. president in 1789. The
(54)   Declaration of Independence was written in 1776. How many years after
the Declaration of Independence did Washington become president?

10. What is the length of $\overline{ST}$?
(Inv. 2)

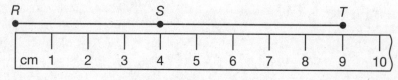

Saxon Math Intermediate 4

11. 4.00
(50) − 2.22

12. 70.5
(50) − 42.3

13. $45.87
(43) + $23.64

*14. $25.42
(43) − $ 7.25

*15. 64
(48) × 5

16. 70
(42) × 6

17. 89
(48) × 4

18. 63
(48) × 7

19. $\frac{63}{7}$
(47)

*20. $8\overline{)15}$
(53)

21. 4.68 + 12.2 + 3.75
(50)

*22. (**Model**) Draw dots and make groups to illustrate 15 ÷ 6.
(53)

23. (**Explain**) Describe the order of operations in this expression and find
(45) the number it equals.

$$\sqrt{64} \div (4 + 4)$$

*24. (**Connect**) Write this addition problem as a multiplication problem:
(27)

$$\$0.75 + \$0.75 + \$0.75 + \$0.75$$

*25. a. Multiple Choice Which of these numbers can be divided by
(55) 5 without leaving a remainder?

A 32 **B** 35 **C** 37 **D** 41

b. (**Explain**) How can you find the answer for part **a** just by
looking?

*26. (**Justify**) One gallon is equal to 128 fluid ounces. Garrett estimates
(40) that four gallons is about 500 fluid ounces. Is Garrett's estimate
reasonable? Explain why or why not.

27. a. Is $2.54 closer to $2 or to $3?
(20,
Inv.4)

b. Is 2.54 closer to 2 or to 3?

28. **a.** What fraction of the large square is shaded?
(Inv. 4, Inv. 5)

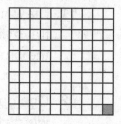

b. The shaded part of the large square represents what decimal number?

c. What percent of the large square is shaded?

*29. **Multiple Choice** Which of these numbers is a composite number and
(55) *not* a prime number?

A 2   **B** 3   **C** 4   **D** 5

30. How many different three-digit numbers can you write using the digits
(3) 8, 3, and 4? Each digit may be used only once in every number you
write. Arrange the numbers in order from least to greatest.

Real-World Connection

The marching band at one school has 36 members. The members can march in any arrangement in which all the rows have the same number of people. Use counters or tiles to form arrays to show all the possible marching arrangements. List each way you find.

Saxon Math Intermediate 4

*1. Drew has fifty-six rolls. Seven rolls will fit on one tray. How many
(52) trays does he need to carry all of the rolls? Write an equation to solve
the problem.

2. One gallon is about 3.78 L. About how many liters is two gallons? Use
(40) words to write the answer.

3. **Estimate** To estimate the sum of $6.87 and $5.92, Socorro rounded
(20) each number to the nearest dollar before adding. Write the numbers
Socorro added and their sum.

*4. **Connect** Write four multiplication/division facts using the numbers 3,
(47) 8, and 24.

*5. **List** What are the seven months of the year that have 31 days?
(54)

*6. **Analyze** Find the eighth multiple of six. Then add one. What is the
(Inv. 3) square root of the answer?

*7. **Represent** Compare these fractions. Draw and shade two congruent
(56) rectangles to show the comparison.

$$\frac{1}{4} \bigcirc \frac{1}{6}$$

*8. **Estimate** In the 2004 presidential election, 4651 residents of the state
(42, 54) of Rhode Island voted for candidate Ralph Nader. Round that number
of residents to the nearest thousand, to the nearest hundred, and to the
nearest ten.

9. a. What is the perimeter of the rectangle shown at
(Inv. 2, right?
Inv. 3)

b. What is its area?

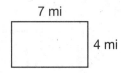
7 mi

4 mi

*10. $10.00   ***11.**   36,024   **12.**   43,675
(43, 52)   − $ 5.46   (52)   − 15,539   (51)   + 52,059

13.   73   **14.**   46   **15.**   84   **16.**   40
(48)   × 9   (48)   × 7   (48)   × 6   (42)   × 5

Name _____

*17. 7)‾48
(53)

18. $\frac{63}{7}$
(46, 47)

*19. 3.75 + 2.5 + 0.4
(50)

*20. 42.25 − 7.5
(50)

*21. **a.** **Multiple Choice** Which of these numbers is a multiple of 10?
(55)

  A 35 **B** 40 **C** 45 **D** 101

  b. How can you find the answer for part **a** just by looking?

22. **a.** A dime is what fraction of a dollar?
(36, Inv. 5)

  b. A dime is what percent of a dollar?

23. (**Represent**) Washington School cost about $12,350,000 to build. Use
(34) words to write that amount of money.

*24. Two factors of 16 are 1 and 16 because 1 × 16 = 16. Find three more
(55) factors of 16.

*25. (**Verify**) Is 16 a prime number? Why or why not?
(55)

*26. (**Conclude**) Refer to figure *ABCD* to answer parts **a** and **b**.
(23, 45)

  a. Which segment appears to be parallel to $\overline{AB}$?

  b. Angle *B* is what type of angle?

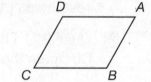

*27. **Multiple Choice** Which of these numbers is a factor of 12?
(55)
  A 0 **B** 6 **C** 8 **D** 24

*28. **Multiple Choice** Which of these numbers is a multiple of 12?
(55)
  A 0 **B** 6 **C** 8 **D** 24

*29. **a.** A penny is what fraction of a dollar?
(36, Inv. 5)

  b. Write the value of a penny as a decimal part of a dollar.

  c. A penny is what percent of a dollar?

*30. Write these numbers in order from greatest to least:
(Inv. 4)

  $\frac{3}{4}$ 0.09 $\frac{2}{5}$ 0.5 $\frac{1}{3}$

Saxon Math Intermediate 4

*1. **Formulate** Marybeth could jump 42 times each minute. At that rate,
(57)   how many times could she jump in 8 minutes? Write an equation to
       solve the problem.

*2. **Analyze** Rodolfo could run 7 miles in 1 hour. At that rate, how many
(57)   miles could Rodolfo run in 3 hours? Make a table to solve.

*3. **Connect** Write four multiplication/division facts using 8, 9, and 72.
(47)

4. What is the sum of $\sqrt{36}$ and $\sqrt{64}$?
(Inv. 3)

*5. Compare: $\frac{1}{3}$ ◯ 50%
(Inv. 5,
56)

*6. **a.** **Estimate** Round 5280 to the nearest thousand.
(42, 54)

   b. Round 5280 to the nearest hundred.

*7. This array of 12 stars shows that 4 and 3 are factors of 12.
(55)   Draw a different array of 12 stars that shows two other
       factors of 12.

*8. **Analyze** Find the fourth multiple of 6. Then find the third multiple of 8.
(55)   Compare these two multiples.

*9. Juan Ponce de León explored the coast of Florida in 1513. In 1800,
(41, 54)   the federal government of the United States moved to Washington,
       DC. Write a *later – earlier = difference* equation and solve it to find the
       number of years that elapsed from 1513 to 1800.

10. A square has one side that is 7 inches long.
(Inv. 2,
Inv. 3)

   a. What is the perimeter of the square?

   b. What is the area of the square?

*11.   70,003   **12.** n **13.** $861.34
(52)   − 36,418   (24, 43)   − 4.32   (43, 51)   + $764.87
                                   _____
                                    2.57

14. 93
(48) × 5

15. 84
(48) × 6

16. 77
(48) × 7

17. 80
(42) × 8

18. $\dfrac{56}{8}$
(47)

19. $7\overline{)65}$
(53)

*20. 45 ÷ 6
(53)

21. 7n = 42
(41)

22. 1.75 + 17.5
(50)

23. **a.** Which segment in this figure is a diameter?
(23, 45)

    b. **Classify** Segments *MW* and *MX* form an angle. What type of angle is it? Explain.

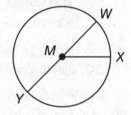

*24. **Represent** Compare these fractions. Draw and shade two congruent
(56) rectangles to show the comparison.

$$\dfrac{2}{3} \bigcirc \dfrac{3}{4}$$

*25. **Represent** Point *X* represents what mixed number and what decimal
(37) number on this number line?

*26. One inch is 2.54 centimeters, so two inches is 2.54 + 2.54 centimeters.
(Inv. 2) A segment that is 3 inches long is how many centimeters long?

*27. Write this addition problem as a multiplication problem:
(27)

$$2.54 + 2.54 + 2.54$$

*28. **a.** Three pennies are what fraction of a dollar?
(36,
Inv. 5)

    b. Write the value of three pennies as a decimal part of a dollar.

    c. Three pennies are what percent of a dollar?

*29. **Multiple Choice** Which of these numbers is a prime number?
(55)
    A 6   **B** 7   **C** 8   **D** 9

Saxon Math Intermediate 4

*30. What is the sum of these lengths? Write three answers using different
(Inv. 2) units.

1 yard + 2 feet + 12 inches

*Real-World
Connection*

Each day Jamaal delivers 30 newspapers in 1 hr 30 min. At this
rate, how many newspapers would he deliver each hour? Explain
your answer.

*1. Chazz pays $7.50 every week for a bus pass. How much does she pay
(57) for 4 weeks of bus passes? Write an equation to solve the problem.

*2. It takes 4 apples to make 1 pint of applesauce. How many apples
(49) does it take to make 5 pints? Make a table to solve the problem.

3. Calvin has to get up at 6 a.m. By what time should he go to bed in
(27) order to get 8 hours of sleep?

*4. ✎ (**Explain**) The store sells paint in quart cans, gallon cans, and 5-
(40) gallon cans. The price per quart is lower with larger cans. Hosni needs 8
quarts of paint. What containers of paint should he buy? Explain.

*5. (**Represent**) Write 8402 in expanded form. Then use words to write
(16, 33) the number.

*6. (**Analyze**) Find the fourth multiple of 7. Then find the sixth multiple of 6.
(Inv. 3, Add these multiples. What is the square root of the answer?

*7. According to this calendar, what is the date of the second
(54) Tuesday in September 2042?

SEPTEMBER 2042						
S	M	T	W	T	F	S
	1	2	3	4	5	6
7	8	9	10	11	12	13
14	15	16	17	18	19	20
21	22	23	24	25	26	27
28	29	30				

8. If $5 + n = 23$, then what number does $n - 5$ equal?
(24)

*9. a. What is the perimeter of this figure? Measurements
(Inv. 2, are in feet.
23)

    b. (**Classify**) Describe each angle an acute, obtuse, or
right.

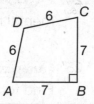

*10. (**Represent**) Compare these fractions. Draw and shade two congruent
(26, 56) circles to show the comparison.

$$\frac{1}{2} \bigcirc \frac{2}{4}$$

Saxon Math Intermediate 4

11. To what mixed number is the arrow pointing?
(37)

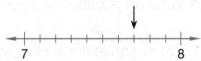

*12. Which segment appears parallel to $\overline{AB}$?
(23)

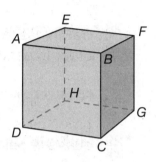

13. 0.47 + 3.62 + 0.85 + 4.54
(50)

14. $3 + $4.39 + $12.62
(43)

15. 36.47 − (3.5 + 12.6)
(45, 50)

*16. $20.00 − (29¢ + $7)
(45, 52)

*17. 41,059 − 36,275
(52)

*18.   768
(58)   ×   3

*19. $2.80
(58)   ×   4

20.   436
(24, 30)   −   z
            252

*21. 5)36
(53)

22. 7)45
(53)

23. 4)35
(53)

24. ✎ **Explain** How can you find the product of 4 × 100 using only
(42, 55) mental math?

*25. **Analyze** Two factors of 20 are 1 and 20 because 1 × 20 = 20.
(55) Find four more factors of 20.

*26. According to the census, the population of South Fork was 6781.
(42, 54)

a. Round 6781 to the nearest thousand.

b. Round 6781 to the nearest hundred.

*27. **Multiple Choice** If $4n = 24$, then which of these equations is *not*
(47) true?

A $\dfrac{24}{4} = n$ \hspace{3cm} B $\dfrac{24}{n} = 4$

C $2n = 12$ \hspace{3.2cm} D $4n = 6$

28. **a.** Seven pennies are what fraction of a dollar?
(36,
Inv. 5)
    b. Write the value of seven pennies as a decimal part of a dollar.

    c. Seven pennies are what percent of a dollar?

*29. **Multiple Choice** Which of these even numbers is a prime number?
(55)
A 2 \hspace{2.5cm} B 4 \hspace{2.5cm} C 6 \hspace{2.5cm} D 8

*30. **Estimate** On a road trip across the country, Kwan drove 387 miles
(58) the first day and 409 miles the second day. If he drives about the same
distance each day, approximately how many miles will Kwan drive in
5 days?

    Saxon Math Intermediate 4

*1. **Analyze** A comfortable walking pace is about 3 miles per hour. How
(57) far would a person walk in 4 hours at a pace of 3 miles per hour? Make
a table to solve the problem.

*2. There were forty-eight pears in all. Six pears were in each box. How
(52) many boxes were there? Write an equation to solve the problem.

3. One mile is about 1.61 km.
(Inv. 2,
Inv. 4)
  a. Use words to write 1.61 km.

  b. Compare: 1 mi ◯ 1 km

*4. **Estimate** To estimate the product of 5 and 193, round 193 to the
(59) nearest hundred before multiplying.

5. Compare: 50% of 16 ◯ $\sqrt{16}$
(Inv. 3,
Inv. 5)

*6. **Analyze** Subtract the third multiple of four from the second multiple
(55) of six. What is the difference?

*7. In 1587, Virginia Dare was the first infant born to English parents in
(54) North America. Write a *later − earlier = difference* equation and solve it
to find the number of years that have elapsed from 1587 to the year of
your birth.

*8. a. **Classify** Which angle in this figure appears to be a
(23, 45) right angle?

  b. Which segment in this figure does not appear to be
  perpendicular to $\overline{AB}$?

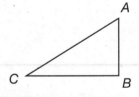

*9. Compare these fractions. Draw and shade two congruent rectangles to
(56) show the comparison.

$$\frac{2}{5} \bigcirc \frac{1}{4}$$

*10. Safara could pack 40 packages in 1 hour. At that rate, how many
(57) packages could she pack in 5 hours?

Saxon Math Intermediate 4 **159**

*11. **Represent** Use digits to write fifteen million, two hundred ten thousand.
(34)

12. **Represent** A town was on a rectangular plot of land 3 miles long and
(Inv. 2, 21) 2 miles wide. Draw the rectangle and show the length of each side.

    a. What is the perimeter of the rectangle?

    b. What is the area?

13. (43, 51)	**14.** (51)	**15.** (50)
$37.75 + $45.95	43,793 + 76,860	48.0 9.7 12.6 5.3 + 236.2

*16. (52)	***17.** (52)	
$50.00 − $42.87	43,793 − 26,860	

*18. 483 × 4   ***19.** 360 × 4   ***20.** 207 × 8
(58)   (58)   (58)

21. 8)‾43‾   **22.** 5)‾43‾   **23.** 7)‾43‾
(53)   (53)   (53)

24. **a.** The thermometer at right shows the temperature at 3 p.m.
(18)   What was the temperature at 3 p.m.?

    b. From 3 p.m. to 6 p.m., the temperature rose 4 degrees.
    What was the temperature at 6 p.m.?

25. **Represent** Use a ruler to draw a line segment 4 in. long. Then draw a
(Inv. 2, 23) parallel segment 10 cm long.

*26. Each engine oil change in Francisco's car requires $3\frac{1}{2}$ quarts of new oil.
(40, 43) That number of quarts is the same as what number of pints?

*27. **Explain** On a playground, a rectangular basketball court measures
(Inv. 2) 58.5 feet long by 42.5 feet wide. What is a reasonable estimate of the
perimeter of the court? Explain your thinking.

Saxon Math Intermediate 4

Name _____

*28. Write each decimal number illustrated, and then write the sum and the
_(Inv. 4, Inv. 5) difference of the numbers.

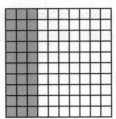 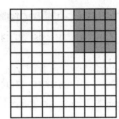

*29. a. Multiple Choice Which of these odd numbers is a composite
₍₅₅₎ number and *not* a prime number?

A 5 **B** 7 **C** 9 **D** 11

b. ✎ **Verify** Explain your answer in part **a.**

30. ✎ **Estimate** J'Neane would like to purchase a pair of in-line skates
₍₅₉₎ and accessories, including a helmet, knee pads, elbow pads, and wrist
guards. The skates cost $59.95, and the total cost of the accessories
is $44.50. What is a reasonable estimate of how much more the skates
cost than the accessories? Explain your thinking.

Formulate Write and solve equations for problems **1** and **2**.

*1. There were two hundred fourteen parrots, seven hundred fifty-two
(1, 33, 51) crows, and two thousand, forty-two blue jays. How many birds were
there in all?

*2. K'Shella used one bag of soil to pot 8 plants. How many bags of soil
(52) would she need to pot 2 dozen plants?

*3. Yachi could paint 12 signs in 1 hour. At that rate, how many signs could
(57) he paint in 3 hours? Make a table to solve this problem.

4. Fifty percent of an hour is how many minutes?
(Inv. 5)

*5. ✏️ **Estimate** Mount St. Helens is a volcano in Washington State. After
(51) erupting in May 1980, the peak of the volcano was 8363 feet above sea
level. During the eruption, the volcano lost 1314 feet of its height. What
is a reasonable estimate of the height of the volcano before its eruption?
Explain your thinking.

*6. Multiple Choice Which of these numbers is *not* a multiple of 2?
(55)

    A 23   **B** 24   **C** 32   **D** 46

7. Write the time "a quarter to seven in the morning" in digital form.
(19)

8. Solve for *n:* $3n = 3 \times 5$
(41)

*9. The product of 6 and 7 is how much greater than the sum of 6
(31) and 7?

10. What is the length of segment *BC?*
(Inv. 2)

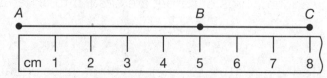

11. Compare: $(32 \div 8) \div 2 \bigcirc 32 \div (8 \div 2)$
(45)

12. $6.49 + $12 + $7.59 + 8¢$
(43)

Saxon Math Intermediate 4

13. 6.5 + 4.75 + 11.3
(50)

14. 12.56 − 4.3
(50)

*15. 350
(58)   × 5

*16. 204
(58)   × 7

*17. 463
(58)   × 6

18. 4)‾3‾7‾
(53)

19. 6)‾3‾9‾
(53)

20. 3)‾2‾8‾
(53)

21. a. A nickel is what fraction of a dollar?
(36,
Inv. 5)

   b. A nickel is what percent of a dollar?

*22. Perfect squares have an odd number of factors. The numbers 9 and 25
(Inv. 3,
55)   are perfect squares. The three factors of 9 are 1, 3, and 9. What are the
   three factors of 25?

23. Compare: 5% ◯ $\frac{1}{2}$
(Inv. 5)

*24. (Classify) Refer to figure ABCD to answer parts **a** and **b.**
(23)

   a. What type of angle are angles *A* and *C*?

   b. What type of angle are angles *B* and *D*?

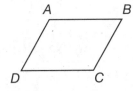

*25. (Analyze) The rectangular room is 5 yards long and 4 yards wide.
(Inv. 2,
Inv. 3)

5 yd

4 yd

   a. How many yards of molding are needed to go around the
   room?

   b. How many square yards of carpet are needed to cover the
   floor?

*26. Multiple Choice If *n* + 10 = 25, then which of these equations is *not*
(24)   true?

   A *n* + 11 = 26

   B *n* + 12 = 27

   C *n* − 5 = 20

   D *n* + 9 = 24

27. **a.** Compare: 8 ÷ (4 ÷ 2) ◯ (8 ÷ 4) ÷ 2
(45, 47)

    b. Look at your answer to part **a.** Does the Associative Property apply to division?

28. **a.** Nineteen pennies are what fraction of a dollar?
(36,
Inv. 5)

    b. Nineteen pennies are what percent of a dollar?

    c. Write the value of nineteen pennies as a decimal part of a dollar.

*29. **(Estimate)** At the restaurant Jackson ordered a meal for $7.95, a
(59)
glass of milk for $1.75, and a dessert for $3.95. Estimate Jackson's restaurant bill.

*30. **a.** **(Conclude)** Name a segment that is parallel to $\overline{EF}$.
(23)

    b. Name a segment that is perpendicular to $\overline{BF}$.

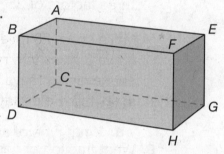

Saxon Math Intermediate 4

*1. (**Explain**) The diameter of Filomena's bicycle tire is 24 inches. What
(21) is the radius of the tire? Explain how you know.

2. There are five apple slices in each school lunch. If 35 students buy a
(49) school lunch, how many apple slices are there? Write an equation for
this problem.

3. a. Two nickels are what fraction of a dollar?
(36,
Inv. 4) **b.** Two nickels are what decimal part of a dollar?

*4. The Gilbreth family drank 39 cups of milk in 3 days. That averages to
(60) how many cups of milk each day?

*5. Maya drove 28 miles to Ariana's house. That afternoon the two friends
(1, 17) drove 3 miles to a restaurant and then drove back to Ariana's house.
That evening Maya drove 28 miles to return home. Altogether, how
many miles did Maya travel that day?

*6. What fraction of this rectangle is *not* shaded?
(61)

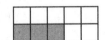

*7. Multiple Choice Which of these numbers is *not* a factor of 10?
(55)   **A** 2   **B** 5   **C** 10   **D** 20

*8. (**Verify**) The loaf of bread was sliced into 6 equal pieces. After 1 piece
(61) was taken, what fraction of the loaf was left?

*9. (**Represent**) Compare these fractions. Draw and shade two congruent
(56) circles to show the comparison.

$$\frac{2}{3} \bigcirc \frac{3}{4}$$

*10. (**Estimate**) Find the sum of 5070 and 3840 by rounding each number
(54, 59) to the nearest thousand before adding.

11. If 60% of the answers were true, then were there more true answers or
(Inv. 5) more false answers?

Name _____

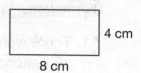

12. **a.** What is the perimeter of this rectangle?
(Inv. 2, Inv. 3)
    b. What is the area of this rectangle?

4 cm

8 cm

13. $62.59
(43, 51)   + $17.47

*14. $5n = 12 + 18$
(61)

*15. $1000 - (110 \times 9)$
(45, 58)

16. $3.675 - 1.76$
(50)

*17. $6.70
(58) $\times$ 4

*18. 703
(58) $\times$ 6

*19. $346
(58) $\times$ 9

*20. $5\overline{)39}$
(53)

*21. $7\overline{)39}$
(53)

22. $4\overline{)39}$
(53)

23. $16 \div 3$
(53)

24. $26 \div 6$
(53)

25. $36 \div \sqrt{36}$
(Inv. 3, 47)

*26. (**Represent**) Point *A* represents what number on this number line?
(Inv. 1)

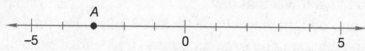

27. Compare:
(33)

    a. 745 ◯ 754

    b. 132 ◯ 99

28. **a.** What fraction of the large square is not shaded?
(Inv. 4, Inv. 5)

    b. The unshaded part of the large square represents what decimal number?

    c. What percent of the large square is not shaded?

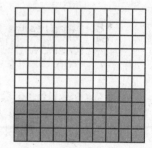

*29. (**Classify**) Name the parallel and perpendicular
(52)   segments in this figure. Describe the angles
    as acute, obtuse, or right.

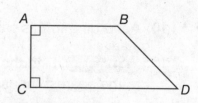

*30. In 1847 the first adhesive postage stamps were sold in the United
(23, 45)   States. In 1873 the first postcards were issued. What is the elapsed
    time in years between those two events?

Saxon Math Intermediate 4

Formulate Write and solve equations for problems **1** and **2**.

*1. There were twice as many peacocks as there were hens. If there were
(52) 12 peacocks, then how many hens were there?

*2. Mae-Ying bought a package of paper priced at $1.98 and 2 pens
(43, 59) priced at $0.49 each. The tax on the entire purchase was 18¢. What
was the total cost of the items? Explain why your answer is reasonable.

3. Raquel's dance class begins at 6 p.m. It takes 20 minutes to drive to
(27) dance class. What time should she leave home to be on time for dance
class?

*4. **Analyze** Glenda drove across the desert at an average speed of
(57) 60 miles per hour. At that rate, how far would she drive in 4 hours?
Make a table to solve the problem.

*5. Two thirds of the race was over. What fraction of the race was left?
(61)

*6. **Estimate** Otieno bought a notebook for $8.87 and paper for $2.91.
(59) Estimate the total by rounding each amount to the nearest dollar, then
add.

*7. In the equation $9 \times 11 = 100 - y$, the letter y stands for what
(61) number?

*8. **Represent** Compare: $\frac{2}{4} \bigcirc \frac{4}{8}$. Draw and shade two congruent circles
(56) to show the comparison.

*9. **Multiple Choice** Recall that a prime number has exactly two factors.
(55) Which of these numbers has exactly 2 factors?

    A 7   **B** 8   **C** 9   **D** 10

10. According to this calendar, July 4, 2014 is what day of the
(54) week?

JULY 2014						
S	M	T	W	T	F	S
		1	2	3	4	5
6	7	8	9	10	11	12
13	14	15	16	17	18	19
20	21	22	23	24	25	26
27	28	29	30	31		

*11. **Connect** Write four multiplication/division facts using the numbers 6,
(47)   3, and 18.

*12. $5 \times 6 \times 7$ ***13.** 4^3
(62)   (62)

14.   476,385   **15.** $20.00   **16.** c
(51) $+ 259,518$ (52) $- \$17.84$ (24) $- 19,434$
                                                        $\overline{45,579}$

*17. $4.17   ***18.** $470   ***19.**   608
(58) $\times 8$ (58) $\times 7$ (58) $\times 4$

20. $4\overline{)29}$ **21.** $8\overline{)65}$ **22.** $5\overline{)29}$
(53)   (53)   (53)

23. $65 \div 7$ **24.** $29 \div 5$ **25.** $65 \div 9$
(53)   (53)   (53)

26. If 40% of the students are boys, then what percent of the students
(Inv. 5)   are girls?

*27. **a.** What is the perimeter of this square shown at right?
(Inv. 2,
Inv. 3)

    b. Use a formula to find the area of the square.

6 in.

*28. **Multiple Choice** What type of angle is each angle of a square?
(23)
     A acute   **B** right   **C** obtuse   **D** straight

*29. This bar graph shows the number of colored candles in a package. Use
(Inv. 6)   the bar graph to answer each question.

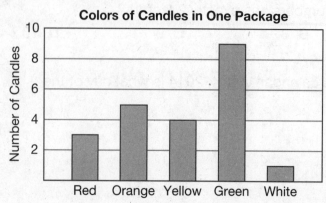

Colors of Candles in One Package

Saxon Math Intermediate 4

Name _____

a. How many red candles were there?

b. There were how many more green candles than orange candles?

*30. **Model** Draw a number line from 1 to 2, and show the locations of $1\frac{1}{2}$,
(37, 50) 1.25, and $1\frac{3}{4}$.

Real-World Connection

A square with 1-inch sides has an area of 1 square inch. A square with 2-inch sides has an area of 4 square inches. Review the squares shown below.

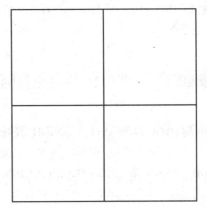

1 × 1 = 1 square inch   2 × 2 = 4 square inches

a. What is the area of a square with sides that are 3 inches long?

b. What is the area of a square with sides that are 4 inches long?

c. What is the area of a square with sides that are 5 inches long?

d. Draw and label each of the squares in parts **a–c**.

Saxon Math Intermediate 4   **169**

1. Three feet equals 1 yard. A car that is 15 feet long is how many
(Inv. 2) yards long?

*****2.** (**Connect**) Write four multiplication/division facts using the numbers 3,
(47) 10, and 30.

*****3.** (**Analyze**) Nevaeh had six quarters, three dimes, and fourteen pennies.
(35) How much money did she have in all?

4. What is the sum of the even numbers that are greater than 10 but less
(1, 10) than 20?

*****5.** (**Estimate**) Round $7.15 and $5.94 to the nearest dollar, and then add.
(59)

*****6.** (**Model**) Erin opened 1 gallon of milk and began filling glasses. Each
(40) glass held 1 cup of milk. Two cups equals a pint. Two pints equals
a quart. Four quarts equals a gallon. How many glasses could
Erin fill? Use containers to solve.

7. To what mixed number is the arrow pointing?
(37)

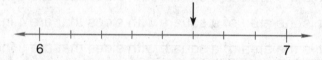

*****8.** The cornbread was cut into 12 equal pieces. Seven of the pieces were
(61) eaten. What fraction of the cornbread was left?

*****9.** The product of 4 and 3 is how much greater than the sum of 4 and 3?
(31, 38)

*****10.** What is the sum of 92 and $\sqrt{9}$?
(Inv. 3,
62)

*****11.** **a.** (**Classify**) What is the name of this polygon?
(Inv. 2,
63)
b. Each side is the same length. What is the perimeter of
this polygon?

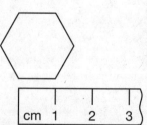

*****12.** Roger picked 56 berries in 8 minutes. At that rate, how many berries
(60) did he pick in 1 minute?

Saxon Math Intermediate 4

Name _____

*13. Chanisse picked 11 berries in 1 minute. At that rate, how many berries
(57) could she pick in 5 minutes?

14. $40.00 − d = $2.43   ***15.** $5 \times n = 15 + \sqrt{25}$
(24, 52)   (Inv. 3, 61)

*16. $6 \times 4 \times 10$ ***17.** 5^3
(62)   (62)

18. $3.5 + 2.45$ **19.** $1.95 − 0.4$
(50)   (50)

20. $1.00 − ($0.36 + $0.57)
(43, 45)

*21. 349×8 ***22.** 7.60×7 **23.** $6\overline{)34}$
(58)   (58)   (53)

24. $8\overline{)62}$ **25.** $5\overline{)24}$ **26.** $\dfrac{63}{7}$
(53)   (53)   (47)

*27. [Explain] Vans will be used to carry 22 soccer players to a game.
(53) Each van can carry 5 players. Write and solve an equation to find the
least number of vans that will be needed. Then explain your answer.

*28. Multiple Choice Which of these numbers is a multiple of 10?
(55)
   A 3   **B** 5   **C** 15   **D** 40

29. **a.** What fraction of the large square is shaded?
(Inv. 4, Inv. 5)
   b. What decimal of the whole grid is not shaded?

   c. What percent of the large square is not shaded?

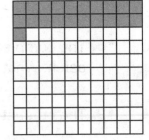

*30. a. (Classify) What polygons form this figure?
(23, 63)

b. Describe the angles and line segments of this figure.

Real-World Connection

Find three classroom objects that are examples of different types of polygons.

a. Name each object.

b. Draw a picture of each object. Each picture should show the number of sides each object has.

c. Label each drawing with the name of the polygon it represents.

*1. A square mile is twenty-seven million, eight hundred seventy-eight
(34) thousand, four hundred square feet. Use digits to write this number.

2. The tree was one hundred thirteen paces away. If each pace was 3 feet,
(49) how many feet away was the tree?

3. Tracey's baseball-card album will hold five hundred cards. Tracey has
(25, 41) three hundred eighty-four cards. How many more cards will fit into the
album? Write an equation.

4. The trip lasted 21 days. How many weeks did the trip last?
(52, 54)

*5. A stop sign has the shape of an octagon. How many sides do seven
(49) stop signs have?

*6. Find the length of this hairpin to the nearest quarter inch.
(39)

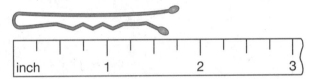

7. Write 406,912 in expanded form. Then use words to write the number.
(16, 33)

*8. One foot equals 12 inches. If each side of a square is 1 foot long, then
(Inv. 2) what is the perimeter of the square in inches?

*9. (Estimate) During a school fundraiser, a group of students worked
(59) for 90 minutes and washed 8 cars. What is a reasonable estimate of the
number of minutes the students spent washing each car? Explain why
your answer is reasonable.

*10. (Represent) Compare: $\frac{3}{6}$ ◯ $\frac{1}{2}$. Draw and shade two congruent circles to
(56) show the comparison.

11. Compare:
(33)
    a. 614 ◯ 609   **b.** 88 ◯ 106

*12. **Explain** Last week Ms. Willyard graded some papers. This week
(11, 30)   she graded 47 more papers. In these two weeks, Ms. Willyard graded
112 papers altogether. How many papers did she grade last week?
Explain why your answer is reasonable.

13. $32.47
(43, 51) + $67.54

14. 51,036
(52)   −   7,648

15. 53.6
(50)   2.9
97.4
8.8
+ 436.1

*16. $5n = 75$
(41)

*17. $3\overline{)84}$
(64)

*18. $4\overline{)92}$
(64)

19. $6\overline{)58}$
(53)

*20. 257
(58)   × 5

*21. $7.09
(58)   × 3

22. $334
(58)   × 9

*23. $2\overline{)36}$
(64)

24. $4n = 36$
(41)

*25. $4^2 + 2^3$
(62)

26. $3.5 - (2.4 - 1.3)$
(43, 45)

*27. Look at these bills. List all of the different ways to pair two bills.
(36)

*28. Three fourths of the game was over. What fraction of the game
(61)   remained?

29. **a.** What fraction of the large square is shaded?
(Inv. 4,
Inv. 5)
b. What decimal number is represented by the shaded part
of the square?

c. What percent of the large square is not shaded?

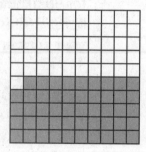

*30. **Multiple Choice** The first two prime numbers are 2 and 3. The next
(55)   two prime numbers are _____.

A 4 and 5   **B** 5 and 6   **C** 5 and 7   **D** 7 and 9

Saxon Math Intermediate 4

Formulate Write and solve equations for problems **1** and **2**.

1. The chef uses 3 eggs for each omelette. How many omelettes can
(52) he make with two dozen eggs?

*2. Aaliyah looked at the clock and realized that her next class would
(25) begin in 27 minutes and end in 72 minutes. How many minutes long is
Aaliyah's next class?

*3. Alvaro is turning three years old today. How many months old is
(54) Alvaro?

*4. **Estimate** Madeline's favorite orange juice is sold in half-gallon
(40, 65) containers. Each month, Madeline estimates that she purchases
7 containers of juice. Estimate the number of gallons of juice
Madeline purchases each month. Explain your reasoning.

*5. Trudy rode her bike 36 miles in 4 hours. She rode at an average
(60) rate of how many miles per hour?

*6. **Analyze** The wagon train traveled at an average rate of 20 miles
(57) per day. At that rate, how many miles would the wagon train travel
in 5 days? Make a table to solve the problem.

*7. a. What fraction of this hexagon is *not* shaded?
(61)

   b. Each side of the hexagon is 1 cm long. What is its
(Inv. 2) perimeter?

*8. **Interpret** The average amount of precipitation received each year
(Inv. 6) in each of four cities is shown in the table below:

Average Annual Precipitation

City and State	Amount (to the nearest inch)
Phoenix, AZ	8
Reno, NV	7
Boise, ID	12
Albuquerque, NM	9

Display the data in a bar graph. Write one statement that describes
the data.

*9. J'Raa started jogging early in the morning and did not stop until he
(27) returned home. How much time did J'Raa spend jogging?

Started jogging   Stopped jogging

a.m.   a.m.

10. Nigel drew a circle with a radius of 18 inches. What was the diameter of
(21) the circle?

11. How long is segment *BC?*
(45)

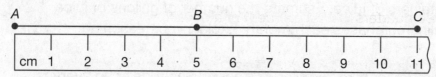

*12. Multiple Choice Which of these words is the answer to a division
(65) problem?

A product   **B** dividend   **C** divisor   **D** quotient

*13. Compare: $27 \div 3^2 \bigcirc 27 \div \sqrt{9}$
(Inv. 3, 62)

14. (43, 51)	**15.** (52)	**16.** (43)
$97.56 + $ 8.49	$60.00 − $54.78	37.64 29.45 3.01 + 75.38

*17. $168 \div 3$ ***18.** $378 \div 7$
(65)   (65)

19. 840×3 **20.** 4×564 ***21.** 304×6
(58)   (58)   (58)

*22. $4\overline{)136}$ ***23.** $2\overline{)132}$ ***24.** $6\overline{)192}$
(65)   (65)   (65)

*25. Explain) Describe the steps for solving the equation and then
(61, 65) solve the equation to find *n.*

$$7n = 50 + 34$$

Saxon Math Intermediate 4

Name _____

*26. $12 \times 7 \times 10$
(62)

27. Dimitri woke up on a cold morning and glanced out the
(18) window at the thermometer. What temperature is shown
on this thermometer?

28. a. Three quarters is what fraction of a dollar?
(36,
Inv. 5)
b. Three quarters is what percent of a dollar?

*29. Draw a quadrilateral. A quadrilateral has how many vertices?
(63)

*30. a. Which side of this quadrilateral is parallel to
(23, 45) side *CB*?

b. Which angle appears to be an obtuse
angle?

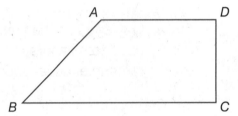

Name _____

Formulate Write and solve equations for problems **1** and **2**.

1. Lobo works 8 hours each day and earns $18 for each hour he works.
(48) What amount of income does Lobo earn each day?

*2. Every third bead on the necklace was red. There were one hundred
(52, 65) forty-one beads in all. How many beads were red? (Make equal groups
of three.)

3. Twenty-five percent of this square is shaded. What percent of
(Inv. 5) the square is not shaded?

*4. **Represent** In one day, Liliana drove 20 kilometers north and then
(25) 15 kilometers south. How far was Liliana from where she started?
Draw a diagram to solve the problem.

5. At 11:45 a.m. Dequon glanced at the clock. His doctor's appointment
(27) was in $2\frac{1}{2}$ hours. At what time was his appointment?

*6. a. **Analyze** In the figure below, we do not state the size of the units
(Inv. 2, used to measure the rectangle. Find the perimeter and area of the
Inv. 3) rectangle. Label your answers with *units* or *square units*.

6 units

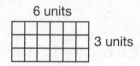

3 units

b. **Represent** The rectangle has 3 rows of 6 squares, showing
that 3 and 6 are factors of 18. Draw a rectangle arranged in two
rows to show two other factors of 18.

*7. **Explain** The car could go 30 miles on 1 gallon of gas. How far
(57) could the car go on 8 gallons of gas? Explain your thinking.

*8. Two sevenths of the crowd cheered wildly. The rest of the crowd stood
(61) quietly. What fraction of the crowd stood quietly?

9. How many different three-digit numbers can you write using the digits
(3, 10) 4, 2, and 7? Each digit may be used only once. Label the numbers you
write as even or odd.

Saxon Math Intermediate 4

Name _____

*10. **(Represent)** Compare: $\frac{1}{2}$ ◯ $\frac{2}{5}$. Draw and shade two congruent
(56)   rectangles to show the comparison.

11. $n + 2 = 3 \times 12$ **12.** $6.42 - (3.3 - 1.5)$
(61)   (45, 50)

*13. $\sqrt{81} + 82 + 3^2$ **14.** $\$10 - 10¢$
(Inv. 3,   (43)
62)

15. $43,016 - 5987$ ***16.** $24 \times 3 \times 10$
(52)   (62)

17. $\$4.86$ **18.** 307 **19.** $\$460$
(58) $\underline{\times \quad 7}$ (58) $\underline{\times \quad 8}$ (58) $\underline{\times \quad 9}$

*20. $2\overline{)152}$ ***21.** $6\overline{)264}$ ***22.** $4w = 56$
(65)   (65)   (41, 64)

*23. $230 \div 5$ ***24.** $91 \div 7$ ***25.** $135 \div 3$
(65)   (64)   (65)

26. **a.** Write 8¢ using a dollar sign and a decimal point.
(20, 35)

     b. Round $11.89 to the nearest dollar.

*27. **(Represent)** Use words to name each number:
(35,
Inv. 4)   **a.** $2\frac{3}{10}$ **b.** 2.3

*28. **a. Multiple Choice** Which two triangles are congruent?
(66)

   A   **B**   **C**   **D**

     b. ✏ **Explain** Explain your answer to part **a.**

*29. **(Represent)** Draw a pentagon. A pentagon has how many vertices?
(63)

*30. (66) 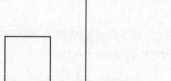 **Conclude** Are all squares similar? Why or why not?

Early Finishers

Real-World Connection

Road signs often have the same shape, but they may not have the same size. Look at the road signs below. Find two signs that are congruent and two other signs that are similar but not congruent.

Saxon Math Intermediate 4

*1. Seventy-five beans were equally divided into five pots. How many
(52, 65) beans were in each pot?

*2. a. (Analyze) Find the perimeter and area of this rectangle. Remember to
(Inv. 2,
Inv. 3) label your answer with *units* or *square units*.

8 units

3 units

b. (Represent) Sketch a rectangle that is four units wide with the same
area as the rectangle in part **a**. What is the perimeter of this new
rectangle?

3. Multiple Choice The server placed a full pitcher of water on the
(40) table. Which of the following is a reasonable estimate of the amount
of water in the pitcher?

A 2 gallons **B** 2 quarts **C** 2 cups **D** 2 ounces

*4. Multiple Choice Which of these numbers is *not* a factor of 12?
(55)
A 6 **B** 5 **C** 4 **D** 3

5. The starting time was before dawn. The stopping time was in the
(27) afternoon. What was the difference in the two times?

Starting time   Stopping time

*6. (Represent) One square mile is 3,097,600 square yards. Use words
(34) to write that number of square yards.

7. a. What fraction of this pentagon is *not* shaded?
(Inv. 5,
61)
b. Is the shaded part of this pentagon more than 50% or
less than 50% of the pentagon?

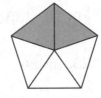

Name _____

8. According to this calendar, what is the date of the last
(54) Saturday in July 2019?

*9. **Estimate** To estimate the product of two factors, a student
(59) rounded one factor down and left the other factor unchanged. Was the
estimate greater than the exact product or less than the exact product?
Give an example to support your answer.

10. **Represent** To what mixed number is the arrow pointing?
(37)

7   8

*11. **Justify** Sofia estimated that the exact product of 4 × 68 is close to
(59) 400 because 68 rounded to the nearest hundred is 100, and 4 × 100 =
400. Was Sofia's estimate reasonable? Explain why or why not.

*12. Compare: 2^3 ◯ 2 × 3
(Inv. 1,
62)

13. $6.25 + $4 + $12.78
(43)

14. 3.6 + 12.4 + 0.84
(50)

15. $30.25   **16.**   149,384   **17.**   409
(24, 52) −   b   (52)   −   98,765   (67)   ×   70
         ———————
          $13.06

18. 5 × $3.46   **19.** $0.79 × 6
(58)   (58)

*20. 10 × 39¢   ***21.** 6)‾90‾   ***22.** 4w = 96
(67)   (64)   (41, 64)

*23. 8)‾456‾   ***24.** 95 ÷ 5   ***25.** 234 ÷ 3
(65)   (64)   (65)

Saxon Math Intermediate 4

*26. Name the shaded part of this rectangle as a fraction and
(Inv. 4) as a decimal.

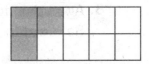

*27. **a. Multiple Choice** Which two figures are congruent?
(66)

A ◭   B △   C ◺   D ◹

     b. ✏ **Conclude** Explain how you know.

28. How much money is $\frac{1}{4}$ of a dollar?
(36)

*29. **Represent** Draw a hexagon. A hexagon has how many vertices?
(63)

*30. **Interpret** The line graph shows the temperature at different times
(Inv. 6) on a winter morning at Hayden's school. Use the graph to answer the
questions that follow.

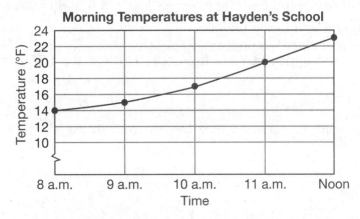

Morning Temperatures at Hayden's School

     a. At what time was the first temperature of the morning recorded?
What was that temperature?

     b. Was the noon temperature warmer or colder than the 10 a.m.
temperature? How many degrees warmer or colder was the
noon temperature?

*Real-World
Connection*

Marla bought a new protein shake with ten times the amount of protein
as her old protein shake.

     a. If the old protein shake has 3.25 grams of protein,
how many grams of protein does Marla's new shake
have?

     b. What equation did you use to solve?

*1. **(Analyze)** Alphonso ran 6 miles per hour. At that rate, how far could
(57) he run in 3 hours? Make a table to solve this problem.

*2. Find the perimeter and area of this rectangle:
(Inv. 2,
Inv. 3)

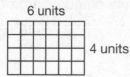

6 units

4 units

3. **(Represent)** Aletta ran 100 meters in twelve and fourteen hundredths
(Inv. 4) seconds. Use digits to write her time.

*4. Taydren drew an octagon and a pentagon. How many sides did the
(63) two polygons have altogether?

*5. 47 × 30   ***6.** 60 × 39   ***7.** 85 × 40
(67)   (67)   (67)

*8. a. Maura ran $\frac{3}{5}$ of the course but walked the rest of the way. What
(Inv. 5, fraction of the course did she walk?
61)

    b. Did Maura run more than 50% of the course or less than 50% of the
course?

9. **(Represent)** To what mixed number is the arrow pointing?
(37)

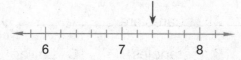

           6   7   8

*10. **(Model)** Draw a number line and show the locations of 0, 1, 2, , $1\frac{2}{3}$
(37) and $2\frac{1}{3}$.

11. **(Represent)** Mount Rainier stands four thousand, three hundred
(33) ninety-two meters above sea level. Use digits to write that number.

*12. Mo'Nique could make 35 knots in 7 minutes. How many knots could
(60) she make in 1 minute?

Saxon Math Intermediate 4

13. Estimate the sum of 6810 and 9030 by rounding each number to the
(59) nearest thousand before adding.

*14. Estimate the sum of $12.15 and $5.95. Then find the exact sum.
(43, 59)

15. $20 − ($8.95 + 75¢)
(43, 45)

16. 23.64 − 5.45
(43)

17.   43¢
(48)   ×   8

18. $3.05
(58)   ×   5

19. $2.63
(58)   ×   7

20. (**Connect**) Rewrite this addition problem as a multiplication problem
(27) and find the answer:

$$64 + 64 + 64 + 64 + 64$$

*21. $5\overline{)96}$
(68)

*22. $7\overline{)156}$
(68)

*23. $3\overline{)246}$
(65)

*24. $\dfrac{216}{6}$
(65)

*25. $4r = 156$
(41, 65)

*26. $195 \div 8$
(68)

*27. (**Model**) Use an inch ruler to find the lengths of segments *AB*, *BC*, and *AC*.
(39, 45)

A   B   C

*28. a. Multiple Choice Which word makes the following sentence untrue?
(63, 66)

All squares are _____.

    A polygons   **B** rectangles   **C** similar   **D** congruent

    b. (**Explain**) Explain your choice.

29. Compare: 2 quarts $\bigcirc$ $\frac{1}{2}$ gallon
(40)

*30. **Interpret** The lengths of three land tunnels in the United States are
(Inv. 6) shown in the graph. Use the graph to answer parts **a–c.**

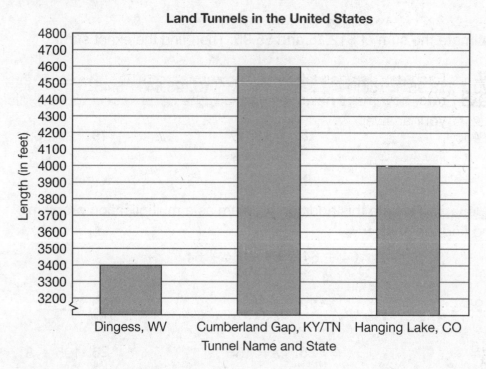

Land Tunnels in the United States

a. Write the names of the tunnels in order from shortest to longest.

b. How many feet longer is the Hanging Lake Tunnel than the Dingess
Tunnel?

c. One mile is equal to 5280 feet. Are the combined lengths of the
tunnels more than or less than 2 miles?

 Saxon Math Intermediate 4

Formulate Write and solve equations for problems **1** and **2**.

*1. Celeste has three hundred eighty-four baseball cards. Will has two
(25, 30) hundred sixty baseball cards. Celeste has how many more cards than
Will?

*2. Forty-two students could ride in one bus. There were 30 buses. How
(49, 67) many students could ride in all the buses?

*3. Kya's house key is 5.2 cm long. How many millimeters long is her
(69) house key?

*4. **Represent** Write a decimal and a fraction (or a mixed number) to
(Inv. 1, 37) represent each point.

*5. **Represent** Copy this hexagon and shade one sixth of it.
(26)

*6. a. This toothpick is how many centimeters long?
(69)

b. This toothpick is how many millimeters long?

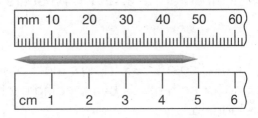

7. Twenty-five percent of the students in a class completed the science
(Inv. 5) project on Thursday. All of the other students in the class completed the
project on Friday. What percent of the students completed the project on
Friday?

8. **Analyze** One yard equals 3 feet. If each side of a square is 1 yard
(Inv. 2, 49) long, then what is the perimeter of the square in feet?

*9.
(59) [Explain] The number of students enrolled at each of three elementary schools is shown in the table below.

Elementary School Enrollment

School	Number of Students
Van Buren	412
Carter	495
Eisenhower	379

Use rounding to make a reasonable estimate of the total number of students enrolled at the three schools. Explain your answer.

*10.
(45, 69) Segment *AB* is 3.5 cm long. Segment *AC* is 11.6 cm long. How long is segment *BC*? Write a decimal subtraction equation and find the answer.

```
A                    B                                              C
●────────────────────●──────────────────────────────────────────────●
```

11.
(57, 60) **a.** Hugo rode 125 miles in 5 hours. His average speed was how many miles per hour?

b. Levi could ride 21 miles in 1 hour. At that rate, how many miles could Levi ride in 7 hours?

*12.
(55) The first three prime numbers are 2, 3, and 5. What are the next three prime numbers?

13.
(20, 59) [Estimate] Claudio's meal cost $7.95. Timo's meal cost $8.95. Estimate the total price for both meals by rounding each amount to the nearest dollar before adding.

*14. 250 ÷ 6
(68)

*15. 100 ÷ 9
(68)

16.
(43)
```
   36.2
    4.7
   15.9
  148.4
   30.5
 +  6.0
```

*17. $\dfrac{256}{8}$
(65)

*18. 4*w* = 60
(41, 64)

19. 9 × $4.63
(58)

*20. 80 × 29¢
(67)

21.
(52)
```
  $10.00
 − $ 1.73
```

22.
(52)
```
  36,428
 − 27,338
```

*23.
(67)
```
    78
 ×  60
```

*24. 4)̄328
(65)

*25. 7)̄375
(68)

*26. 5)̄320
(65)

Saxon Math Intermediate 4

27. $a + 5 = 25 + 25$
(61)

*28. **Explain** Solve the equation below and describe the steps in the
(43, 45) order you completed them.

$$4.7 - (3.6 - 1.7)$$

*29. a. Find the perimeter of this rectangle in millimeters.
(Inv. 2, Inv. 3)
 b. Find the area of this rectangle in square centimeters.

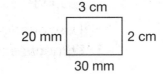

*30. Multiple Choice Each angle of this triangle is ___.
(23)
  A acute   **B** right
  C obtuse   **D** straight

Formulate Write and solve equations for problems **1** and **2**.

*1. There were 150 seats in the cafeteria. If 128 seats were filled, how
(31)   many seats were empty?

*2. **Analyze** Anaya ran 100 meters in 12.14 seconds. Marion ran
(Inv. 4, 100 meters in 11.98 seconds. Marion ran 100 meters how many
43)   seconds faster than Anaya?

3. Forty-two million is how much greater than twenty-four million?
(31, 34)

4. Keenan bought his lunch Monday through Friday. If each lunch cost
(49) $1.25, how much did he spend on lunch for the week?

*5. Find the perimeter and area of this rectangle:
(Inv. 2,
Inv. 3)

                                    5 units
                            ┌─┬─┬─┬─┬─┐
                    4 units │ │ │ │ │ │
                            ├─┼─┼─┼─┼─┤
                            │ │ │ │ │ │
                            ├─┼─┼─┼─┼─┤
                            │ │ │ │ │ │
                            ├─┼─┼─┼─┼─┤
                            │ │ │ │ │ │
                            └─┴─┴─┴─┴─┘

*6. ✏ **Explain** Re'Bekka read 30 pages a day on Monday, Tuesday, and
(22)   Wednesday. She read 45 pages on Thursday and 26 pages on Friday.
       How many pages did she read in all? Explain why your answer is
       reasonable.

*7. a. **Represent** One half of the cabbage seeds sprouted. If 74 seeds
(Inv. 5, were planted, how many sprouted? Draw a picture to solve the
70)   problem.

b. What percent of the seeds sprouted?

8. **Represent** Show all of the different ways these bills can be arranged
(36)   in a row.

*9. **Represent** What is $\frac{1}{6}$ of 60? Draw a picture to solve the problem.
(70)

Saxon Math Intermediate 4

*10. (57) **Analyze** Driving at a highway speed limit of 65 miles per hour, how far can a truck travel in 3 hours? Make a table to solve this problem.

*11. (60, 65) **Formulate** If a truck traveled 248 miles in 4 hours, then the truck traveled an average of how many miles each hour? Write an equation to solve this problem.

*12. (69) **a.** What is the diameter of this shirt button in centimeters?

b. What is the radius of this shirt button in millimeters?

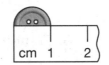

*13. (45, 69) Segment *AB* is 2.7 cm long. Segment *BC* is 4.8 cm long. How long is segment *AC*? Write a decimal addition equation and find the answer.

$$A \qquad\qquad B \qquad\qquad\qquad\qquad C$$

14. (43) $8 + $9.48 + 79¢

15. (50) 5.36 + 2.1 + 0.43

16. (52)
$100.00
− $ 59.47

17. (52)
37,102
− 18,590

18. (Inv. 3, 62) $\sqrt{49} \times 2^3$

*19. (67) $1.63 × 40

*20. (67) 60 × 39

21. (58) 7 × $2.56

*22. (68) 3)‾89‾

*23. (65) 9)‾234‾

24. (64) $\dfrac{90}{6}$

*25. (68) 243 ÷ 7

*26. (41, 65) 5*m* = 355

27. (2) 7 + *n* = 28

28. (35, Inv. 4) **Represent** Write twelve and three tenths as a mixed number and as a decimal number.

*29. (55) **Multiple Choice** Which of these numbers is a factor of both 12 and 20?

A 3   **B** 4   **C** 5   **D** 6

*30. **Represent** Draw a triangle that has one right angle.
(23)

Real-World Connection

Leroy's class took a field trip to the aquarium. A total of 35 students and adults went on the trip. Five sevenths of the group were students.

a. How many students went on the field trip?

b. Draw a diagram to show that your answer is reasonable.

Saxon Math Intermediate 4

* 1. A rectangular ceiling is covered with square tiles. The ceiling is 40 tiles
<small>(Inv. 3, 67)</small> long and 30 tiles wide. In all, how many tiles are on the ceiling?

2. There were two hundred sixty seats in the movie theater. All but forty-three
<small>(30)</small> seats were occupied. How many seats were occupied?

3. At the grand opening of a specialty food store, five coupons were
<small>(49, 58)</small> given to each customer. One hundred fifteen customers attended the
grand opening. How many coupons were given to those customers
altogether?

* 4. A recipe for making fruit punch calls for a cup of pineapple juice for
<small>(40)</small> each quart of fruit punch. How many cups of pineapple juice are
needed to make a gallon of fruit punch?

* 5. (**Analyze**) What is the value of 5 pennies, 3 dimes, 2 quarters, and
<small>(35)</small> 3 nickels?

* 6. a. (**Represent**) On the last Friday in May, one fourth of the 280
<small>(Inv. 5, 70)</small> students in a school were away on a field trip. How many
students were on the field trip? Draw a picture to solve the
problem.

b. What percent of the students were on the field trip?

* 7. (**Represent**) What is $\frac{1}{2}$ of 560? Draw a picture to solve the problem.
<small>(70)</small>

* 8. a. The line segment shown below is how many centimeters long?
<small>(69)</small>

b. The segment is how many millimeters long?

*9. The first four multiples of 9 are 9, 18, 27, and 36. What are the first four
(55) multiples of 90?

10. (Represent) Compare: $\frac{2}{3}$ ◯ $\frac{2}{5}$. Draw and shade two congruent
(56) rectangles to show the comparison.

*11. Badu can ride her bike an average of 12 miles per hour. At that
(57) rate, how many miles could she ride in 4 hours? Make a table to
solve this problem.

12. (43, 51) $375.48 $+ $536.70	**13.** (51) 367,419 + 90,852	**14.** (50) 42.3 57.1 28.9 96.4 + 38.0

15. (52) $20.00 − $19.39	**16.** (52) 310,419 − 250,527	

17. (58) $6.08 × 7	**18.** (67) 86 × 40	**19.** (48) 59¢ × 8

*20. 3)$\overline{180}$ ***21.** 8)$\overline{241}$ ***22.** 5)$\overline{323}$
(71)   (71)   (68)

*23. 184 ÷ 6   ***24.** 423 ÷ 7   ***25.** $\sqrt{36} + 4^2 + 10^2$
(71)   (71)   (Inv. 3, 62)

26. 9 + m = 27 + 72   **27.** 6n = 90
(61)   (41, 64)

28. (Model) Use an inch ruler to find the lengths of segments *AB, BC,*
(39) and *AC.*

        A   B   C

*29. If the diameter of a coin is 2 centimeters, then its radius is how many
(21, 69) millimeters?

Name _____

*30. **Estimate** From 7 a.m. until noon, the employees in a customer
(71)   service department received 147 phone calls. What is a reasonable
         estimate of the number of calls that were received each hour? Explain
         how you found your answer.

Early Finishers

Real-World Connection

Maddox has a roll of film with 32 photos and another roll with
12 photos. He developed both rolls of film. He decided to put all of his
photos into two scrapbooks. Each scrapbook will hold 20 pictures.

   a. How many pictures does Maddox have altogether?

   b. Will Maddox be able to place all of his photos into the two
       scrapbooks? Explain your answer.

1. Christie's car travels 18 miles on each gallon of gas. How many miles
(57) can it travel on 10 gallons of gas?

*2. (Analyze) Alejandro's front yard was 50 feet wide. Each time he
(Inv. 2, 52) pushed the mower along the length of the yard, he mowed a path
24 inches wide. To mow the entire yard, how many times did Alejandro
need to push the mower along the length of the yard?

*3. A gift of $160 is to be divided equally among 8 children. What amount
(64, 71) of money will each child receive?

4. Soccer practice lasts for an hour and a half. If practice starts at
(27) 3:15 p.m., at what time does it end?

*5. (Represent) One third of the team's 36 points were scored by
(70) Chinara. How many points did Chinara score? Draw a picture to
help you solve the problem.

6. Find the perimeter and area of the rectangle at right.
(Inv. 2, Inv. 3)

4 units

3 units

*7. (Estimate) This key is 60 mm long. The key is how many centimeters
(69) long?

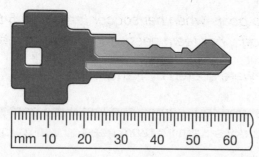

mm 10 20 30 40 50 60

*8. According to this calendar, the year 1902 began on what
(54) day of the week?

DECEMBER 1901

S	M	T	W	T	F	S
1	2	3	4	5	6	7
8	9	10	11	12	13	14
15	16	17	18	19	20	21
22	23	24	25	26	27	28
29	30	31				

Saxon Math Intermediate 4

*9. Jocelyn is the first person in line at the school cafeteria. Antonio, Bryan,
(72)   and Caroline are standing in line behind Jocelyn. In how many different
        orders could Antonio, Bryan, and Caroline be arranged behind Jocelyn?
        Name the ways.

10. A meter equals 100 centimeters. If each side of a square is 1 meter
(Inv. 2)   long, then what is the perimeter of the square in centimeters?

*11. List the first four multiples of 90.
(55)

12. $1.68 + 32¢ + $6.37 + $5
(43)

13. 4.3 + 2.4 + 0.8 + 6.7
(43)

14. ✏️ **Explain** Find $10 − ($6.46 + $2.17). Describe the steps you used.
(43, 45)

15. 5 × 4 × 5   **16.** 359 × 70   **17.** 50 × 74
(62)   (67)   (67)

*18. 2)‾161‾   ***19.** 5)‾400‾   ***20.** 9)‾462‾
(71)   (71)   (68)

21. $\frac{216}{3}$ ***22.** 159 ÷ 4   ***23.** $\frac{490}{7}$
(65)   (68)   (71)

24. $\frac{126}{3}$ ***25.** 360 ÷ $\sqrt{36}$ **26.** 5n = 120
(65)   (Inv. 3,   (41, 65)
                          71)

*27. **Analyze** Use the information below to answer parts **a** and **b**.
(72)

*Kamili scored two goals when her soccer team won 5 to 4 on November 3.
To make the playoffs, her team needs to win two of the next three games.*

a. How many goals were scored by Kamili's teammates?

b. Kamili's team has won four games and lost three games. Altogether,
how many games does Kamili's team need to win to make the
playoffs?

28. a. **Classify** Angles C and D of this polygon are right
(23)   angles. Which angle appears to be an obtuse
           angle?

b. **Classify** Which segments are perpendicular?

c. **Classify** Which segments are parallel?

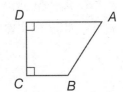

*29. **Multiple Choice** Which two of these figures appear to be congruent?
(66)

A   B   C   D

*30. (Represent) The average weights of some animals are shown in the
(Inv. 6) table. Make a bar graph to display the data.

Average Weights of Animals

Animal	Weight (in pounds)
Domestic Rabbit	8
Otter	13
Ringtail Monkey	6
Chicken	7

Saxon Math Intermediate 4

*1. (**Represent**) Half of the 48 pencils were sharpened. How many were
(Inv. 5, 70) *not* sharpened? What percent of the pencils were not sharpened?
Draw a picture to solve the problem.

*2. (**Represent**) What number is $\frac{1}{4}$ of 60? Draw a picture to solve the
(70) problem.

*3. Use this information to answer parts **a–c:**
(52, 72)

> *Thirty students are going on a field trip. Each car can hold*
> *five students. The field trip will cost each student $5.*

   a. How many cars are needed for the field trip?

   b. Altogether, how much money will be needed?

   c. Diego has saved $3.25. How much more does he need to go on
   the field trip?

4. (**Analyze**) During the summer, the swim team practiced $3\frac{1}{2}$ hours a day.
(27) If practice started at 6:30 a.m., at what time did it end if there were no
breaks?

5. One gallon of water will be poured into 1-quart bottles.
(40) How many 1-quart bottles will be filled?

1 gal   1 qt

*6. Each side of a regular polygon has the same length. A regular hexagon
(69) is shown below. How many millimeters is the perimeter of this
hexagon?

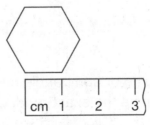

7. A mile is five thousand, two hundred eighty feet. The Golden Gate
(31, 52) Bridge is four thousand, two hundred feet long. The Golden Gate
Bridge is how many feet less than 1 mile long?

Name _____

*8. **Multiple Choice** Which of these numbers is *not* a multiple of 90?
(55)

    A 45   **B** 180   **C** 270   **D** 360

9. What number is halfway between 300 and 400?
(Inv. 1)

10. $37.56 - 4.2$ **11.** $4.2 + 3.5 + 0.25 + 4.0$
(50)   (50)

12. $\$100.00$ **13.** $251{,}546$ **14.** n
(52) $-\ \$\ 31.53$ (52) $-\ \ \ 37{,}156$ (24) $+\ 423$
                                                             618

15. $\$3.46$ **16.** 96 **17.** $\$0.59$
(58) $\times\ \ \ \ \ 7$ (67) $\times\ 30$ (58) $\times\ \ \ \ \ \ 8$

*18. $7\overline{)633}$ ***19.** $5\overline{)98}$ ***20.** $3\overline{)150}$
(71)   (68)   (71)

*21. $329 \div 6$ ***22.** $274 \div 4$ ***23.** $247 \div 8$
(68)   (68)   (71)

24. $\sqrt{25} \times m = 135$ **25.** $z - 476 = 325$ **26.** $6a = 12 + 6$
(41, 65)   (24)   (61)

*27. **Connect** Segment *AB* is 2.3 cm long. Segment *BC* is 3.5 cm long.
(45, 69) How long is segment *AC*? Write a decimal addition problem and find
the answer.

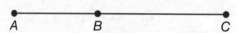

      A   *B*   *C*

*28. **Conclude** Which transformation would position $\triangle ABC$
(73) on $\triangle ABD$?

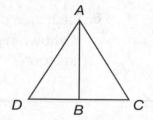

29. **Estimate** Using rounding or compatible numbers, which numbers
(59) would you choose to estimate the exact product of 25×25? Explain
your reasoning.

    Saxon Math Intermediate 4

Name _____

*30. ✏️ **Interpret** This pictograph shows the maximum speeds that
(Inv. 6) animals can run for a short distance. Use the pictograph to answer the
questions that follow.

Animal	Maximum Speed (in miles per hour)
Warthog	🐎 🐎 🐎
Wild turkey	🐎 🐎
Lion	🐎 🐎 🐎 🐎 🐎
Elephant	🐎 🐎 🐎
Zebra	🐎 🐎 🐎 🐎

Key: 🐎 = 10 miles per hour

a. Which animals can run at a speed of at least 30 miles per hour?

b. A squirrel can run at a maximum speed of 12 miles per hour. About
how many times greater is the maximum speed of a lion? Explain
your reasoning.

c. Some athletes can run at a maximum speed of about 28 miles per
hour for short distances. Could some athletes run faster than an
elephant? Explain your answer.

*Real-World
Connection*

Mr. Mikel drew the figure shown below. His students said the answer
was "flip." What questions did Mr. Mikel ask the students?

1. Milagro volunteered for sixty-two hours last semester. Michael
(1, 17) volunteered for seven hours. Mitsu and Michelle each volunteered for
twelve hours. Altogether, how many hours did they volunteer?

*2. The Matterhorn is fourteen thousand, six hundred ninety-one feet high.
(31, 52) Mont Blanc is fifteen thousand, seven hundred seventy-one feet high.
How much taller is Mont Blanc than the Matterhorn?

3. There are 25 squares on a bingo card. How many squares are on
(49) 4 bingo cards?

*4. (Analyze) Ninety-six books were placed on 4 shelves so
(70) that the same number of books were on each shelf. How
many books were on each shelf?

96 books

*5. One half of the 780 fans stood and cheered. How many fans stood and
(Inv. 5, 70) cheered? What percent of the fans stood and cheered?

6. How many years is ten centuries?
(54)

*7. (Estimate) A package of José's favorite trading cards costs $1.75.
(59) What is a reasonable estimate of the number of packages José could
purchase with $10.00? Explain your answer.

*8. What fraction of this set is not shaded?
(74)

9. This 2-liter bottle contains how many milliliters of juice?
(40)

10. a. What is the perimeter of the rectangle shown at
(Inv. 2, right?
Inv. 3)

b. How many 1-inch squares would be needed to cover
this rectangle?

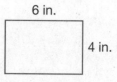

6 in.

4 in.

Saxon Math Intermediate 4

Name _____

*11. **Predict** How many millimeters are equal to 10 centimeters? Use the
(32) table to decide.

Millimeters	10	20	30	40	50
Centimeters	1	2	3	4	5

12. Which transformation(s) would position △STR on △PQR?
(73)

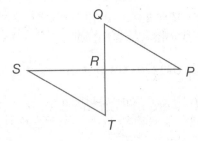

13. $6.15 − ($0.57 + $1.20)
(43, 45)

14. 43,160 − 8459
(52)

*15. 8 × 8 × 8
(62)

16. $3.54 × 6
(58)

17. 80 × 57
(67)

*18. 704 × 9
(58)

*19. 9)‾354‾
(68)

*20. 7)‾285‾
(71)

*21. 5)‾439‾
(68)

*22. 515 ÷ 6
(68)

*23. $\dfrac{360}{4}$
(71)

24. 784 ÷ 8
(65)

*25. $\sqrt{36} + n = 6^2$
(Inv. 3, 62)

26. 462 − y = 205
(24)

27. 50 = 5r
(41)

*28. **Conclude** Find the next number in this counting sequence:
(3)

..., 90, 180, 270, ____, ...

*29. **Explain** Sierra's arm is 20 inches long. If Sierra swings her arm in a
(21) circle, what will be the diameter of the circle? Explain your answer.

*30. **Multiple Choice** Which of these numbers is a prime number?
(55)

 A 1   **B** 2   **C** 4   **D** 9

Saxon Math Intermediate 4   **203**

1. Pears cost 59¢ per pound. How much would 4 pounds of pears cost?
(49)

2. Find the perimeter and area of this rectangle:
(Inv. 2,
Inv. 3)

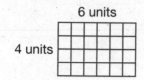

6 units

4 units

*3. (Connect) There were three hundred sixty books on the floor. Da-Xia
(70) put one fourth of the books on a table.

    a. How many books did Da-Xia put on the table?

    b. How many books were still on the floor?

4. What percent of the books in problem **3** were left on the floor?
(Inv. 5)

*5. (Represent) To what decimal number is the arrow pointing? What
(37) mixed number is this?

2   3

*6. (Estimate) Two hundred seventy-two students attend one elementary
(59) school in a city. Three hundred nineteen students attend another
elementary school. Estimate the total number of students attending
those schools by rounding the number of students attending each
school to the nearest hundred before adding.

*7. What fraction of this set is shaded?
(74)

*8. One quart of milk is how many ounces?
(40)

9. One quart is a quarter of a gallon. So one quart is what percent of
(40,
Inv. 5) a gallon?

Saxon Math Intermediate 4

*10. **Interpret** Use the information in the bar graph below to answer parts
(Inv. 6) **a** and **b**.

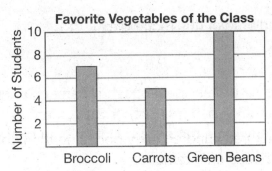

Favorite Vegetables of the Class

a. Carrots are the favorite vegetable of how many students?

b. Altogether, how many students said broccoli or carrots are their
favorite vegetable?

*11. **Represent** The 8 a.m. temperature was −5 degrees Fahrenheit.
(18) By 3 p.m., the temperature had increased 10 degrees. What was the
3 p.m. temperature?

*12. **Conclude** Describe the number of degrees and the
(75) direction of a turn that would move this letter B to an
upright position.

13. $86.47
(43, 51) + $47.98

14. 36.7
(50) − 18.5

15. 2358
(51) 4715
317
2103
+ 62

*16. 8)716
(68)

*17. 2)161
(71)

18. 7)434
(65)

*19. 513 ÷ 6
(68)

*20. $\frac{270}{9}$
(71)

21. $\frac{267}{3}$
(65)

22. $n − 7.5 = 21.4$
(24, 50)

23. $6.95
(58) × 8

24. 46
(67) × 70

25. 460
(58) × 9

26. $3a = 30 + 30$
(61)

27. $3^2 − 2^3$
(62)

*28. A quarter turn is 90°. How many degrees is a three-quarter turn?
(75)

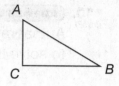
29. **Conclude** **a.** Which segment appears to be
(23, 66) perpendicular to segment *BC*?

b. Draw a triangle similar to, but not congruent to,
△*ABC*.

A
C *B*

30. ✏️ **Explain** During their professional baseball careers, pitcher
(52) Nolan Ryan struck out 5714 batters. Pitcher Steve Carlton struck out
4136 batters. How many more batters did Nolan Ryan strike out?
Explain why your answer is reasonable.

*Real-World
Connection*

Alba glanced at the clock and saw that it was 3:00 p.m. When Alba
glanced at the clock again, it was 3:45 p.m.

a. During this time, how many degrees did the minute
hand turn?

b. Draw a picture to solve the problem.

Saxon Math Intermediate 4

*1. (**Analyze**) Brett can type at a rate of 25 words per minute.
(57) At that rate, how many words can he type in 5 minutes? Make a table to solve this problem.

*2. Shakia has five days to read a 200-page book. If she wants to
(52, 71) read the same number of pages each day, how many pages should she read each day?

*3. (**Estimate**) Jira ordered a book for $6.99, a dictionary for $8.99, and a
(43, 59) set of maps for $5.99. Estimate the price for all three items. Then find the actual price.

4. Patrick practiced the harmonica for 7 weeks before his recital. How
(49) many days are equal to 7 weeks?

5. One third of the books were placed on the first shelf. What fraction of
(61) the books were not placed on the first shelf ?

*6. (**Represent**) To what decimal number is the arrow pointing? What
(Inv. 1) mixed number is this?

*7. In the word HIPPOPOTAMI, what fraction of the letters are Ps?
(74)

*8. Multiple Choice Deunoro ran a 5-kilometer race. Five kilometers is
(Inv. 2) how many meters?

   A 5 m   **B** 50 m   **C** 500 m   **D** 5000 m

9. What is the perimeter of this triangle?
(Inv. 2)

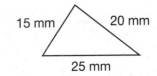

*10. (**Estimate**) Altogether, 117 students attend 6 different grades of a
(76) small elementary school. About the same number of students attend each grade. What is a reasonable estimate of the number of students in each grade? Explain your answer.

*11. (Connect) The length of segment *AB* is 3.6 cm. The length of segment
(45, 69) *AC* is 11.8 cm. What is the length of segment *BC*? Write and solve a
decimal addition equation and a decimal subtraction equation.

A ●————————— B ●——————————————————————— C ●

12. $25 − ($19.71 + 98¢)
(43, 45)

13. 12 + 13 + 5 + n = 9 × 8
(2, 24)

14. $5.00 − $2.92
(43)

15. 36.21 − 5.7
(50)

16. 5 × 6 × 9
(62)

17. 50 × 63
(67)

18. 478 × 6
(58)

*19. 3)‾435
(76)

*20. 7)‾867
(76)

*21. 5)‾$13.65
(76)

22. 453 ÷ 6
(68)

*23. 543 ÷ 4
(76)

*24. $4.72 ÷ 8
(76)

25. n + 6 = 120
(24)

26. 4w = 132
(41, 65)

*27. 4 + 8 + 7 + 6 + 4 + n + 3 + 6 + 5 = 55
(2)

*28. (Predict) Mieko was facing east. If Mieko turned 90° clockwise, in
(75) which direction would she be facing?

29. If the diameter of a playground ball is one foot, then its radius is how
(21) many inches?

*30. (Conclude) Which transformations would move △*ABC*
(73) to position *RST*?

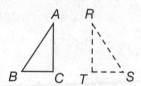

Saxon Math Intermediate 4

*1. Use the information in the pictograph below to answer parts **a–c.**
(40, Inv. 6)

Consumed by Matt in One Day	
Water	🥛🥛🥛🥛🥛🥛
Tea	🥛
Milk	🥛🥛🥛🥛
Juice	🥛🥛🥛

Key: 🥛 = 1 cup = 8 ounces

a. How many pints of liquid did Matt drink in 1 day?

b. Matt drank twice as much water as he did what other beverage?

c. He drank exactly 1 quart of which beverage?

*2. (Analyze) There were 4 rooms. One fourth of the 56 guests gathered in
(Inv. 5, 70) each room. How many guests were in each room? What percent of the
guests were in each room?

3. (Estimate) Which of these arrows could be pointing to 2500?
(Inv. 1)

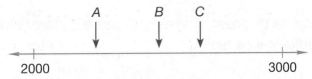

*4. (Estimate) Zoe estimated the sum of 682 + 437 + 396 by first
(59) rounding each addend to the nearest hundred. What was Zoe's
estimate of the actual sum?

*5. What fraction of this set is shaded?
(74)

*6. (Connect) Jevonte weighed 9 pounds when he was born. How many
(77) ounces is that?

*7. a. **Estimate** The segment below is how many centimeters long?
(69)

b. The segment is how many millimeters long?

cm 1 2 3 4 5 6

*8. **Represent** A company was sold for $7,450,000. Use words to
(33) write that amount of money.

9. If each side of a hexagon is 1 foot long, then how many inches is its
(Inv. 2,
63) perimeter?

10.   93,417   **11.**   42,718   **12.**   1307
(51)   + 8,915   (24, 52) −   k   (51)   638
                                 26,054   5219
                                                       138
                                                    +   16
13. $100.00   **14.** 405,158
(41, 52) − $ 86.32   (52) − 396,370

15. 567 × 8   **16.** 30 × 84¢   **17.** $2.08 × 4
(58)   (67)   (58)

*18. 4)$15.00   ***19.** 936   ***20.** 8)4537
(76)   (76) ───   (76)
                               6

*21. 452 ÷ 5   **22.** 378 ÷ 9   ***23.** 960 ÷ 7
(71)   (65)   (76)

24. $\sqrt{16} \times n = 100$ **25.** $5b = 10^2$
(Inv. 3,   (61, 62)
41)

*26. **Represent** To what decimal number is the arrow pointing? What
(Inv. 1) mixed number is this?

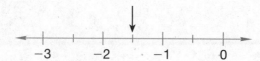

*27. **Conclude** Mona turned a quarter turn clockwise, and then she turned
(75) two more quarter turns clockwise. Altogether, Mona turned how many
degrees?

210

Saxon Math Intermediate 4

Name _____

28. Find the perimeter and area of the rectangle shown
(Inv. 2, Inv. 3) at right.

5 units

3 units

29. The relationship between feet and inches is shown in the table below:
(3, 32)

Inches	12	24	36	48	60
Feet	1	2	3	4	5

a. **Generalize** Write a rule that describes the relationship.

b. **Predict** How many inches are equal to 12 feet?

*30. **Verify** The weight of an object on the moon is about $\frac{1}{6}$ of its weight on
(77) Earth. Obi's golden retriever weighs 84 pounds. What would the golden
retriever weigh on the moon?

Real-World Connection

The great white shark is found in oceans all over the world. It is the
world's largest predatory fish. The average weight of the great white is
2500 pounds.

a. Does the average great white shark weigh more or less than a ton?
Explain your answer.

b. Does the average great white shark weigh more or less than
two tons? Explain your answer.

1. Jarell bought pencils on sale for 5 cents each. He spent 95 cents. How
(52, 64) many pencils did Jarell buy?

2. **Estimate** Clanatia went to the store with $9.12. She spent $3.92.
(25, 30) About how much money did Clanatia have left?

3. Pamela listened to half of a 90-minute tape. How many minutes of the
(70) tape did she hear?

*4. One fourth of the guests gathered in the living room. What fraction
(Inv. 5, of the guests did not gather in the living room? What percent of the
61) guests did not gather in the living room?

*5. If one side of an equilateral triangle is 3 centimeters long, then what is
(69, 78) its perimeter in

    a. centimeters?   **b.** millimeters?

*6. **Represent** To what decimal number is the arrow pointing? What
(Inv. 1) mixed number is this?

*7. **Analyze** Half of a gallon is a half gallon. Half of a half gallon is a
(40, 74) quart. Half of a quart is a pint. Half of a pint is a cup. A cup is what
fraction of a quart?

*8. A baby deer is called a fawn. Most fawns weigh about 3 kilograms
(77) when they are born. How many grams is that?

*9. **Explain** Isabella estimated the product of 389 × 7 to be 2800.
(59) Explain how Isabella used rounding to make her estimate.

*10. **Multiple Choice** It is late afternoon. When the minute
(27, 75) hand turns 360°, what time will it be?

    A 11:25 a.m.   **B** 5:56 a.m.

    C 4:56 p.m.   **D** 5:56 p.m.

    Saxon Math Intermediate 4

*11. **Represent** Compare: $\frac{3}{4}$ ◯ $\frac{4}{5}$. Draw and shade two congruent
(56) rectangles to show the comparison.

12. 4.32 − 2.5
(50)

13. 3.65 + 5.2 + 0.18
(50)

14. $50.00 − $42.60
(50)

15. $17.54 + 49¢ + $15
(43)

*16. 2)$\overline{567}$
(76)

*17. 6)$\overline{\$34.56}$
(76)

*18. 4)$\overline{978}$
(76)

19. 398 × 6
(58)

20. 47 × 60
(67)

21. 8 × $6.25
(58)

*22. 970 ÷ $\sqrt{25}$
(Inv. 3, 76)

*23. $\frac{372}{3}$
(76)

24. 491 ÷ 7
(71)

25. 8n = 120
(41, 65)

26. $f \times 3^2 = 108$
(62, 65)

27. 7 + 8 + 5 + 4 + n + 2 + 7 + 3 = 54
(2)

*28. Find the perimeter and area of this rectangle:
(Inv. 2, Inv. 3)

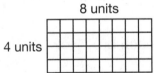

8 units

4 units

*29. Name the transformation(s) that would move △ABC to position WXY.
(73)

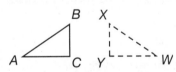

*30. The first four multiples of 18 are 18, 36, 54, and 72. What are the first
(55) four multiples of 180?

*1. **Interpret** Use this circle graph to answer parts **a–d.**
(Inv. 6, 74)

How Franz Spent His Day

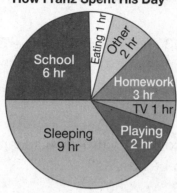

a. What is the total number of hours shown in the graph?

b. What fraction of Franz's day was spent watching TV?

c. If Franz's school day starts at 8:30 a.m., at what time does it end?

d. **Multiple Choice** Which two activities together take more than half of Franz's day?

  A sleeping and playing   B school and homework

  C school and sleeping   D school and playing

2. One fifth of the 60 eggs were placed in each box. How
(70) many eggs were placed in each box?

3. **Estimate** Which of these arrows could be pointing to 2250?
(Inv. 1)

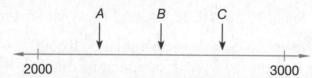

*4. **Estimate** Find a reasonable estimate of $4.27, $5.33, and $7.64 by
(59) rounding each amount to the nearest dollar before adding.

*5. a. What fraction of this set is *not* shaded?
(74)

b. What decimal of this set is shaded?

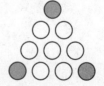

Saxon Math Intermediate 4

*6. Kurt drove across the state at 90 kilometers per hour. At that rate,
(57) how far will Kurt drive in 4 hours? Make a table to solve the problem.

7. **Verify** Is the product of 3 and 7 a prime number? How do you
(55) know?

*8. a. What is the perimeter of this square?
(Inv. 2,
Inv. 3) **b.** If the square were to be covered with 1-inch squares,
how many squares would be needed?

5 inches

*9. **Represent** Draw the capital letter E rotated 90° clockwise.
(73)

10. $20.10
(43, 51)   − $16.45

11. $98.54
(43, 51)   + $ 9.85

12. 380×4
(58)

13. 97×80
(67)

*14. $5\overline{)3840}$
(76)

15. 8.63×7
(58)

16. $4.25 − 2.4$
(50)

*17. $8\overline{)\$70.00}$
(76)

*18. $6\overline{)3795}$
(76)

19. $4p = 160$
(41, 71)

20. $\dfrac{\sqrt{64}}{\sqrt{16}}$
(Inv. 3)

21. $\dfrac{287}{7}$
(65)

*22. $10 \times (6^2 + 2^3)$
(45, 62)

23. **Analyze** Find the perimeter of this rectangle
(Inv. 2,
69)   **a.** in centimeters.

   b. in millimeters.

1.5 cm

0.8 cm

24. The thermometer shows the outside temperature on a cold,
(18) winter day in Cedar Rapids, Iowa. What temperature does
the thermometer show?

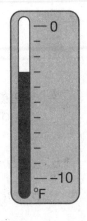

*25. Mulan spun completely around twice on a skateboard. How many
₍₇₅₎ degrees did Mulan spin?

*26. a. (**Conclude**) Which of these letters does *not* have a line
₍₇₉₎ of symmetry?

T N V W

b. Which of these letters has rotational symmetry?

*27. a. Multiple Choice Sketch each of the triangles below. Which of
₍₇₈₎ these triangles does *not* exist?

    A a scalene right triangle   **B** an isosceles right triangle

    C an equilateral right triangle   **D** an equilateral acute triangle

b. ✎ (**Justify**) Explain why the triangle you chose does not
exist.

*28. (**Analyze**) How many different amounts of money could you make
₍₂₂₎ using any two of the four coins shown below? Name the amounts.

*29. (**Estimate**) Cora estimated the quotient of 261 ÷ 5 to be 50. Explain
₍₆₅₎ how Cora used a compatible number to make her estimate.

Saxon Math Intermediate 4

Name _____

*30. (25) **Formulate** Write and solve a subtraction word problem for the equation $175 - t = 84$.

 Early Finishers
Real-World Connection

a. Draw a capital letter that has rotational symmetry and line symmetry.

b. Draw a capital letter that has line symmetry but does *not* have rotational symmetry.

c. What is the difference between the two figures you have drawn?

1. If the chance of rain is 30%, then is it more likely that it will rain or that
(Inv. 5) it will not rain?

*2. (Analyze) Monty ran the race 12 seconds faster than Ivan. Monty ran
(31) the race in 58 seconds. Ivan ran the race in how many seconds?

3. The whole rectangle is divided into 5 equal parts.
(70) Each part is what percent of the rectangle?
(*Hint:* Divide 100 by 5.)

4. (Analyze) How many 6-inch-long sticks can be cut from a 72-inch-long
(52) stick?

*5. Multiple Choice One fifth of the leaves had fallen. What fraction of
(61) the leaves had *not* fallen?

 A $\frac{2}{5}$ **B** $\frac{3}{5}$ **C** $\frac{4}{5}$ **D** $\frac{5}{5}$

6. (Estimate) Which of these arrows could be pointing to 5263?
(Inv. 1)

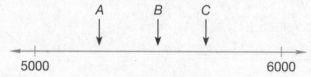

*7. What fraction of the months of the year have 31 days?
(54, 74)

*8. The prefix *kilo-* means what number?
(77)

9. (Explain) Cleon would like to estimate the difference between $579
(52) and $385. Explain how Cleon could use compatible numbers to make
an estimate.

*10. The triangle at right is equilateral.
(Inv. 2, 78)
  a. How many millimeters is the perimeter of the
      triangle?

  b. (Classify) Describe the angles.

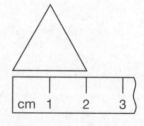

Saxon Math Intermediate 4

Name _____

11. Three liters equals how many milliliters?
(40)

*12. Wilma runs 5 miles every day. At that rate, how many days would it take
(60) her to run 40 miles? Make a table to solve the problem.

13. $2n = 150$
(41, 65)

14. $24.25 - (6.2 + 4.8)$
(45, 50)

15. 103,279
(51) $+ \ 97,814$

16. $36.14
(43, 51) $+ \ \$27.95$

17. 39,420
(52) $- \ 29,516$

18. $60.50
(24, 52) $- \quad\quad n$
  $\overline{\quad\ \$43.20}$

19. 604
(58) $\times \quad 9$

20. 87
(67) $\times \quad 60$

21. $6.75
(58) $\times \quad 4$

*22. $3\overline{)618}$
(80)

*23. $5\overline{)\$21.50}$
(76, 80)

*24. n
(24, 52) $+ \ 1467$
  $\overline{\quad 2459}$

*25. $\dfrac{600}{4}$
(80)

26. $543 \div 6$
(71)

27. $472 \div 8$
(65)

*28. $9w = 9^2 + (9 \times 2)$
(61, 62)

*29. Divide mentally: $5\overline{)3000}$
(80)

*30. a. (Represent) Draw a triangle that is congruent to this
(66, 79) isosceles triangle. Then draw its line of symmetry.

b. Draw the triangle when it is rotated 180°.

1. Cecilia skated 27 times around the rink forward and 33 times around the rink
(1) backward. How many times did she skate around the rink altogether?

2. Nectarines cost 68¢ per pound. What is the price for 3 pounds of
(49) nectarines?

*3. **Analyze** In bowling, the sum of Amber's score and Bianca's score
(72) was equal to Consuela's score. If Consuela's score was 113 and
Bianca's score was 55, what was Amber's score?

*4. One third of the 84 students were assigned to each room. How many
(70) students were assigned to each room? Draw a picture to explain how
you found your answer.

5. Round 2250 to the nearest thousand.
(54)

*6. In the word ARIZONA, what fraction of the letters are *not* As?
(74)

*7. **Multiple Choice** The African elephant weighed 7 tons. How many
(77) pounds is that?

    A 7000   **B** 140   **C** 14,000   **D** 2000

*8. **Estimate** The tip of this shoelace is how many millimeters long?
(69)

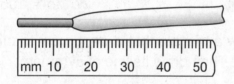

*9. **Conclude** Choose the more reasonable measure for parts **a** and **b**.
(40, 77)

    a. a new box of cereal: 2 lb or 2 oz

    b. a full pail of water: 1 pt or 1 gal

*10. According to this calendar, what is the date of the last
(54) Tuesday in February 2019?

FEBRUARY 2019						
S	M	T	W	T	F	S
					1	2
3	4	5	6	7	8	9
10	11	12	13	14	15	16
17	18	19	20	21	22	23
24	25	26	27	28		

    Saxon Math Intermediate 4

Name _____

11. **Represent** Forty-two thousand, seven hundred is how much greater
(31, 52) than thirty-four thousand, nine hundred?

12. Find the perimeter and area of this rectangle:
(Inv. 2,
Inv. 3)

10 units

5 units

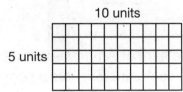

*13. **Analyze** Sh'Reese was riding north. Then she turned 90° to the left.
(75) After turning, in what direction was Sh'Reese riding? Explain how you
know.

14. 6743 − (507 × 6)
(52, 58)

15. $70.00 − $63.17
(43)

16. 3 × 7 × 0
(62)

17. $8.15 × 6
(58)

18. 67¢ × 10
(67)

19. 4.5 + 0.52 + 1.39
(50)

*20. 2)$12.16
(76, 80)

*21. 6)4321
(80)

*22. 8)4800
(80)

*23. 963 ÷ √9
(Inv. 3,
76)

*24. 5³ ÷ 5
(62, 65)

*25. $6.57 ÷ 9
(76)

26. 4n = 200
(41, 71)

27. 7d = 105
(41, 65)

28. 473
(17, 24) 286
+ n
943

29. 1 + 12 + 3 + 14 + 5 + 26
(1)

*30. The bar graph shows the average life span in years of several animals.
(Inv. 6) Use the graph to solve parts **a–c.**

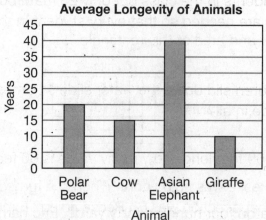

a. Write the names of the animals in order from longest to shortest average life span.

b. What fraction of the average life span of an Asian elephant is the average life span of a polar bear?

c. When compared to the average life span of a giraffe, how many times greater is the average life span of an Asian elephant?

Real-World Connection

a. Use the angle measurement tool you created in the activity to draw a polygon. Use all the angles on your tool at least once.

b. For each angle of the polygon, label the type of angle as obtuse, right, or acute.

c. Then label each angle with the number of degrees.

Saxon Math Intermediate 4

Formulate Write and solve equations for problems **1–4.**

1. There were 35 students in the class but only 28 math books. How many
(31) more math books are needed so that every student in the class has a
math book?

2. Each of the 7 children slid down the water slide 11 times. How many
(49) times did they slide in all?

*3. A bowling lane is 60 feet long. How many yards is 60 feet?
(Inv. 2,
52)

*4. Wei carried the baton four hundred forty yards. Eric carried it eight
(1, 51) hundred eighty yards. Jesse carried it one thousand, three hundred
twenty yards, and Bernardo, carried it one thousand, seven hundred
sixty yards. Altogether, how many yards was the baton carried?

5. One third of the members voted "no." What fraction of the members
(61) did not vote "no"?

*6. **Explain** Marissa would like to estimate the sum of 6821 + 4963.
(59) Explain how Marissa could use rounding to make an estimate.

7. What fraction of the days of the week start with the letter S?
(74)

*8. Together, Bob's shoes weigh about 1 kilogram. Each shoe weighs
(77) about how many grams?

*9. **Interpret** Use the line graph below to answer parts **a–c.**
(Inv. 6)

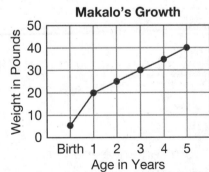

Makalo's Growth

a. About how many pounds did Makalo weigh on his second
   birthday?

Name _____

b. About how many pounds did Makalo gain between his third and fifth birthdays?

c. Copy and complete this table using information from the line graph:

Makalo's Growth

Age	Weight
At birth	6 pounds
1 year	
2 years	

10. If 65% of the lights are on, then what percent of the lights are off?
(Inv. 5)

*11. (**Analyze**) Kerry is thinking about names for a baby girl. She likes Abby
(39) or Bekki for the first name and Grace or Marie for the middle name. What combinations of first and middle names are possible with these choices?

*12. The table shows the number of vacation days Carson earns at work:
(Inv. 8)

Days Worked	Vacation Days Earned
30	1
60	2
90	3
120	4
150	5
180	6

a. (**Generalize**) Write a word sentence that describes the relationship of the data.

b. (**Predict**) Use the word sentence you wrote to predict the number of vacation days Carson will earn by working 300 days.

Saxon Math Intermediate 4

Name _____

13. $\$60.75$
(43, 51) $+ \$95.75$

14. $\$16.00$
(43, 52) $- \$15.43$

15. 3.15
(50) $- 3.12$

16. 320
(67) $\times\ 30$

17. 465
(58) $\times\ 7$

18. $\$0.98$
(58) $\times\ \ \ 6$

19. $425 \div 6$
(71)

*20. $\$6.00 \div 8$
(76)

*21. $625 \div 5$
(76)

22. $3r = 150$
(41, 71)

23. $10^2 + t = 150$
(24, 62)

24. $1 + 7 + 2 + 6 + 9 + 4 + n = 37$
(2)

25. **a.** If the 3-inch square is covered with 1-inch squares, how
(Inv. 3) many of the 1-inch squares are needed?

b. What is the area of the larger square?

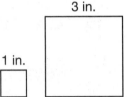

26. **a.** What is the perimeter of this triangle?
(Inv. 2, 78)

b. Is the triangle a right triangle, an acute triangle, or an obtuse triangle?

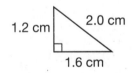

*27. **a.** (Conclude) Which of these letters has only one line of symmetry?
(79)

Q R H T

b. Which of these letters has rotational symmetry?

*28. Write the capital letter P rotated 90° counterclockwise.
(75)

*29. **Multiple Choice** Three of these triangles are congruent. Which
(66) triangle is *not* one of the three congruent triangles?

A   B   C   D

*30. The radius of this circle is 1.2 cm. What is the diameter
(21, 43) of the circle?

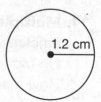

1.2 cm

Real-World Connection

In science Nam learned that a bee's honeycomb is a tessellation of hexagons. Nam is putting tile in his bathroom, and he wants to use a tessellation design on the floor. He decides to use 6-inch square tiles to cover part of the floor.

a. Using the measurements of the rectangle below, how many 6-inch tiles does he need?

b. Choose a different shape, and then draw a different tessellation that Nam could use on his bathroom floor.

2 feet

5 feet

Saxon Math Intermediate 4

*1. Multiple Choice To prepare for a move to a new building, the
(49, 67) employees of a library spent an entire week packing books in boxes.
On Monday the employees packed 30 books in each of 320 boxes.
How many books did those boxes contain?

   A 9600 books   **B** 960 books   **C** 320 books   **D** 350 books

2. The movie was 3 hours long. If it started at 11:10 a.m., at what time did
(27) it end?

3. ✏️ (Explain) Jonathan is reading a 212-page book. If he has finished
(25, 30) 135 pages, how many pages does he still have to read? Explain why
your answer is reasonable.

4. Khalil, Julian, and Elijah each scored one third of the team's
(70) 42 points. Copy and complete the diagram at right to show
how many points each person scored.

42 points

5. (Estimate) A family has $4182 in a savings account. Round the
(54) number of dollars in the account to the nearest thousand.

*6. ✏️ (Explain) The shirt was priced at $16.98. The tax was $1.02. Sam
(83) paid the clerk $20. How much money should Sam get back? Explain
your thinking.

*7. What fraction of the letters in the following word are Is?
(74)

   S U P E R C A L I F R A G I L I S T I C E X P I A L I D O C I O U S

8. Compare: $3 \times 4 \times 5 \bigcirc 5 \times 4 \times 3$
(Inv. 1,
62)

9. $m - 137 = 257$
(24)

10. $n + 137 = 257$
(24)

11. $1.45 + 2.4 + 0.56 + 7.6$
(50)

12. $5.75 - (3.12 + 0.5)$
(45, 50)

*13. **(Analyze)** Use the information below to answer parts **a–c.**
(72)

    In the first 8 games of this season, the Rio Hondo football team won 6 games and lost 2 games. They won their next game by a score of 24 to 20. The team will play 12 games in all.

    a. In the first nine games of the season, how many games did Rio Hondo win?

    b. Rio Hondo won its ninth game by how many points?

    c. What is the greatest number of games Rio Hondo could win this season?

14. 638
(67) × 50

15. 472
(58) × 9

16. $6.09
(58) × 6

*17. 3)921
(80)

*18. 5)678
(76)

*19. 4)2400
(80)

20. $12.60 ÷ 5
(76)

21. $14.34 ÷ 6
(76)

*22. $46.00 ÷ 8
(76)

23. $9^2 = 9n$
(61, 62)

24. $5w = 5 \times 10^2$
(61, 62)

25. The names of one fourth of the months begin with the letter J. What
(Inv. 5) percent of the months begin with the letter J?

*26. a. **(Model)** Use a ruler to find the perimeter of the rectangle
(Inv. 2, at right in millimeters.
69)

    b. **(Analyze)** Draw a rectangle that is similar to the rectangle in part **a** and whose sides are twice as long. What is the perimeter in centimeters of the rectangle you drew?

27. Barton turned around three times. How many degrees did Barton turn?
(75)

28. Rachel wants to determine if two right triangles are congruent, so
(73) she moves △1 to the position of △2 to see if they match. Name two transformations Rachel uses to move △1.

Saxon Math Intermediate 4

29. Below we show an equilateral triangle, an isosceles triangle, and
(78, 79) a scalene triangle. Name the triangle that does not have reflective
symmetry.

*30. Four students wrote their names on slips of paper. The names were
(36) then placed in a paper bag and picked one at a time.

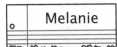 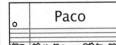 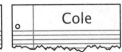 

List the different ways the second, third, and fourth names could have
been chosen if Cole's name was chosen first.

*Real-World
Connection*

Before taxes were calculated, Crystal spent $34.00 on school supplies.
After adding tax, she paid the clerk $37.40.

a. What was the tax on Crystal's purchase?

b. How many cents per dollar of tax did Crystal pay?

*1. If it is not a leap year, what is the total number of days in January,
(54) February, and March?

2. A tailor made each of 12 children a pair of pants and 2 shirts. How
(49) many pieces of clothing did the tailor make?

*3. Ariel did seven more chin-ups than Burke did. If Ariel did eighteen
(31) chin-ups, how many chin-ups did Burke do?

4. Kadeeja drove 200 miles on 8 gallons of gas. Her car averaged how
(60) many miles on each gallon of gas?

*5. Melinda paid the clerk $20.00 for a book that was priced at $8.95. The
(83) tax was 54¢. How much money should she get back?

*6. a. Which two prime numbers are factors of 15?
(55)

   b. (Explain) Is 15 a prime number? Why or why not?

7. If each side of an octagon is 1 centimeter long, what is the octagon's
(69) perimeter in millimeters?

8. (Represent) One third of the 18 marbles were blue. How many
(70) of the marbles were blue? Draw a picture to solve the problem.

9. a. (Analyze) The Mendez family hiked 15 miles in 1 day. At that
(57) rate, how many miles would they hike in 5 days? Make a table to
   solve the problem.

   b. (Formulate) Write an equation to represent the data in the table.

*10. (Explain) Mylah picked 3640 peaches in 7 days. She picked an
(60, 80) average of how many peaches each day? Explain why your answer is
   reasonable.

*11. a. (Analyze) Zachary did 1000 push-ups last week. He did 129 of
(74, 84) those push-ups last Wednesday. What fraction of the 1000 push-ups
did Zachary do last Wednesday?

b. (Represent) Write the answer to part **a** as a decimal number.
Then use words to name the number.

*12. (Explain) Suppose that an object on Earth has a known mass of
(77) 80 kilograms. Will the mass of that object be less than, more than, or the
same as on the other planets in our solar system? Explain your answer.

13. $4.56 - (2.3 + 1.75)$
(45, 50)

14. $\sqrt{36} + n = 7 \times 8$
(Inv. 3, 61)

15. $3 \times 6 \times 3^2$
(62)

16. $462 \times \sqrt{9}$
(Inv. 3, 58)

17. $7^2 - \sqrt{49}$
(Inv. 3, 62)

18. $\begin{array}{r} 36 \\ \times\ 50 \\ \hline \end{array}$
(67)

19. $\begin{array}{r} \$4.76 \\ \times\ \ \ \ 7 \\ \hline \end{array}$
(58)

20.
(2)
$\begin{array}{r} 4\ \ 17 \\ 3 \\ 2 \\ 7 \\ 6 \\ 8 \\ +\ n \\ \hline 47 \end{array}$

21. $\dfrac{524}{4}$
(76)

*22. $6\overline{)4200}$
(80)

23. $5\overline{)\$26.30}$
(76)

24. $2n = \$3.70$
(41, 76)

25. $786 \div 3$
(76)

*26. $4902 \div 7$
(80)

*27. Write 0.321 as a fraction.
(84)

28. Find the perimeter and area of this square:
(Inv. 2, Inv. 3)

3 yards

3 yards

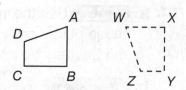
29. Which transformations would move figure *ABCD* to
(73) position *WXYZ*?

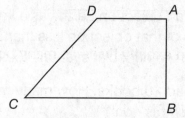

30. **Estimate** Which angle in this figure looks like it measures about 45°?
(23, 81)

The Republic of Malta is a group of small islands in the Mediterranean
Sea. It is directly south of Sicily and north of Libya. From 1972 to 1994,
the currency used in the Republic of Malta included a 2-mil coin, a
3-mil coin, and a 5-mil coin. A mil was $\frac{1}{1000}$ (or 0.001) of a lira, another
Maltese money amount.

*Real-World
Connection*

a. Write the value of each mil coin in both decimal and fraction form
as it relates to the lira.

b. Use words to name each fraction in part **a.**

c. If you were to add a 2-mil coin, a 3-mil coin, and a 5-mil coin
together, how many mils would you have?

d. How many lira would equal the total in part **c?** Write the total as a
decimal and than as a fraction in lowest terms.

*1. **(Interpret)** Use the information in the graph below to answer parts **a–c.**
(49,
Inv. 6)

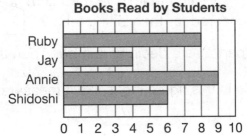

Books Read by Students

Ruby
Jay
Annie
Shidoshi

0 1 2 3 4 5 6 7 8 9 10

a. Which student has read exactly twice as many books as Jay?

b. Shidoshi's goal is to read 10 books. How many more books does he need to read to reach his goal?

c. If the books Annie has read have an average of 160 pages each, how many pages has she read?

*2. Dala saw some pentagons. The pentagons had a total of 100 sides.
(52, 63) How many pentagons did Dala see?

*3. Mariah bought a rectangular piece of land that was 3 miles long and
(Inv. 3, 2 miles wide. Fifty percent of the land could be farmed. How many
Inv. 5) square miles could be farmed?

*4. Max bought 10 pencils for 24¢ each. The tax was 14¢. What was the
(83) total cost of the pencils?

*5. **Multiple Choice** A full pitcher of orange juice contains about how
(40) much juice?

   A 2 ounces   **B** 2 liters   **C** 2 gallons   **D** 2 cups

6. **(Represent)** Draw a triangle that has two perpendicular sides. What
(23, 78) type of triangle did you draw?

7. a. **(Represent)** One fourth of the 48 gems were rubies. How many of
(Inv. 5, the gems were rubies? Draw a picture to solve the problem.
70)

   b. What percent of the gems were not rubies?

*8. a. **Represent** One thousand fans attended the game, but only
^(74, 84) 81 fans cheered for the visiting team. What fraction of the fans who
attended the game cheered for the visiting team?

b. Write the answer in part **a** as a decimal number. Then use words to
name the number.

9. $46.01 - (3.68 + 10.2)$
^(45, 50)

10. $728 + c = 1205$
⁽²⁴⁾

11. 36×10 **12.** 100×42 **13.** $\$2.75 \times 1000$
⁽⁸⁵⁾   ⁽⁸⁵⁾   ⁽⁸⁵⁾

14. $\$3.17$ **15.** 206 **16.** 37
⁽⁵⁸⁾ $\underline{\times \quad\ 4}$ ⁽⁵⁸⁾ $\underline{\times \quad\ 5}$ ⁽⁶⁷⁾ $\underline{\times\ 40}$

17. $3\overline{)492}$ **18.** $5\overline{)860}$ **19.** $6m = \$9.30$
⁽⁷⁶⁾   ⁽⁷⁶⁾   ^(41, 76)

20. $168 \div 2^3$ ***21.** $\$20.00 \div 8$ ***22.** $1600 \div \sqrt{16}$
^(62, 65)   ^(76, 80)   ^(Inv. 3, 80)

23. Find the perimeter and area of this rectangle:
^(Inv. 2, Inv. 3)

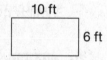

10 ft

6 ft

*24. a. **Verify** Which of these letters has two lines of symmetry?
⁽⁷⁹⁾

HAPPY

b. Which of these letters has rotational symmetry?

*25. **Estimate** Which angle in this figure looks like it measures about
^(23, 81) 135°?

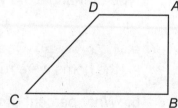

Saxon Math Intermediate 4

Name _____

*26. Multiple Choice Luz wants to cover a floor with tiles. Which of these
(82) tile shapes will *not* tessellate, or will not completely cover the floor?

A △   B ☐   C ⬠   D ⬡

*27. The table shows the relationship between meters and centimeters:
(Inv. 8)

Number of Meters	1	2	3	4	5
Number of Centimeters	100	200	300	400	500

a. **Formulate** Write a formula to represent the relationship.

b. **Predict** Use your formula to find the number of centimeters in
10 meters.

28. In Dodge City, Kansas, the average maximum temperature in January
(18) is 41°F. The average minimum temperature is 19°F. How many degrees
cooler is 19°F than 41°F?

29. The Peace River is 1210 miles long, and its source is in British Columbia.
(52) The Red River is 1290 miles long, and its source is in New Mexico.
Which river is longer?

*30. Model Draw a number line from 6 to 7 divided into tenths. On it show the
(Inv. 1) locations of 6.1, $6\frac{3}{10}$, 6.6, and $6\frac{9}{10}$.

1. It takes Tempest 20 minutes to walk to school. At what time should she
(27) start for school if she wants to arrive at 8:10 a.m.?

*2. A container and its contents weigh 125 pounds. The contents of the
(25, 30) container weigh 118 pounds. What is the weight of the container?

*3. Anjelita is shopping for art supplies and plans to purchase a sketchpad
(83) for $4.29, a charcoal pencil for $1.59, and an eraser for 69¢. If the
amount of sales tax is 43¢ and Anjelita pays for her purchase with a
$10 bill, how much change should she receive?

4. According to this calendar, October 30, 1904,
(54) was what day of the week?

OCTOBER 1904						
S	M	T	W	T	F	S
						1
2	3	4	5	6	7	8
9	10	11	12	13	14	15
16	17	18	19	20	21	22
23	24	25	26	27	28	29
30	31					

*5. (**Explain**) From 3:00 p.m. to 3:45 p.m., the minute hand of a clock
(75) turns how many degrees? Explain your thinking.

6. Round three thousand, seven hundred eighty-two to the nearest
(34, 54) thousand.

7. The limousine weighed 2 tons. How many pounds is 2 tons?
(77)

*8. (**Represent**) One fifth of the 45 horses were pintos. How many of the
(70) horses were pintos? Draw a picture to illustrate the problem.

9. What percent of the horses in problem **8** were pintos?
(Inv. 5,
70) (*Hint:* Find $\frac{1}{5}$ of 100%.)

100%

10. (**Represent**) Which point on the number line below could represent
(Inv. 1) 23,650?

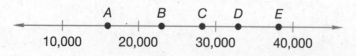

Saxon Math Intermediate 4

Name _____

*11. (Connect) Write each decimal number as a fraction:
(Inv. 4, 84)
   a. 0.1   **b.** 0.01   **c.** 0.001

12. $36.47
(43, 51) + $ 9.68

13. $30.00
(52)   − $13.45

14.   6
(17)   8
      17
      23
    110
      25
  + 104

15.   476
(58) ×   7

16.   804
(58) ×   5

17. $12.65 - (7.43 - 2.1)$
(45, 50)

18. $5^2 + 5^2 + n = 10^2$
(61, 62)

19. (Represent) Write each of these numbers with words:
(35, Inv. 4)

   a. $2\frac{1}{10}$ **b.** 2.1

*20. 100 × 23¢
(85)

*21. 60 × 30
(86)

*22. 70 × $2.00
(86)

*23. 3)$6.27
(76, 80)

24. 7)820
(76)

25. 6)333
(68)

26. $625 \div \sqrt{25}$
(Inv. 3, 76)

*27. $4000 \div 2^3$
(62, 80)

28. $2w = 1370$
(41, 76)

29. Find the perimeter and area of this square.
(Inv. 2, Inv. 3)

                                      10 m

*30. a. (Analyze) Some combinations of shapes will fit together
(63, 82)   to cover a flat surface. What two types of polygons are
    used in the pattern at right?

    b. Does this tessellation have line symmetry?

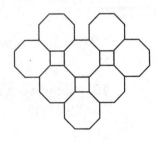

*1. **(Analyze)** Use the following information to answer parts **a–c.**
(27, 72)

Freeman rode his bike 2 miles from his house to Didi's house. Together they rode 4 miles to the lake. Didi caught 8 fish. At 3:30 p.m. they rode back to Didi's house. Then Freeman rode home.

    a. Altogether, how far did Freeman ride his bike?

    b. It took Freeman an hour and a half to get home from the lake. At what time did he get home?

    c. Didi caught twice as many fish as Freeman. How many fish did Freeman catch?

*2. Saraj bought some feed priced at $12.97. Tax was 91¢. He paid with a
(83) $20 bill. How much change should he receive?

3. **(Estimate)** Find a reasonable sum of 4876 and 3149 by rounding each
(59) number to the nearest thousand and then adding.

4. **(Estimate)** What is the perimeter of a pentagon if each side is
(Inv. 2, 63) 20 centimeters long? Explain your reasoning.

*5. **(Estimate)** Find the length of this segment to the nearest quarter inch:
(39)

6. **(Represent)** One half of the 18 players were on the field. How many
(70) players were on the field? Draw a picture to illustrate the problem.

7. A dime is $\frac{1}{10}$ of a dollar. What fraction of a dollar is a penny?
(36)

8. A dime is what percent of a dollar?
(Inv. 5)

Saxon Math Intermediate 4

Name _____

9. Find 13^2 by multiplying 13×13.
(87)

10. **Represent** One millimeter is $\frac{1}{1000}$ of a meter. Write that number as
(84) a decimal number. Then use words to write the number.

*11.   31
(87) $\times\, 21$

*12.   32
(87) $\times\, 31$

*13.   13
(87) $\times\, 32$

*14.   11
(87) $\times\, 11$

*15.   12
(87) $\times\, 14$

*16. 30×800
(86)

17. $7\overline{)1000}$
(76)

18. $3\overline{)477}$
(76)

19. $5\overline{)2535}$
(80)

20. $\$64.80 \div 9$
(76, 80)

21. $716 \div 4$
(76)

22. $8x = 352$
(41, 65)

*23. How many different three-digit numbers can you write using the digits
(36) 1, 5, and 0? Each digit may be used only once, and the digit 0 may not
be used in the hundreds place.

*24. Find the perimeter and area of this rectangle:
(Inv. 3,
86)

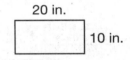

20 in.

10 in.

*25. **Represent** Draw an equilateral triangle with sides 2 cm long.
(78)

26. What is the perimeter in millimeters of the triangle you drew in
(Inv. 2,
69) problem **25?**

*27. a. **Conclude** In this polygon, which side appears to be parallel to
(23, 81)   side AB?

   b. **Estimate** Which angle looks as if it might measure
   110°?

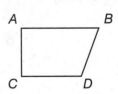

Saxon Math Intermediate 4   **239**

28. This graph shows the relationship between Rudy's age and Neelam's
(Inv. 8) age. How old was Neelam when Rudy was 4 years old?

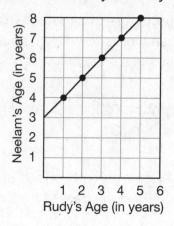

29. **Represent** Each grid represents a decimal number.
(Inv. 4)

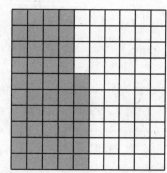 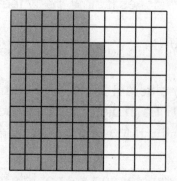

Write each decimal number. Then write the sum and the difference of
those numbers.

30. **Estimate** A mail carrier worked from 8 a.m. to noon and from 1 p.m.
(76) to 4 p.m. During those times, the carrier delivered mail to 691 homes.
About how many deliveries did the carrier make each hour? Explain
your answer.

*Real-World
Connection*

Murals are pictures painted on walls. In 2005, archaeologists revealed
the last wall of a room-sized mural that was painted more than
2000 years ago in the ancient Mayan city of San Bartolo, Guatemala.

a. Estimate the area of a mural that measures 23 feet by 84 feet.

b. Find the actual area of a mural with the measurements given.

c. How close was your estimate to the actual area?

Saxon Math Intermediate 4

*1. (Interpret) Taryn packed 6 table-tennis balls in each package. There
(88) were 100 table-tennis balls to pack.

    a. How many packages did he fill?

    b. How many table-tennis balls were left over?

*2. Write the formula for the area of a square. Then find the area of a
(62, 87) square with sides 12 inches long.

*3. (Estimate) Paola bought four pretzels priced at 59¢ each. The
(83) sales tax was 16¢. Estimate the total cost of the pretzels. Explain your
thinking.

4. Twenty-four inches is how many feet?
(Inv. 2)

*5. **a.** Segment *YZ* is how many millimeters long?
(45, 69)
    b. Segment *YZ* is how many centimeters long?

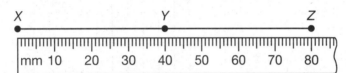

6. Jorge finished eating breakfast at the time shown on the
(27) clock. He finished eating lunch 5 hours 20 minutes later.
What time did Jorge finish eating lunch?

7. (Represent) Write the number 7528 in expanded form. Then use
(16, 33) words to write the number.

*8. **a.** (Represent) One fifth of the 25 band members missed the note.
(Inv. 5, 70) How many band members missed the note? Draw a picture to
illustrate the problem.

    b. What percent of the band members missed the note?

*9. Nikki cut a rectangular piece of paper along a diagonal to
(73) make two triangles. What transformation can Nikki use to
find out if the triangles are congruent?

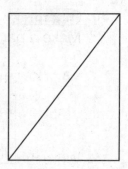

10. $6.35 + $14.25 + $0.97 + $5
(43, 51)

*11. 4.60 − (1.4 + 2.75)   **12.** $10.00 − (46¢ + $1.30)
(43, 50)   (43, 45)

*13. 28 × 1000   ***14.**   13   ***15.**   12
(85)   (87)   × 13   (87)   × 11

16. $8.67   ***17.**   31   ***18.**   12
(58)   ×   9   (87)   × 31   (87)   × 31

19. 7)3542   **20.** 6)$33.00   **21.** 8)4965
(80)   (76, 80)   (80)

22. 482 ÷ 5   **23.** 2700 ÷ 9   **24.** 2700 ÷ √9
(68)   (80)   (Inv. 3, 80)

25. 7 + 7 + n = 7²   **26.** 3n = 6²
(61, 62)   (61, 62)

*27. a. (Represent) Draw an obtuse triangle.
(78)

 b. (Explain) Describe the segments of the obtuse angle. Explain
your thinking.

28. The classroom was 40 feet long and 30 feet wide. How
(Inv. 3, 86) many 1-foot square floor tiles were needed to cover the
floor?

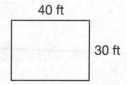

*29. a. In polygon *ABCD,* which side appears to be parallel to
(23) side *AD?*

 b. (Classify) Describe the angles.

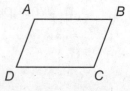

Saxon Math Intermediate 4

*30. **Interpret** This table shows the heights of several tall buildings.
(Inv. 6) Make a bar graph to display the data.

Tall Buildings in the United States

Building	Location	Height (stories)
The Pinnacle	Chicago, IL	48
Interstate Tower	Charlotte, NC	32
Two Union Square	Seattle, WA	56
28 State Street	Boston, MA	40

Real-World Connection

George's Peach Pit Stop sells peaches in paper packages. Each package holds 25 peaches. George has an order for 346 peaches.

a. How many packages can be filled?

b. How many packages will he actually need?

c. How many peaches will be in the partially filled package?

Saxon Math Intermediate 4 **243**

*1. (Interpret) The coach divided 33 players as equally as possible into
(88) 4 teams.

    a. How many teams had exactly 8 players?

    b. How many teams had 9 players?

2. (Justify) On the package there were two 39¢ stamps, two 20¢
(1, 43) stamps, and one 15¢ stamp. Altogether, how much did the stamps
on the package cost? Explain why your answer is reasonable.

3. Daniella read 20 pages each day. How many pages did she read in
(49, 67) 2 weeks?

4. In the first track meet of the season, Wyatt's best triple jump measured
(Inv. 2) 36 feet. What was the distance of that jump in yards?

*5. What is the perimeter of this isosceles triangle in
(Inv. 2, 69) centimeters?

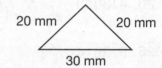

20 mm   20 mm

30 mm

*6. Multiple Choice Which of these tallies represents a prime number?
(55, Inv. 7)

  A 卌 ||| **B** 卌 卌

  C 卌 卌 | **D** 卌 卌 ||

*7. Multiple Choice About how much liquid is in this medicine
(40) dropper?

  A 2 milliliters   **B** 2 liters

  C 2 pints   **D** 2 cups

8. Solve for n: $87 + 0 = 87 \times n$
(61)

     Saxon Math Intermediate 4

Name _____

*9. **Represent** One third of the 24 students finished early. How
(70)   many students finished early? Draw a picture to illustrate the
          problem.

10. What percent of a dollar is a quarter?
(Inv. 5)

11. $478.63   **12.**   137,140   **13.** $60.00
(43, 51) + $ 32.47   (52) − 129,536   (52) − $24.38

*14. 70 × 90   **15.**   11   ***16.**   12
(86)   (87) × 13   (87) × 12

17. $4.76   ***18.**   21   ***19.**   21
(58)   ×   8   (87) × 13   (87) × 21

20. 4)3000   **21.** 5n = 635   **22.** 7)426
(80)   (41, 76)   (71)

23. 8)3614   **24.** $\dfrac{2736}{6}$
(76)   (76)

25. How much is one fourth of $10.00?
(70)

*26. **Represent** Draw and shade circles to show that $1\frac{1}{2}$ equals $\frac{3}{2}$.
(89)

*27. **a.** **Represent** Draw a rectangle that is 5 cm long and 4 cm wide.
(Inv. 2,
Inv. 3)
    b. What is the perimeter and area of the rectangle you drew?

*28. **a.** **Conclude** In this polygon, which side appears to be
(23, 79)   parallel to side *BC*?

    b. Copy this figure and draw its line of symmetry.

    c. Does this figure have rotational symmetry?

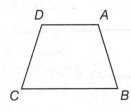

*29. (Analyze) Which two-digit number less than 20 is a multiple of both
(55) 4 and 6?

*30. (Interpret) This circle graph shows the results of an election for class
(Inv. 6) president. Use the graph to answer the questions that follow.

Class Election Results

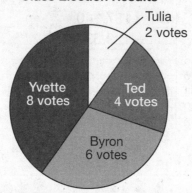

Tulia
2 votes

Yvette
8 votes

Ted
4 votes

Byron
6 votes

a. Which candidate won the election? How many votes did that
candidate receive?

b. Altogether, how many votes were cast in the election?

c. Which number is greater: the number of votes received by the
winner, or the sum of the number of votes received by all of the
other candidates?

Saxon Math Intermediate 4

*1. **Interpret** The line graph shows the average monthly temperatures
(Inv. 6) during spring in Jacksonville, Florida. Use the graph to answer the
questions that follow.

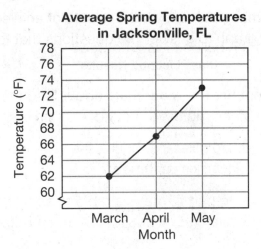

Average Spring Temperatures in Jacksonville, FL

a. What is the average temperature during March in Jacksonville, Florida? During April? During May?

b. Write a sentence that compares the average March temperature to the freezing temperature of water.

c. In Salt Lake City, Utah, the average May temperature is 14 degrees cooler than the average May temperature in Jacksonville, Florida. What is the average May temperature in Salt Lake City?

2. The 3-pound melon cost $1.44. What was the cost per pound?
(52)

3. Jin spun all the way around in the air and dunked the basketball. Jin
(75) turned about how many degrees?

*4. Shunsuke bought a pair of shoes priced at $47.99. The sales tax was
(83) $2.88. Shunsuke gave the clerk $60.00. How much change should he receive?

5. **Analyze** If the perimeter of a square is 1 foot, how many inches long
(Inv. 2) is each side?

*6. a. The mass of a dollar bill is about 1 gram. Use this information to
(77) estimate the number of dollar bills it would take to equal 1 kilogram?

Name _____

b. Would the mass of a dollar bill still be about 1 gram on the moon? Why or why not?

7. a. (Represent) One fourth of the 64 balloons were red. How many
(Inv. 5, 70) balloons were red? Draw a picture to illustrate the problem.

b. What percent of the balloons was not red?

*8. a. T'Marra knew that her trip would take about 7 hours. If she left
(27) at half past nine in the morning, around what time should she arrive?

b. If T'Marra traveled 350 miles in 7 hours, then she traveled an average of how many miles each hour?

c. Using your answer to part **b,** make a table to show how far T'Marra would travel at her average rate in 1, 2, 3, and 4 hours.

*9. (Explain) On the last Wednesday in May, school buses
(88) will transport 116 students on a field trip. Each bus can seat 40 passengers. How many buses will be needed to transport the students, 8 teachers, and 13 adult volunteers? Explain your answer.

10. Compare: 3049 ◯ 3049.0
(33)

*11. (Estimate) Shakura purchased a birthday present for each of
(22) two friends. Including sales tax, the cost of one present was $16.61 and the cost of the other present was $14.37. What is a reasonable estimate of the total cost of the presents? Explain your answer.

*12. (Represent) Manuel is deciding what to wear. He must choose
(83) between blue pants and black pants, and between a red shirt, a green shirt, and a yellow shirt. Draw a tree diagram to show all of the different ways to combine two pairs of pants and three shirts.

*13. Eighty-eight horseshoes are enough to shoe how many horses?
(52, 64)

*14. a. (Conclude) Triangles *ABC* and *DEF* are congruent. Which
(73, 78) transformations would move △*ABC* to the same position as △*DEF*?

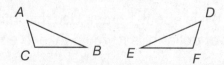

Saxon Math Intermediate 4

b. Multiple Choice Which of these words does *not* describe triangles *ABC* and *DEF*?

    A similar   **B** obtuse   **C** scalene   **D** isosceles

15. Find $0.625 - (0.5 + 0.12)$. Describe the steps in order.
(45, 50)

16. Mentally find the product of 47×100.
(85)

17.   328   ***18.**   43   ***19.**   25
(58) $\times$ 4   (87) $\times$ 32   (90) $\times$ 35

20. $5\overline{)4317}$ **21.** $8\overline{)\$40.00}$ **22.** $6\overline{)3963}$
(76)   (80)   (80)

23. $3a = 426$ **24.** $2524 \div 4$ ***25.** 60×700
(76)   (76)   (86)

26. (Represent) Draw and shade circles to show that $2\frac{1}{2}$ equals $\frac{5}{2}$.
(89)

27. $4 + 3 + 27 + 35 + 8 + n = 112$
(2)

*28. a. Segment *BC* is 1.7 cm long. How many centimeters long is
(69)   segment *AB*?

         A   *B*   *C*

         cm   1   2   3   4

b. Write a decimal addition problem that is illustrated by the lengths of segments *AB*, *BC*, and *AC*.

*29. a. Name a pair of parallel edges in the figure at
(45)   right.

b. Name a pair of perpendicular edges.

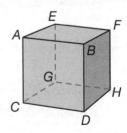

*30. Before multiplying two numbers, Ashley estimated the product. After
(90) multiplying the numbers, she used the estimate to check her work. Explain
how Ashley can estimate the product of 32 × 57.

*Real-World
Connection*

a. Describe the error Julio made on his homework.

$$\begin{array}{r} 67 \\ \times\ 38 \\ \hline 536 \\ 201 \\ \hline 737 \end{array}$$

b. What is the correct answer?

Saxon Math Intermediate 4

*1. (**Analyze**) Three quarters, four dimes, two nickels, and seven pennies
(35)   is how much money?

*2. (**Analyze**) Colvin separated the 37 math books as equally as possible
(88)   into 4 stacks.

   a. How many stacks had exactly 9 books?

   b. How many stacks had 10 books?

*3. (**Explain**) Gregory paid $1 for a folder and received 52¢ in change. If
(83)   the tax was 3¢, how much did the folder cost without tax? Explain your
       thinking.

4. Ryan wrote each of his 12 spelling words five times. In all, how many
(49)   words did he write?

5. (**Estimate**) In the 2004 presidential election, 5992 voters in Blaine
(59)   County, Idaho, voted for candidate John Kerry, and 4034 voters voted
       for candidate George Bush. Estimate the total number of votes those
       two candidates received and explain your estimate.

6. What is the tally for 10?
(Inv. 7)

7. Name the shaded part of this square
(Inv. 4)   **a.** as a fraction.

   b. as a decimal number.

8. (**Represent**) One sixth of the 48 crayons is in the box. How many
(70)   crayons are in the box? Draw a picture to illustrate the problem.

*9. Segment *AB* is 32 mm long. Segment *BC* is 26 mm long. Segment
(45, 69)   *AD* is 91 mm long. How many millimeters long is segment *CD*?

A   *B*   *C*   *D*

*10. Which digit in 6.125 is in the hundredths place?
(91)

11. (**Estimate**) If a pint of water weighs about one pound, then about how
(40, 77)   many pounds does a quart of water weigh?

*12. 4.32 − 0.432
(91)

13. $5^2 + \sqrt{25} + n = 30$
(Inv. 3, 62)

14. $6.08
(58) $\times$ 8

*15. 47
(90) $\times$ 24

*16. 36
(90) $\times$ 62

17. 53 × 30
(67)

*18. 63 × 37
(90)

19. 100 × 32
(85)

20. $4\overline{)3456}$
(76)

21. $8n = 6912$
(76)

22. $7\overline{)$50.40}$
(76, 80)

*23. **Represent** Draw and shade circles to show that $1\frac{1}{4}$ equals $\frac{5}{4}$.
(89)

*24. a. **Represent** Draw a square with sides 4 cm long.
(21, Inv. 5)

   b. Shade 50% of the square you drew. How many square centimeters did you shade?

*25. **Represent** Write twenty-one thousandths as a fraction and as a
(84) decimal number.

*26. **Explain** Emma mixed two quarts of orange juice from frozen
(40, 88) concentrate. She knows 1 quart is equal to 32 fluid ounces. The small juice glasses Emma is filling each have a capacity of 6 fluid ounces. How many juice glasses can Emma fill? Explain your answer.

*27. **Multiple Choice** Use the polygons below to answer parts **a–c.**
(63, 79)
A △ B ⏢ C ▢ D ⏢

   a. Which of these polygons has no lines of symmetry?

   b. Which two of these polygons have rotational symmetry?

   c. Which polygon is *not* a quadrilateral?

*28. How many degrees does the minute hand of a clock turn in half
(75) an hour?

*29. Compare: 4.2 ◯ 4.200
(91)

*30. Use the pictograph below to answer parts **a–c.**
(Inv. 6)

Animal	Typical Weight (in pounds)
Alligator	🔔—🔔 🔔—
Porpoise	🔔— 🔔
Wild Boar	🔔—🔔—🔔—🔔—🔔—🔔
Seal	🔔—🔔—🔔—🔔

Key: 🔔—🔔 = 100 pounds

a. What amount of weight does each symbol represent?

b. Write the typical weights of the animals in order from least to greatest.

c. ✏️ **Connect** Write a sentence that compares the weights of two animals.

Early Finishers

Real-World Connection

Gas is sold in amounts to the tenth of a penny, which is the same as the thousandth of a dollar. Gus's Grand Gas Station is selling gas for $2.679 per gallon.

a. Which digit is in the thousandths place? Which digit is in the tenths place?

b. Which is more: 2.679 or 2.67?

c. If you were to buy ten gallons of gas, how much would you spend? If you were to pay $30 for the gas, what would your change be?

*1. (Analyze) Use this information to answer parts **a–c**.
(72, 88)
  Lanisha invited 14 friends over for lunch. She plans to make 12 tuna sandwiches, 10 bologna sandwiches, and 8 chicken sandwiches.

  a. How many sandwiches will Lanisha make in all?

  b. Including Lanisha, each person can have how many sandwiches?

  c. If Lanisha cuts each tuna sandwich in half, how many halves will there be?

2. Five pounds of grapes cost $2.95. What is the cost per pound?
(53)

*3. If each side of a hexagon is 4 inches long, what is the perimeter of the
(Inv. 2, hexagon in feet?
63)

4. (Represent) Nine million, four hundred thousand is how much greater
(31, 52) than two million, seven hundred thousand?

*5. Three brands of whole grain cereal cost $4.68, $4.49, and $4.71.
(30) Arrange these prices in order from least to greatest.

*6. (Estimate) Lauren saw that a package of 50 blank CDs costs $9.79.
(58) Estimate the cost for Lauren to buy 100 blank CDs. Explain your
  answer.

7. Name the shaded part of the large square
(Inv. 4)
  a. as a fraction.

  b. as a decimal number.

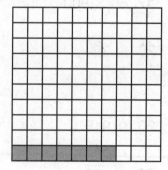

8. (Represent) Use words to write $7572\frac{1}{8}$.
(35)

*9. (Represent) At Kelvin's school, one fifth of the 80 fourth grade
(70) students ride the bus to and from school each day. How many
  fourth grade students ride the bus? Draw a picture to illustrate
  the problem.

Saxon Math Intermediate 4

Name _____

10. How many different three-digit numbers can you write using the digits
(3) 9, 1, and 5? Each digit may be used only once in every number you
write.

11. Franca's trip only lasted for a couple of hours. According to the clocks
(27) shown below, exactly how long did the trip take?

Began   Finished

*12. ✎ Justify James traveled 301 miles in 7 hours. He traveled an
(60) average of how many miles per hour? Explain why your answer is
reasonable.

*13. Martino bought 3 folders priced at $1.99 each. Sales tax was 33¢. He
(83) paid with a $20 bill. How much money should he get back?

14. $25 + $2.75 + $15.44 + 27¢
(43, 51)

*15. $m + 0.26 = 6.2$ **16.** $100 − $89.85
(91)   (43, 52)

17. 60×900 **18.** 42×30 **19.** 21×17
(86)   (67)   (87)

*20. $\begin{array}{r} 36 \\ \times\ 74 \\ \hline \end{array}$ ***21.** $\begin{array}{r} 48 \\ \times\ 25 \\ \hline \end{array}$ **22.** $\begin{array}{r} \$4.79 \\ \times\ \ \ \ 6 \\ \hline \end{array}$
(90)   (90)   (58)

23. $9\overline{)918}$ **24.** $5r = 485$
(80)   (41)

25. $6\overline{)482}$ **26.** $50.00 \div 8$
(53)   (76)

27. $2100 \div 7$ **28.** $0.875 − (0.5 + 0.375)$
(80)   (45, 50)

Name _____

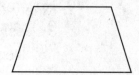

*29. **Classify** This polygon is what type of quadrilateral?
(92)   How do you know?

*30. **Represent** Draw and shade rectangles to show that $1\frac{2}{3}$ equals $\frac{5}{3}$.
(89)

Real-World Connection

Stephanie's class has to identify polygons for math class.

a. Draw and label a picture for each of the following shapes that
her class could use as examples: square, rectangle, rhombus,
trapezoid, and parallelogram.

b. Explain why each drawing fits its name.

Saxon Math Intermediate 4

Name _____

*1. Ninety-one students are divided as equally as possible among
(88) 3 classrooms.

    a. How many classrooms have exactly 30 students?

    b. How many classrooms have 31 students?

*2. a. (Analyze) In 1970 it cost 6¢ to mail a letter. How much did it cost to
(49)   mail twenty letters in 1970?

    b. How much does it cost to mail twenty letters today?

3. (Represent) Point A represents what number on this number
(Inv. 1) line?

                        A

          0   100   200

4. George Washington was born in 1732. How old was he when he
(54) became the first president of the United States in 1789?

5. A $1 bill weighs about 1 gram. How much would a $5 bill weigh?
(77)

*6. Draw a quadrilateral that has two pairs of parallel sides.
(92)

7. Name the shaded part of the large square
(Inv. 4)
    a. as a fraction.

    b. as a decimal number.

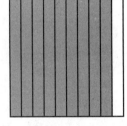

8. (Estimate) Jon used rounding and decided that 54,000 was a good
(93) estimate of the product 58 × 87. Was Jon's estimate reasonable?
Explain why or why not.

*9. (Represent) One half of the 32 chess pieces were still on the board.
(70) How many chess pieces were still on the board? Draw a picture to
illustrate the problem.

10. Miriam left home at 10:30 a.m. She traveled for 7 hours. What time was
(27) it when she arrived?

11. Maureo traveled 42 miles in 1 hour. If he kept going at the same speed,
(57, 67) how far would he travel in 20 hours?

Name _____

*12. Violet gave the cashier $40 for a toaster that cost $29.99 plus $1.80 in
(83) tax. What was her change? Write one equation to solve the problem.

*13. Alvin faced the sun as it set in the west, then turned 90°
(75) counterclockwise and headed home. In what direction was
Alvin heading after the turn?

14. $n + 8 + 2 + 3 + 5 + 2 = 24$
(2)

15. $4.12 - (3.6 + 0.2 + 0.125)$
(45, 91)

16. $18 - 15.63
(43, 52)

17. $15.27 + 85.75
(43, 51)

18. $2^3 \times \sqrt{25}$
(Inv. 3, 62)

19. 30×90
(86)

20. 7.50×8
(58)

*21. $\begin{array}{r} 49 \\ \times\ 62 \\ \hline \end{array}$
(90)

*22. $\begin{array}{r} 54 \\ \times\ 23 \\ \hline \end{array}$
(90)

23. $\begin{array}{r} 74 \\ \times\ 40 \\ \hline \end{array}$
(67)

24. $4\overline{)\$6.36}$
(76)

25. $5\overline{)800}$
(80)

26. $473 \div 8$
(53)

27. $3m = 1800$
(41, 80)

*28. Estimate the quotient when 1520 is divided by 5. Then find the exact quotient.
(53, 93)

*29. (**Represent**) Draw and shade circles to show that $2\frac{1}{4}$ equals $\frac{9}{4}$.
(89)

30. Find the perimeter and area of this rectangle.
(Inv. 2, Inv. 3)

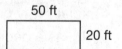

50 ft

20 ft

Saxon Math Intermediate 4

1. Joel gave the clerk a $5 bill to pay for a half gallon of milk that cost
(83) $1.06 and a box of cereal that cost $2.39. How much change should he receive?

*2. Eighty-one animals live at the zoo. One third of them are not mammals.
(70, 94) The rest are mammals. How many mammals live at the zoo? (*Hint:* First find the number of animals that are not mammals.)

3. Ciante planted 8 rows of apple trees. There were 15 trees in each row.
(49) How many trees did she plant?

4. A ruble is a Russian coin. If four pounds of bananas costs one hundred
(52, 65) and fifty-six rubles, what is the cost in rubles of each pound of bananas?

*5. a. This scale shows a mass of how many grams?
(77)

  b. **Explain** Would this fruit have the same mass on another planet? Explain why.

*6. Felix is ten years younger than Zatravian. Zatravian wrote this formula
(94) for finding Felix's age: $F = Z - 10$. Find F when Z is 27.

7. Name the shaded part of the large square
(Inv. 4)
  a. as a fraction.

  b. as a decimal number.

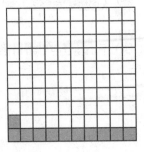

*8. Estimate the product of 32 and 48. Then find the exact product.
(93)

9. (**Represent**) Bactrian camels have 2 humps. One third of the
(70)   24 camels were Bactrian. How many camels were Bactrian? Draw
       a picture to illustrate the problem.

10. A quart is a quarter of a gallon. A quart is what percent of a gallon?
(40,
Inv. 5)

*11. (**Classify**) For each statement, write either "true" or "false."
(92)
       a. Every square is also a rectangle.

       b. Every rectangle is also a square.

*12. a. (**Represent**) Four hundred seventy-one of the one thousand
(Inv. 4,   students in the school were girls. Girls made up what fraction of
84)   the students in the school?

       b. (**Represent**) Write your answer for part **a** as a decimal number.
       Then use words to name the number.

*13. Which digit in 1.875 is in the tenths place?
(91)

*14. If $y = 2x - 3$, what is y when x is 5?
(94)

15. Tyler traveled 496 miles in 8 hours. He traveled an average of how
(60)   many miles per hour?

*16. Find $8.3 - (1.74 + 0.9)$. Describe the steps in order.
(45, 91)

17. 63×1000
(85)

18. $80 \times 50¢$
(86)

19. 37
(17)   81
       45
       139
       7
       15
     + 60

*20. 52
(90) $\times 15$

*21. 36
(90) $\times 27$

22. $2\overline{)714}$
(76)

23. $6\overline{)789}$
(53, 76)

24. $3n = 624$
(41, 80)

25. $5 + w = 5^2$
(61, 62)

*26. (**Represent**) Draw and shade rectangles to show that $1\frac{2}{5}$ equals $\frac{7}{5}$.
(89)

Saxon Math Intermediate 4

Name _____

27. A room is 5 yards long and 4 yards wide. How many square yards of
(Inv. 3) carpeting are needed to cover the floor?

28. The radius of this circle is 15 millimeters. The diameter of
(21, 69) the circle is how many centimeters?

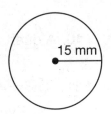

15 mm

*29. a. (Verify) Which of these letters has two lines of symmetry?
(79, 81)

V W X Y Z

b. (Verify) Which two letters have rotational symmetry?

c. Multiple Choice The angle formed by the letter V measures about
how many degrees?

A 45°   **B** 90°   **C** 135°   **D** 180°

*30. Rihanne and Kendra sat across the table from each other in the café.
(73) When Rihanne was finished looking at the one-page menu, she moved
it over to Kendra's side of the table so Kendra could read it. Which two
transformations did Rihanne use to move the menu?

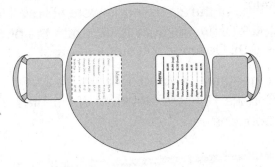

*Real-World
Connection*

A long mountain trail has an upward elevation of 4780 feet.

a. If you were to hike the trail five hours each day for four days,
how many feet would be the average elevation gain each day?

b. What would be the average elevation gain for each hour of
hiking?

*1. **Interpret** Use this tally sheet to answer parts **a–c.**
(Inv. 7)

Results of Class Election

Candidate	Tally
Irma	~~IIII~~ II
Hamish	~~IIII~~ I
Thanh	~~IIII~~ III
Marisol	~~IIII~~ ~~IIII~~ II

a. Who was second in the election?

b. Who received twice as many votes as Hamish?

c. Altogether, how many votes were cast?

2. Write these amounts in order from greatest to least:
(Inv. 4)

$1.45 $2.03 $0.99 $1.48

3. **Formulate** The Osage River in Kansas is 500 miles long. The
(25, 41) Kentucky River is 259 miles long. How many miles longer is the Osage
River? Write and solve an equation.

*4. **Represent** Two fifths of the 20 balloons were yellow. How many
(95) balloons were yellow? Draw a picture to illustrate the problem.

*5. Tim is 5 years younger than DeMario. DeMario is 2 years older
(94) than Lucinda. Lucinda is 11 years old. How old is Tim?
How did you find your answer?

6. Name the shaded part of this group
(Inv. 4,
74) **a.** as a fraction.

b. as a decimal number.

7. The fraction $\frac{1}{10}$ equals 10%. What percent of the group in problem **6** is
(Inv. 5) shaded?

Saxon Math Intermediate 4

Name _____

*8. Estimate the product of 88 and 59. Then find the exact product.
(93)

9. Sue's birthday is May 2. Her birthday will be on what day of
(54) the week in the year 2045?

MAY 2045						
S	M	T	W	T	F	S
	1	2	3	4	5	6
7	8	9	10	11	12	13
14	15	16	17	18	19	20
21	22	23	24	25	26	27
28	29	30	31			

*10. Point *W* represents what number on this number line?
(94)

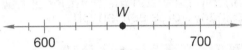

600   700

11. $32.63 + $42 + $7.56
(43, 51)

12. $86.45 − ($74.50 + $5)
(43, 45)

13. 83 × 40
(67)

14. 1000 × 53
(85)

15. $9^2 - \sqrt{81}$
(Inv. 3, 62)

*16.   32
(90)   × 16

*17.   67
(90)   × 32

18. $8.95
(58)   ×   4

19. 3)‾625‾
(80)

20. 4)‾714‾
(53, 76)

21. 6)‾1385‾
(80)

22. $\dfrac{900}{5}$
(80)

23. 3748 ÷ 9
(76)

24. 8*m* = $28.56
(41, 76)

*25. (**Represent**) This circle shows that $\frac{2}{2}$ equals 1. Draw a circle that shows
(89) that $\frac{3}{3}$ equals 1.

26. Find the perimeter and area of this rectangle.
(Inv. 2, Inv. 3)

50 mi

40 mi

*27. a. Draw a quadrilateral that is congruent to the quadrilateral
(66, 79)   at right. Then write the name for this type of quadrilateral.

    b. Draw the line of symmetry on the figure you created.

*28. Compare: 0.05 ◯ 0.050
(91)

*29. ✎ Explain Kelly ran and jumped 9 ft 6 in. How many inches did
(Inv. 2,
94) Kelly jump?

*30. The table shows the relationship between the number of hours Aidan
(Inv. 8) works and the amount of money he earns.

Number of Hours Worked	Income Earned (in dollars)
1	19
2	38
3	57
4	76
5	95

    a. ✎ Generalize Generalize Write a word sentence that describes the
relationship of the data.

    b. ✎ Predict Aidan works 40 hours each week. What is a reasonable
estimate of the amount of income he earns each week? Explain
your answer.

Saxon Math Intermediate 4

*1. (Analyze) Freddie is 2 years older than Francesca. Francesca is twice
(94) as old as Chloe. Chloe is 6 years old. How old is Freddie?

*2. (Analyze) What is the total number of days in the first three months of
(54) a leap year?

*3. It costs $1.52 to mail the package. Nate put three 37¢ stamps on
(94) the package. How much more postage does Nate need to mail the
package?

*4. Thirty-two desks were arranged as equally as possible in 6 rows.
(88)
   a. How many rows had exactly 5 desks?

   b. How many rows had 6 desks?

*5. (Represent) Two thirds of the 21 riders rode their horses bareback. How
(95) many riders rode bareback? Draw a picture to illustrate the problem.

*6. a. What decimal number names the shaded part of the large
(Inv. 4, square at right?
Inv. 5)

   b. What decimal number names the part that is not shaded?

   c. What percent of the square is shaded?

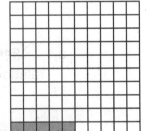

*7. (Explain) Near closing time, 31 children and adults are waiting in
(88) line to board a ride at an amusement park. Eight people board the
ride at one time. How many people will be on the last ride of the day?
Explain your answer.

8. Round 3874 to the nearest thousand.
(54)

9. (Estimate) Alicia opened a liter of milk and poured half of it into a
(40, pitcher. About how many milliliters of milk did she pour into the pitcher?
Inv. 5) What percent of the milk was still in the container?

Name _____

10. The sun was up when Mark started working. It was dark when he
(27) stopped working later in the day. How much time had gone by?

Started   Stopped

*11. For five days Pilar recorded the high temperature. The temperatures
(96) were 79°F, 82°F, 84°F, 81°F, and 74°F. What was the average high
temperature for those five days?

12. ✏️ **Explain** Leena drove 368 miles in 8 hours. If she drove the same
(60) number of miles each hour, how far did she drive each hour? Explain
how you found your answer.

13. 496,325
(51) +   3,680

14. $36.00
(52) − $30.78

15. $12.45
(22) $ 1.30
 $ 2.00
 $ 0.25
 $ 0.04
 $ 0.32
+ $ 1.29

*16. 26
(90) × 24

*17. 25
(90) × 25

18. $8m = \$16.40$
(41, 80)

19. 60×300
(86)

20. $\$8.56 \times 7$
(58)

21. $7\overline{)845}$
(80)

22. $9\overline{)1000}$
(76)

23. $\dfrac{432}{6}$
(65)

*24. **Represent** Draw and shade a circle that shows that $\frac{4}{4}$ equals 1.
(89)

25. The wall was 8 feet high and 12 feet wide. How many square feet of
(Inv. 3) wallpaper were needed to cover the wall?

26. **Analyze** Below are Tene's scores on the first seven games. Refer to
(94, 96) the scores below to answer parts **a–c.**

85, 85, 100, 90, 80, 100, 85

a. Rearrange the scores so that the scores are in order from lowest to
highest.

Saxon Math Intermediate 4

b. In your answer to part **a,** which score is the middle score in the list?

c. In the list of game scores, which score occurs most frequently?

*27. [✏️ Estimate] What is a reasonable estimate of the number in each
(59, 65) group when 912 objects are separated into 3 equal groups? Explain why your estimate is reasonable.

*28. According to many health experts, a person should drink 64 ounces
(52) of water each day. If Shankeedra's glass holds 8 ounces of water, how many glasses of water should she drink in one day?

*29. Arthur told his classmates that his age in years is a single-digit odd
(10) number greater than one. He also told his classmates that his age is not a prime number. How old is Arthur?

*30. If $y = 3x - 1$, what is y when x is 2?
(94)

Real-World Connection

Mylah decided she wanted to grow three peanut plants for her science class. After five months, one of her plants is 1 ft 6 in. tall. The second plant is 1 ft 2 in. tall, and the third is 10 inches tall.

a. Convert the heights of the first two peanut plants to inches, and then find the average height of all of Mylah's plants (in inches).

b. Convert the average to feet and inches.

*1. **Interpret** Use the information in this circle graph to answer parts **a–d.**
(Inv. 6)

Activities of 100 Children at the Park

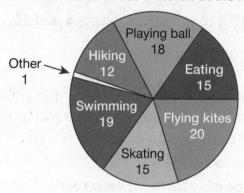

Playing ball
18

Hiking
12

Other → 1

Eating
15

Swimming
19

Flying kites
20

Skating
15

a. Altogether, how many children were at the park?

b. How many children were *not* swimming?

c. How many children were either hiking or skating?

d. How many more children were flying kites than were swimming?

*2. **Represent** Three fourths of the one thousand gold coins were
(95) special gold coins called doubloons. How many doubloons were
there? Draw a picture to illustrate the problem.

*3. What percent of the gold coins in problem **2** was doubloons?
(Inv. 5, 95)

4. Write each mixed number as a decimal:
(84)

a. $3\frac{5}{10}$ b. $14\frac{21}{1000}$ c. $9\frac{4}{100}$

*5. Estimate the product of 39 and 406. Then find the exact
(93) product.

*6. If $y = 4x - 2$, what is y when x is 4?
(94)

*7. Write these fractions in order from least to greatest:
(Inv. 9)

$$\frac{3}{4} \qquad \frac{1}{2} \qquad \frac{5}{8}$$

  Saxon Math Intermediate 4

Name _____

8. Compare: 2 thousand ◯ 24 hundred
(33)

Refer to the rectangle at right to answer problems **9** and **10**.

9. What is the perimeter of the rectangle
(Inv. 2,
69)   **a.** in millimeters?

    b. in centimeters?

10. What is the area of the rectangle
(Inv. 3,
86)   **a.** in square millimeters?

    b. in square centimeters?

30 mm
10 mm

11. Santos figured the trip would take seven and a half hours. He left
(27)   at 7 a.m. At what time does he think he will arrive?

*12. (Analyze) What is the average (mean) number of days per month in the
(96)   first three months of a common year?

13. 25 × 40
(67)

14. 98¢ × 7
(48)

15. $\sqrt{36} \times \sqrt{4}$
(Inv. 3)

16. $\dfrac{3^3}{3}$
(62)

17.   36
(90)   × 34

*18.   35
(90)   × 35

19.   4
(2)   2
       1
       3
       4
       7
       2
       2
       3
       4
     + x
     ——
      42

20. 8m = $70.00
(41, 76)

21. 6)‾1234‾
(80)

22. 800 ÷ 7
(65)

23. 487 ÷ 3
(65)

24. $2.74 + $0.27 + $6 + 49¢
(43)

25. 9.487 − (3.7 + 2.36)
(45, 50)

*26. (Represent) Draw and shade circles to show that $2\frac{1}{3}$ equals $\frac{7}{3}$.
(89)

*27. (**Analyze**) Listed below are the number of points Amon scored in his
(97) last nine basketball games, which range from 6 to 10. Refer to these
scores to answer parts **a–e.**

8, 7, 7, 8, 6, 10, 9, 10, 7

a. What is the mode of the scores?

b. What is the median of the scores?

c. What is the range of the scores?

d. What is the mean of the scores?

e. Are there any outliers?

28. Each school day, Brent's second class begins at 9:00 a.m. What
(81) kind of angle is formed by the minute hand and the hour hand of a
clock at that time?

*29. (**Explain**) Thirty-one students are entering a classroom. The desks
(58) in the classroom are arranged in rows with 7 desks in each row. If the
students fill the first row of desks, then fill the second row of desks,
and so on, how many full rows of students will there be? How many
students will sit in a row that is not full? Explain your answer.

*30. Melvin was reading a book. When he finished reading every other page,
(73) Melvin flipped the page. Turning a page is like which transformation?

Saxon Math Intermediate 4

*1. Use this information to answer parts **a–c.**
(72, 94)

> *In the Lerma family there are 3 children. Juno is 10 years old.*
> *Joaquin is 2 years younger than Jovana. Joaquin is 4 years older*
> *than Juno.*

    a. How old is Joaquin?

    b. How old is Jovana?

    c. When Joaquin is 16 years old, how old will Jovana be?

*2. D'Andra bought an artichoke and 6 pounds of carrots for $2.76. If the
(94) artichoke cost 84¢, how much did 1 pound of carrots cost? (*Hint:* First
find the cost of all the carrots.)

3. Compare. Write >, <, or =.
(33)
    a. 206,353 $\bigcirc$ 209,124   **b.** 518,060 $\bigcirc$ 518,006

4. Write these numbers in order from greatest to least:
(33)

        89,611   120,044   102,757   96,720

5. (**Represent**) Write each mixed number as a decimal:
(84)
    a. $5\dfrac{31}{1000}$ **b.** $16\dfrac{7}{10}$ **c.** $5\dfrac{7}{100}$

*6. (**Represent**) Three fifths of the team's 40 points were scored in
(95) the first half. How many points did the team score in the first half?
Draw a picture to illustrate the problem.

*7. One fifth is 20%. What percent is three fifths?
(Inv. 5,
95)

8. (**Represent**) Use words to write 7.68.
(Inv. 4)

9. (**Represent**) Use words to write 76.8.
(Inv. 4)

*10. **Explain** Armondo estimated that the exact product of 78 and 91
(93)   was close to 720. Did Armondo make a reasonable estimate? Explain
    why or why not.

11. **Connect** Name the number of shaded squares below
(Inv. 4)

    a. as a mixed number.

    b. as a decimal.

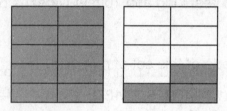

*12. There were 24 people in one line and 16 people in the other line. What
(96)   was the average number of people per line?

13. Makayla's school day ends 5 hours 20 minutes after the
(27)   time shown on the clock. What time does Makayla's
    school day end?

14. Mr. Romano could bake 27 dozen whole wheat muffins in 3 hours.
(60)

    a. How many dozen whole wheat muffins could he bake in 1 hour?

    b. How many dozen whole wheat muffins could he bake in 5 hours?
    (*Hint:* Multiply the answer to part **a** by 5.)

15. 3.65 + 4.2 + 0.625
(50)

16. $13.70 − $6.85
(43, 51)

17. 26 × 100
(85)

18. 9 × 87¢
(48)

19. 14 × 16
(90)

20. 15^2
(62, 90)

21. $\dfrac{456}{6}$
(65)

22.   47
(67) × 60

Saxon Math Intermediate 4

Name _____

23. $6x = 4248$
(80)

24. $1\overline{)163}$
(76)

25. $5\overline{)\$49.00}$
(76, 80)

*26. This table represents the equation $y = 2x + 3$ and
(94) shows the values of y when x is 2 and when x is 3.
What is y when x is 4?

$y = 2x + 3$	
x	**y**
2	7
3	9
4	?

27. How many one-foot-square tiles are needed to cover the
(Inv. 3, 85) floor of a room that is 15 feet long and 10 feet wide?

*28. Find the median and mode of this set of numbers:
(97)

$$1, 1, 2, 3, 5, 8, 13$$

*29. What geometric shape is a globe?
(98)

*30. **a.** What is the geometric name for this solid?
(63, 98)

   b. How many faces does this solid have?

   c. Describe the angles.

*1. Fifty-three family photographs are being arranged in a photo album.
(88) The album has 12 pages altogether, and 6 photographs can be placed
on each page.

    a. How many full pages of photographs will be in the album?

    b. How many photographs will be on the page that is not full?

    c. How many pages in the album will be empty?

2. (**Estimate**) Abraham Lincoln was born in 1809. How old was he when
(54) he issued the Emancipation Proclamation in 1863?

*3. (**Analyze**) The parking lot charges $1.25 to park a car for the first hour.
(94) It charges 75¢ for each additional hour. How much does it cost to park
a car in the lot for 3 hours?

*4. (**Represent**) Two thirds of the team's 45 points were scored in the
(95) second half. How many points did the team score in the second half?
Draw a picture to illustrate the problem.

*5. Something is wrong with the sign at right. Draw two
(35) different signs that show how to correct the error.

JUICE
BARS
0.75¢ each

6. (**Analyze**) What is the value of 3 $10 bills, 4 $1 bills, 5 dimes, and
(35) 2 pennies?

7. (**Represent**) Use words to write 6412.5.
(Inv. 4)

8. (**Estimate**) Last year 5139 people attended an outdoor jazz
(59) festival. This year 6902 people attended the festival. Estimate the
total attendance during those years and explain why your estimate
is reasonable.

9. a. Cooper opened a 1-gallon bottle of milk and poured out 1 quart.
(40, How many quarts of milk were left in the bottle?
Inv. 5)

    b. What percent of the milk was left in the bottle?

10. Look at the coins below. List all of the different amounts you could
(36) make using exactly two coins.

*11. Estimate the product of 39 and 41. Then find the exact product.
(93)

12. Felicia slowly gave the doorknob a quarter turn counterclockwise. How
(75) many degrees did she turn the doorknob?

*13. Five full buses held 240 students. What was the average number of
(96) students per bus?

14. $68.57
(43, 51) + $36.49

15. $100.00
(52) − $ 5.43

16. 15
(17)   24
        36
        75
        21
         8
        36
    + 420

17. 12
(87) × 12

18. $5.08
(58) ×   7

19. 50²
(62, 86)

20. √144
(Inv. 3)

21. 12.08 − (9.61 − 2.4)
(45, 50)

22. 49 × 51
(90)

23. 33 × 25
(90)

24. $\frac{848}{8}$
(80)

25. 9w = 6300
(80)

*26. (**Represent**) Draw and shade circles to show that $2\frac{2}{3}$ equals $\frac{8}{3}$.
(89)

*27. (**Represent**) Draw a rectangle that is three inches long and one inch
(21, Inv. 3) wide. Then find the perimeter and the area.

*28. This table represents the equation $y = 3x + 1$ and shows
(94) the values of y when x is 3 and when x is 4. What is y
when x is 5?

$y = 3x + 1$	
x	**y**
3	10
4	13
5	?

*29. **Classify** Refer to this triangular prism for parts **a** and
(23, 99) **b.**

   a. Describe the angles as acute, right, or obtuse.

   b. Which faces are parallel?

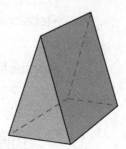

*30. This pyramid has a square base. How many vertices does
(98) the pyramid have?

1. One hundred fifty feet equals how many yards?
(Inv. 2, 71)

2. Tammy gave the clerk $6 to pay for a book. She received 64¢ in
(83) change. Tax was 38¢. What was the price of the book?

3. DaJuan is 2 years older than Rebecca. Rebecca is twice as old as
(94) Dillon. DaJuan is 12 years old. How old is Dillon? (*Hint:* First find
Rebecca's age.)

4. Write each decimal as a mixed number:
(84)
    a. 3.295   **b.** 32.9   **c.** 3.09

*5. a. (**Represent**) Three fourths of the 84 contestants guessed
(Inv. 5, 95)   incorrectly. How many contestants guessed incorrectly?
    Draw a picture to illustrate the problem.

    b. What percent of the contestants guessed incorrectly?

6. These thermometers show the average
(18, 97) daily minimum and maximum temperatures
in North Little Rock, Arkansas, during the
month of January. What is the range of the
temperatures?

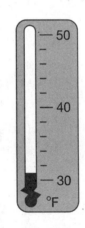 

7. a What is the diameter of this circle?
(21)

    b. What is the radius of this circle?

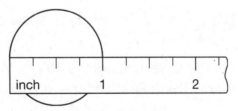

8. (**Represent**) Use words to write 8.75.
(Inv. 4)

Name _____

*9. **Estimate** Three students each made a different estimate of the
(93) quotient 2589 ÷ 9. Paulo's estimate was 30, Ka'Dentia's estimate was 300, and Carter's estimate was 3000. Which student made the best estimate? Explain your answer.

*10. The first five odd counting numbers are 1, 3, 5, 7, and 9.
(10, 97)

Find the mean and the median of these five numbers.

*11. What geometric shape is a roll of paper towels?
(98)

*12. **a. Multiple Choice** Which of these polygons is a parallelogram?
(92)

    A   B   C   D

b. Which polygons appear to have at least one obtuse angle?

c. Which polygon does not appear to have any perpendicular sides?

13. $16.25 − ($6 − 50¢)
(43, 45)

14. $5 \times 7 \times 9$ **15.** $7.83 × 6   **16.** 54×1000
(62)   (58)   (85)

17. $\begin{array}{r} 45 \\ \times\ 45 \\ \hline \end{array}$ **18.** $\begin{array}{r} 32 \\ \times\ 40 \\ \hline \end{array}$ **19.** $\begin{array}{r} 46 \\ \times\ 44 \\ \hline \end{array}$
(90)   (67)   (90)

20. $6\overline{)3625}$ **21.** $5\overline{)3000}$ **22.** $7n = 987$
(80)   (80)   (41, 76)

23. $\dfrac{10^3}{\sqrt{25}}$ **24.** $13.76 ÷ 8   **25.** $\dfrac{234}{4}$
(Inv. 3, 62)   (76)   (68)

*26. **Represent** Draw and shade a circle to show that $\frac{8}{8}$ equals 1.
(56)

27. The perimeter of the square at right is 40 cm. What is the
(Inv. 2, Inv. 3) area of this square? (*Hint:* First find the length of each side.)

     Saxon Math Intermediate 4

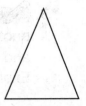

*28. **Represent** Draw a triangle that is similar to this isosceles
(66, 79) triangle. Then draw its line of symmetry.

*29. a. Compare: 0.25 ◯ 0.250
(91)
  b. Compare: $0.25 ◯ 0.25¢

*30. One of these nets could be cut out and folded to form a cube. The
(99) other will not form a cube. Which net will form a cube?

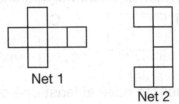

Net 1

Net 2

Real-World Connection

a. Use a ruler to sketch the front, top, sides, and bottom of a pyramid, cone, and cube.

b. In your sketches, what do the dashed lines represent?

*1. (Inv. 6, 101) **Interpret** Use the information in the table below to answer parts **a–c.**

Average Yearly Rainfall

City	Rainfall (in inches)
Boston	43
Chicago	36
Denver	16
Houston	48
San Francisco	20

a. Which cities listed in the table average less than 2 feet of rain per year?

b. In one year Houston received 62 inches of rain. This was how much more than its yearly average?

c. Copy and complete the bar graph below to show the information in the rainfall table.

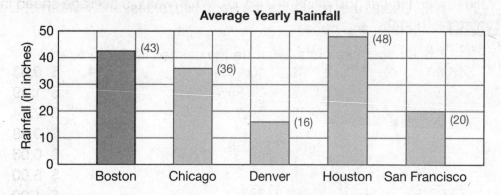

Average Yearly Rainfall

*2. (95) **Represent** Five sixths of the 288 marchers were out of step. How many marchers were out of step? Draw a picture to illustrate the problem.

*3. (35) **Represent** Something is wrong with this sign. Draw two different signs that show how to correct the error.

WATER
.99¢
per gallon

4. (21, 69) What is the radius of this circle in millimeters?

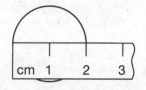

*5. _(Inv. 10) ✏️ Conclude The chance of rain is 60%. Is it more likely that it will rain or that it will not rain? Explain your answer.

*6. ₍₉₃₎ Estimate the product of 88 and 22. Then find the actual product.

7. ₍₄₉₎ Apples were priced at 53¢ per pound. What was the cost of 5 pounds of apples?

8. _(16, 33) Represent Write the number 3708 in expanded form. Then use words to write the number.

9. _(Inv. 2) The top of a doorway is about two meters from the floor. Two meters is how many centimeters?

*10. ₍₉₄₎ Four pounds of pears cost $1.20. What did 1 pound of pears cost? What did 6 pounds of pears cost?

11. ₍₆₀₎ Mike drove his car 150 miles in 3 hours. What was his average speed in miles per hour?

12. ₍₅₂₎

$46.00
− $45.56

13. ₍₅₂₎

10,165
− 856

14. _(43, 51)

$ 0.63
$ 1.49
$12.24
$ 0.38
$ 0.06
$ 5.00
+ $ 1.20

*15. _(62, 86) 70^2

16. ₍₉₀₎ 71×69

17. _(76, 80) $4\overline{)\$30.00}$

18. ₍₆₈₎ $3\overline{)263}$

19. ₍₇₆₎ $5x = 4080$

20. ₍₆₅₎ $\dfrac{344}{8}$

21. ₍₆₇₎

37
× 60

22. ₍₉₀₎

56
× 42

23. ₍₅₈₎

$5.97
× 8

24. _(45, 50) $10.000 − (4.468 − 2.3)$

*25. ₍₉₇₎ Find the mean, median, mode, and range of this set of numbers:

3, 1, 4, 1, 6

*26. (**Represent**) Draw and shade circles to show that 2 equals $\frac{4}{2}$.
(89)

*27. a. (**Represent**) Draw a square with sides 4 cm long.
(21,
Inv. 3)
    b. Find the perimeter and the area of the square you drew.

*28. (**Conclude**) Which of these nets can be folded to form a pyramid?
(100)

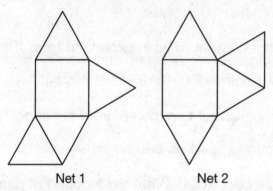

Net 1   Net 2

*29. If $y = 6x - 4$, what is y when
(94)
    a. x is 5?   **b.** x is 8?

*30. In this pattern of loose tiles, there are triangles and squares:
(66, 78)

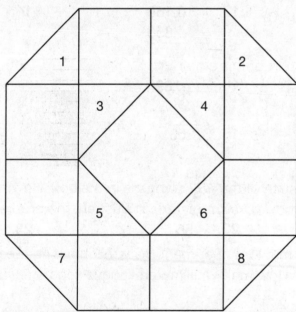

    a. What transformation could be performed on triangle 7 to see if it is congruent to triangle 4?

    b. What transformation could be performed on triangle 1 to see if it is congruent to triangle 3?

Saxon Math Intermediate 4

Name _____

Early Finishers
Real-World Connection

Use the table below to answer parts **a–c.**

Airline	Flight Time
Airline A	2 hours 45 minutes
Airline B	3 hours 15 minutes
Airline C	6 hours 35 minutes

a. Maria is taking Airline A, and her flight leaves at 9:00 a.m. What time will she arrive at her destination?

b. How much longer is the flight time for Airline B than Airline A?

c. If Carol took Airline C and arrived at her destination at 10:00 p.m., what time did her flight leave?

*1. **(Analyze)** All 110 books must be packed in boxes. Each box will hold
(88)   8 books.

    a. How many boxes can be filled?

    b. How many boxes are needed to hold all the books?

*2. **(Formulate)** What number is five more than the product of six and
(94)   seven? Write an expression.

*3. **(Explain)** Trevor paid $7 for the tape. He received a quarter and
(83)   two dimes as change. Tax was 42¢. What was the price of the tape?
    Explain how you found your answer.

*4. **a.** **(Represent)** Four fifths of the 600 gymnasts did back
(70, 95)   handsprings. How many gymnasts did back handsprings? Draw
    a picture to illustrate the problem.

    b. What percent of the gymnasts did not do back handsprings?

5. **(Explain)** Mrs. Tyrone is arranging 29 desks into rows. If she
(88)   starts by putting 8 desks in each row, how many desks will be in
    the last row? Explain how you know.

6. **(Analyze)** What is the value of two $100 bills, five $10 bills, four $1
(35)   bills, 3 dimes, and 1 penny?

7. **a.** Find the length of this line segment in millimeters.
(69)

    b. Find the length of the segment in centimeters. Write the answer as a
    decimal number.

8. **(Represent)** Use words to write 12.67.
(Inv. 4)

*9. **a.** Round 3834 to the nearest thousand.
(54, 102)

    b. Round 38.34 to the nearest whole number.

Saxon Math Intermediate 4

Name _____

10. The diameter of a circle is 1 meter. What is the radius of the circle in
(Inv. 2, centimeters?
21)

*11. Find the sum of two hundred eighty-six thousand, five hundred fourteen
(34, 51) and one hundred thirty-seven thousand, two.

12. Seven pairs of beach sandals cost $56. What is the cost of one pair?
(94) What is the cost of ten pairs?

*13. There were 36 children in one line and 24 children in the other line.
(96) What is the average number of children per line?

*14. If the arrow is spun once, what is the probability that it
(Inv. 10) will stop in sector C?

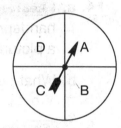

15. 7.486 − (6.47 + 0.5)   **16.** 40 × 50
(45, 50)   (86)

17. 41 × 49   **18.** $2^3 \times 5 \times \sqrt{49}$
(90)   (Inv. 3,
                                       62)

*19.   32   ***20.**   38
(90)   × 17   (67)   × 40

21. 7 + 4 + 6 + 8 + 5 + 2 + 7 + 3 + k = 47
(2)

*22. 8)360   ***23.** 4)810   ***24.** 7)356
(65)   (80)   (65)

*25. 6n = $4.38   **26.** 7162 ÷ 9   **27.** $\frac{1414}{2}$
(76)   (76)   (80)

*28. Draw and shade circles to show that 2 equals $\frac{8}{4}$.
(89)

*29. The basketball player was 211 centimeters tall. Write the height of the
(Inv. 2) basketball player in meters.

30. How many square yards of carpeting are needed to cover the floor of a
(Inv. 3, classroom that is 15 yards long and 10 yards wide?
85)

1. (Analyze) Find an even number between 79 and 89 that can be divided
(64) by 6 without a remainder.

2. How many minutes is 3 hours?
(19, 49)

*3. Victor has $8. Dana has $2 less than Victor. How much money do they
(94) have altogether?

*4. (Represent) Write each fraction or mixed number as a decimal
(84) number:

     a. $\frac{3}{10}$ **b.** $4\frac{99}{100}$ **c.** $12\frac{1}{1000}$

*5. (Represent) Five eighths of the 40 students wore school colors.
(95) How many students wore school colors? Draw a picture to illustrate
the problem.

6. a. What is the diameter of this circle in centimeters?
(21, 69)

     b. What is the radius of this circle in centimeters?

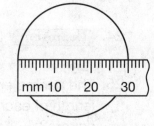

7. The radius of a circle is what percent of the diameter?
(21,
Inv. 5)

8. Estimate the product of 49 and 68. Then find the actual product.
(93)

*9. (Explain) Pavan has filled a pitcher with iced tea for two guests and
(88) himself. The capacity of the pitcher is two quarts. How many 10-ounce
glasses of iced tea can be poured from the pitcher? Explain your answer.

*10. In row 1 there were 6 students, in row 2 there were 4 students, in
(96) row 3 there were 6 students, and in row 4 there were 4 students. What
was the average number of students per row?

*11. Gretchen paid $20 for five identical bottles of fruit juice. She received
(94) $6 in change. What was the price of one bottle of juice?

Saxon Math Intermediate 4

*12. (Analyze) Find the median, mode, and range of Vonda's game scores.
(97) (Since there is an even number of scores, the median is the average of the two middle scores.)

100, 80, 90, 85, 100, 90, 100, 100

13. $3.85
(58) × 7

14. 48
(90) × 29

15. 16
(17) 15
23
8
217
20
6
+ 317

16. 5
(2) 4
3
7
2
5
8
1
4
+ n
45

17. 60^2
(62, 86)

18. 59 × 61
(90)

19. $\dfrac{400}{5}$
(71)

20. 6)582
(65)

21. 9)$37.53
(76)

22. 7)420
(65)

23. 7.500 − (3.250 − 0.125)
(43, 45)

*24. (Represent) Draw and shade circles to show that $3\frac{3}{4}$ equals $\frac{15}{4}$.
(89)

25. The perimeter of this square is 20 inches. What is the
(Inv. 2, Inv. 3) length of each side of the square? What is the area of the square?

*26. Write a fraction equal to 1 with a denominator of 8.
(103)

*27. (Explain) If two dot cubes are rolled together, which outcome is
(Inv. 10) more likely: dots totaling 12 or dots totaling 7? Explain your answer.

*28. Songhi measured the paper in her notebook and found that it was
(Inv. 2, 102) 28 cm long. Write the length of her paper in meters.

*29. (Estimate) Round $12\frac{5}{12}$ to the nearest whole number.
(103)

*30. **a.** (Classify) What is the geometric name for the shape
(23, 98)   of a cereal box?

   b. How many edges does this box have?

   c. Describe the angles.

**Real-World
Connection**

Eight students have decided to paint a rectangular mural in the school
cafeteria. Five of Mrs. Lowery's students and three of Mr. Rushing's
students will be painting equal sections for the mural.

   a. Draw a diagram representing how much of the mural each class
   will paint.

   b. Are Mrs. Lowery's or Mr. Rushing's students painting more than
   half of the mural?

   c. Explain your answer for part **b.**

       Saxon Math Intermediate 4

*1. **a.** If the perimeter of a square is 280 feet, how long is each side of the
(Inv. 2)   square?

    b. What is the area?

*2. There are 365 days in a common year. How many full weeks are there
(54, 88) in 365 days?

*3. Nia passed out crayons to 6 of her friends. Each friend received
(88, 94) 3 crayons. There were 2 crayons left for Nia. How many crayons
did Nia have when she began?

*4. (**Represent**) Three fifths of the 60 trees in the orchard were more than
(95) 10 feet tall. How many trees were more than 10 feet tall? Draw a
picture to illustrate the problem.

  5. **a.** Find the length of this line segment in millimeters.
(69)

    b. Find the length of the line segment in centimeters. Write the answer
as a decimal number.

mm 10	20	30	40	50

cm 1   2   3   4   5

*6. What fraction name for 1 is shown by this circle?
(103)

*7. Round $350,454 to the nearest thousand, to the nearest hundred, and
(20, 54) to the nearest ten.

*8. Copy this number line. Then make a dot at $\frac{1}{2}$ and label the dot point *A*.
(37, 102) Make a dot at 1.3 and label the dot point *B*. Make a dot at $1\frac{7}{10}$ and label
the dot point *C*.

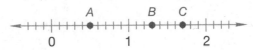

*9. (104) **Represent** Change the improper fraction $\frac{5}{4}$ to a mixed number. Draw a picture to show that the improper fraction and the mixed number are equal.

*10. (Inv. 6) **Interpret** The bar graph shows the number of students in fourth grade at Sebastian's school. Use the graph to answer the questions that follow.

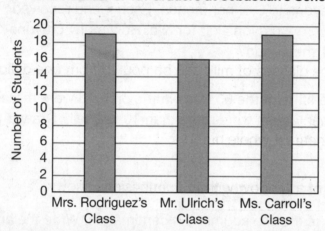

The Number of 4th Graders at Sebastian's School

a. How many fewer students are in Mr. Ulrich's class than in Ms. Carroll's class or in Mrs. Rodriguez's class?

b. Altogether, how many fourth grade students does the bar graph represent?

c. Which measure of the data is greater: the range or the median? Explain your answer.

11. (49, 67) The baker used 30 pounds of flour each day to make bread. How many pounds of flour did the baker use in 73 days?

12. (96) The chef used 132 pounds of potatoes every 6 days. On average, how many pounds of potatoes were used each day?

13. (43) $6.52 + $12 + $1.74 + 26¢

14. (50) 3.65 + 2.7 + 0.454 + 2.0

15. (43, 45) $80 − ($63.72 + $2)

16. (52) 37,614 − 29,148

17. (61) 9w = 9 · 26

*18. (62) 3^4

Saxon Math Intermediate 4

19. 24 × 1000
(85)

20. 79¢ × 6
(48)

21.   50
(86) × 50

22.   51
(90) × 49

23.   47
(90) × 63

24. 4)810
(76)

25. 5)490
(65)

26 6)362
(65, 68)

27. 1435 ÷ √49
(Inv. 3, 80)

***28.** How many 8-ounce glasses of milk can be poured from one gallon
(40) of milk?

***29.** Round $16\frac{5}{8}$ to the nearest whole number.
(103)

***30.** Estimate the area of a window with the dimensions shown.
(Inv. 3)

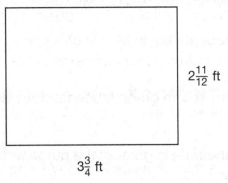

$2\frac{11}{12}$ ft

$3\frac{3}{4}$ ft

Real-World Connection

Joyce went fishing for crustaceans with her brothers and caught $2\frac{1}{4}$ pounds of crab, $1\frac{1}{4}$ pounds of lobster, and $2\frac{3}{4}$ pounds of shrimp.

a. Write each mixed number as an improper fraction.

b. Use fraction manipulatives or diagrams to show each amount and then find the total number of pounds of crustaceans that Joyce caught.

c. Which crustacean did Joyce catch the most pounds of?

1. How many 6¢ erasers can be bought with 2 quarters?
(88)

2. Two quarters are what percent of a dollar?
(Inv. 5)

3. D'Jmon has $8. Parisa has $2 more than D'Jmon. How much money
(94) do they have altogether?

*4. (**Represent**) Three fourths of the 20 students in a class participate
(95) in an after-school activity. What number of students participate?
Draw a picture to illustrate and solve the problem.

*5. (**Justify**) If one card is drawn from a standard deck of playing cards,
(Inv. 10) is it more likely that the card will be a "number card" or a "face card"?
Explain your answer.

*6. Write a fraction equal to one that has a denominator of 10.
(103)

7. (**Represent**) Write 86.743 with words.
(84)

*8. (**Estimate**) There are many ways to make an estimate. Describe two
(59) different ways to estimate the difference of 496 subtracted from 605.

*9. Change each improper fraction to a whole number or a mixed number:
(104)
   a. $\frac{9}{5}$ **b.** $\frac{9}{3}$ **c.** $\frac{9}{2}$

*10. (**Estimate**) Soon after James Marshall discovered gold at John Sutter's
(94, 105) mill in California on January 24, 1848, the "gold rush" began. If 2400
people came in 10 days, about how many came each day? About how
many people came in 1 week?

11. Find the length of this segment to the nearest tenth of a centimeter.
(69) Write the length as a decimal number.

*12. A miner bought 6 bags of flour for $4.20 per bag and 8 pounds of salt
(94) for 12¢ per pound. How much money did the miner spend?

   Saxon Math Intermediate 4

*13. a. Which digit in 86.743 is in the tenths place?

(91, 102)

     b. Is 86.74 closer to 86.7 or 86.8?

*14. Draw a trapezoid.

(92)

15. $4.867 - (2.8 + 0.56)$

(45, 50)

16. 30^2

(62, 86)

17. 54×29

(90)

*18. $10\overline{)230}$

(105)

19. $7\overline{)2383}$

(80)

*20. $372 \div 10$

(105)

21. $8c = \$5.76$

(41)

22.

(17)

    12
    26
    13
    35
  110
     8
+ 15

23.   351,426

(51) + 449,576

24. $50.00

(52) − $49.49

25. $12.49

(48) ×   8

26.   73

(90) × 62

*27. a. A field is 300 feet long and 200 feet wide. How many

(Inv. 2)   feet of fencing would be needed to go around the
    field?

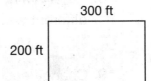

    b. **Explain** Is this problem about perimeter or area?
How do you know?

*28. Which letters in **MATH** have one line of symmetry? Which have two lines

(79) of symmetry? Which have rotational symmetry?

*29. Which transformation can make the digit 6 look like the digit 9?

(73)

*30. **Interpret** Use this chart to answer parts **a–c.**
(101)

Mileage Chart

	Atlanta	Boston	Chicago	Kansas City	Los Angeles	New York City	Wash., D.C.
Chicago	674	963		499	2054	802	671
Dallas	795	1748	917	489	1387	1552	1319
Denver	1398	1949	996	600	1059	1771	1616
Los Angeles	2182	2979	2054	1589		2786	2631
New York City	841	206	802	1198	2786		233
St. Louis	541	1141	289	257	1845	948	793

a. The distance from Los Angeles to Boston is how much greater than the distance from Los Angeles to New York City?

b. Heather is planning a trip from Chicago to Dallas to Los Angeles to Chicago. How many miles will her trip be?

c. There are three empty boxes in the chart. What number would go in these boxes?

Real-World Connection

There are 728 students in the auditorium. Ten students can fit in each row. The students are to fill as many rows as possible.

  a. Divide 728 by 10.

  b. How many rows are filled?

  c. How many rows are only partly filled? Why?

Saxon Math Intermediate 4

*1. Use this information to answer parts **a–c.**
(94)

> *Nara has 6 cats. Each cat eats half of a can of food each day. Cat food costs 47¢ per can.*

   a. How many cans of cat food are eaten each day?

   b. How much does Nara spend on cat food per day?

   c. How much does Nara spend on cat food in a week?

*2. a. Sketch a right triangle. Label the vertices *A*, *B*, and *C*, so that *C*
(63)   is at the right angle.

   b. Name two segments that are perpendicular.

   c. Name two segments that intersect but are not perpendicular.

   d. Can a triangle have two parallel sides?

*3. (**Represent**) Four students are planning a race. Draw a tree diagram to
(39) show all of the different ways that Quinton, Katelyn, and Nafuna can finish the race if Rita wins the race. Then list all the possible combinations.

| Quinton | Katelyn | Nafuna | Rita |

4. If the perimeter of a square classroom is 120 feet, then how long is
(Inv. 3, 86) each side of the classroom? What is the area of the classroom?

*5. (**Represent**) Math was the favorite class of five sevenths of the
(95) 28 students. Math was the favorite class of how many students? Draw a picture to illustrate the problem.

*6. (**Analyze**) Something is wrong with this sign. Draw
(99) two different signs to show how to correct the error.

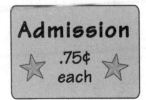

Admission

.75¢ each

7. If the radius of a circle is $1\frac{1}{2}$ inches, then what is the diameter of the
(21, 39) circle?

8. (**Represent**) Use words to write 523.43.
(Inv. 4)

9. (93) <u>Estimate</u> Colin used rounding to estimate the product of 61 and 397. What estimate did Colin make? Explain your answer.

*10. (104) Change each improper fraction to a whole number or a mixed number:

    a. $\dfrac{10}{10}$ **b.** $\dfrac{10}{5}$ **c.** $\dfrac{10}{3}$

*11. (94) LaTonya went to the fair with $20. She paid $6.85 for a necklace and $4.50 for lunch. Then she bought bottled water for 75¢. How much money did she have left?

*12. (83) <u>Explain</u> Clara bought two dolls priced at $7.40 each. The tax was 98¢. She paid the clerk with a $20 bill. How much change did she get back? Explain why your answer is reasonable.

13. (60) The big truck that transported the Ferris wheel could go only 140 miles in 5 hours. What was the truck's average speed in miles per hour?

*14. (103) Compare: $\dfrac{49}{100} \bigcirc \dfrac{1}{2}$

*15. (20, 102) **a.** <u>Estimate</u> Round $12.25 to the nearest dollar.

    b. Round 12.25 to the nearest whole number.

*16. (91, 102) **a.** Which digit in 36.47 is in the tenths place?

    b. <u>Estimate</u> Is 36.47 closer to 36.4 or to 36.5?

17. (50)
$$\begin{array}{r} 73.48 \\ 5.63 \\ + 17.9 \\ \hline \end{array}$$

18. (52)
$$\begin{array}{r} \$65.00 \\ - \$29.87 \\ \hline \end{array}$$

19. (52)
$$\begin{array}{r} 24{,}375 \\ - 8{,}416 \\ \hline \end{array}$$

20. (58)
$$\begin{array}{r} \$3.68 \\ \times \quad 9 \\ \hline \end{array}$$

21. (90) 89×91

22. (76) $3\overline{)3210}$

*23. (105) $10\overline{)4300}$

24. (76) $6\overline{)\$57.24}$

25. (65) $765 \div 9$

*26. (105) $563 \div 10$

*27. (106) Find the value of n^2 when n is 90.

Saxon Math Intermediate 4

Name _____

*28. Find the value of $\frac{m}{\sqrt{m}}$ when m is 36.
(106)

*29. a. Multiple Choice The sum of $6\frac{3}{4}$ and $5\frac{3}{5}$ is between which two
(59)   numbers?

   A 5 and 7   **B** 30 and 40   **C** 0 and 2   **D** 11 and 13

   b. Explain your answer for part **a.**

*30. The African bush elephant is the heaviest land mammal on Earth. Even
(77)   though it eats only twigs, leaves, fruit, and grass, an African bush
       elephant can weigh 7 tons. Seven tons is how many pounds?

*1. **Justify** Hayley bought 5 tickets for $2.75 each. She paid for them
(83) with a $20 bill. How much change should she receive? Explain why
your answer is reasonable.

2. If fifty cents is divided equally among 3 friends, there will be some
(88) cents left. How many cents will be left?

3. What is the difference when four hundred nine is subtracted from
(30) nine hundred four?

*4. **Represent** Two fifths of the 45 stamps were from Brazil. How many
(95) stamps were from Brazil? Draw a picture to illustrate the problem.

*5. a. Find the length of this line segment in millimeters.
(69)
b. Find the length of the segment in centimeters.

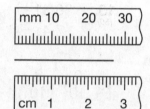

*6. a. The pizza was cut into 10 equal slices. The entire sliced
(Inv. 5, pizza shows what fraction name for 1?
103)
b. One slice of the pizza is what percent of the whole
pizza?

*7. Multiple Choice If a number cube is tossed once,
(Inv. 10) which of these is the most likely outcome?

A 1   **B** 3
C a number greater than 1   **D** a number less than 3

8. **Estimate** Round 5167 to the nearest thousand.
(54)

*9. Change the improper fraction $\frac{9}{4}$ to a mixed number.
(104)

*10. Multiple Choice Which of these fractions is *not* equal to 1?
(103)
A $\frac{12}{12}$ **B** $\frac{11}{11}$ **C** $\frac{11}{10}$ **D** $\frac{10}{10}$

Saxon Math Intermediate 4

Name _____

11. In the summer of 1926, there were only 17 stores in the town. Today
(48, 72) there are 8 times as many stores in the town. How many stores are in
the town today?

12. The wagon train took 9 days to make the 243-mile journey. What was
(96) the average number of miles traveled per day?

*__**13.**__ ✏️ **Explain** On Saturday Jacinda played outside for $1\frac{1}{2}$ hours and
(107) played board games for $2\frac{1}{2}$ hours. Altogether, how much time did
Jacinda spend playing outside and playing board games? Explain
how you found your answer.

*__**14.**__ **Estimate** Round $8\frac{21}{100}$ to the nearest whole number.
(37, 59)

15.   36.31
(50) − 7.4

*__**16.**__ $\frac{5}{8} + \frac{2}{8}$
(107)

17.   6
(2)   5
   4
   3
  $+ n$
  ‾‾‾‾
   25

*__**18.**__ $\frac{9}{10} - \frac{2}{10}$
(107)

*__**19.**__ $3\frac{2}{5} + 1\frac{1}{5}$
(107)

20. 27×32
(90)

21. 62×15
(90)

22. $7^2 + \sqrt{49}$
(Inv. 3, 62)

*__**23.**__ $10\overline{)460}$
(105)

24. $9\overline{)\$27.36}$
(76, 80)

25. $6w = 2316$
(41, 76)

26. $1543 \div 7$
(80)

*__**27.**__ $532 \div 10$
(105)

28. $\frac{256}{8}$
(65)

*__**29.**__ **a.** How many square feet of shingles are needed to cover a rectangular
(Inv. 3, 86) roof that is 40 feet wide and 60 feet long?

b. Is this problem about area or perimeter? How do you know?

30. Shaun walked $2\frac{1}{5}$ miles on Monday. He walked $3\frac{4}{5}$ miles on Wednesday.
(107) How many more miles did Shaun walk on Wednesday than on Monday?

*1. **Analyze** Cody bought 8 pounds of oranges. He gave the storekeeper a
(94) $5 bill and received $1.96 in change. What did 1 pound of oranges cost?
What is the first step in solving this problem?

2. After baking a dozen raisin muffins, Ethan ate two muffins for a snack.
(94) Then he placed half of the remaining muffins in the freezer. How many
muffins did Ethan place in the freezer?

3. What number is six less than the product of five and four?
(94)

4. Two thirds of the 12 guitar strings were out of tune. How many guitar
(95) strings were out of tune? Draw a picture to illustrate the problem.

*5. What is the probability that a rolled dot cube will stop with exactly two
(Inv. 10) dots on top?

*6. Write a fraction equal to 1 and that has a denominator of 5.
(103)

7. **Represent** Use words to write $397\frac{3}{4}$.
(35)

8. Estimate the sum of 4178 and 6899 by rounding both numbers to the
(59) nearest thousand before adding.

*9. Change each improper fraction to a whole number or a mixed number:
(104)
  a. $\frac{7}{3}$ **b.** $\frac{8}{4}$ **c.** $\frac{9}{5}$

*10. The hiking club went on hikes of 8 miles, 15 miles, 11 miles, and
(96) 18 miles. What was the average length of the club's hikes?

*11. For the first 3 hours, the hikers hiked at 3 miles per hour. For the next
(57, 94) 2 hours, they hiked at 4 miles per hour. If the total trip was 25 miles,
how far did they still have to go?

12. What percent of a quart is a pint?
(40,
Inv. 5)

13. $41.6 + 13.17 + 9.2$ **14.** $h + 8.7 = 26.47$
(50) (50)

*15. $6\frac{3}{8} + 4\frac{2}{8}$ ***16.** $4\frac{7}{10} - 1\frac{6}{10}$
(107) (107)

Saxon Math Intermediate 4

*17. We may write 48 as 40 + 8. Use the Distributive Property to find 5(40 + 8).
(108)

*18. (Analyze) Two fifths of the students rode the bus, and one fifth
(107) traveled by car. What fraction of the students either rode the bus or
traveled by car?

19. $0.48 × 5
(48)

20. 80^2
(62, 86)

21. $\sqrt{25} × \sqrt{25}$
(Inv. 3)

22. $4d = \$6.36$
(41, 76)

*23. $10)\overline{520}$
(105)

24. $\dfrac{175}{5}$
(65)

*25. What is the perimeter and area of this square?
(Inv. 2,
Inv. 3)

10 in.

*26. If a 3 in. by 4 in. rectangle is cut from the square in problem **25,** then
(Inv. 3,
108) what is the perimeter and area of the remaining figure?

*27. The tabletop was 76 cm above the floor. The tabletop was how many
(69, 102) meters above the floor?

*28. (Interpret) Use the line graph to answer parts **a–c.**
(Inv. 6,
97)

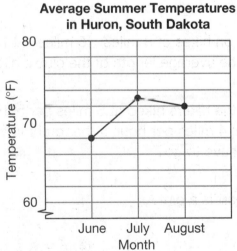

**Average Summer Temperatures
in Huron, South Dakota**

a. Write the names of the months in order from warmest to coolest.

b. How many degrees warmer is the average temperature during July than the average temperature during June?

c. Write a sentence that explains how the mean temperature compares to the median temperature.

*29. There were $3\frac{4}{5}$ potpies in the chef's kitchen. Then the chef removed $1\frac{3}{5}$
(107) of the potpies. How many potpies remained in the chef's kitchen?

*30. Multiple Choice The mixed numbers $5\frac{3}{8}$ and $7\frac{4}{5}$ do not have common
(103) denominators, but we know their sum is between which two numbers?

   A 14 and 16   **B** 12 and 14

   C 10 and 12   **D** 5 and 8

Real-World Connection

Cardinal Elementary is preparing the stage for a school play. The stage will be covered with hay. The rectangular stage has a length of 12 feet and a width of 14 feet.

   a. How much area must be covered with hay?

   b. The perimeter of the stage will be outlined with grass. Use the formula $2(l + w)$ to find the number of feet the grass will cover.

Saxon Math Intermediate 4

1. Interpret The pictograph shows the number of motor vehicles that
(Inv. 6) were driven past Sylvia's home during 1 hour. Use the pictograph to
answer the questions that follow.

Type of Vehicle	Number of Vehicles
Cars	◯ ◯ ◯ ◯ ◯ ◯
Trucks	◯ ◯
Mopeds	◖
Motorcycles	◯ ◖

Key: ◯ = 4 vehicles

a. What kind of vehicle was driven past Sylvia's home two times?

b. Write a word sentence that compares the number of trucks to the
number of cars.

c. Suppose ten bicyclists rode past Sylvia's house. In the pictograph,
how many symbols would be needed to show the number of
bicycles? Explain your answer.

*2. What number is six less than the sum of seven and eight? Write an
(94) expression.

*3. Nell read three tenths of 180 pages in one day. How many pages did
(95) she read in one day?

4. The thermometer shows the temperature of a warm
(18) October day in Buffalo, New York. What temperature
does the thermometer show?   67°F

5. A circular disc, divided into 8 equal pieces, represents what fraction
(103) name for 1?

6. **a.** What is the diameter of this dime?
(21, 69)

b. What is the radius of the dime?

c. What is the diameter of the dime in centimeters?

7. There are 11 players on a football team, so when two teams play, there
(32) are 22 players on the field at one time. Across the county on a Friday
night in October, many games are played. The table shows the number
of players on the field for a given number of games. How many players
are on the field in 5 games? 10 games?

Number of games	1	2	3	4	5
Number of players	22	44	66	88	?

8. Rick left home in the afternoon at the time shown on the
(19) clock and arrived at a friend's house 15 minutes later. At
what time did Rick arrive at his friend's house?

*9. **Represent** Change the improper fraction $\frac{5}{2}$ to a mixed number. Draw
(104) a picture that shows that the improper fraction and the mixed number
are equal.

*10. Use the information below to answer parts **a** and **b**.
(94, 96)

*Chico did 12 push-ups on the first day. On each of the next four
days, he did two more push-ups than he did the day before.*

a. Altogether, Chico did how many push-ups in five days?

b. What was the average number of push-ups Chico did per day?

Saxon Math Intermediate 4

*11. The dashes in this polygon divide the figure into
(Inv. 3, 79) two rectangles.

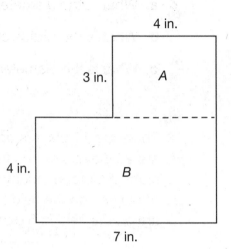

4 in.

3 in.   A

4 in.   B

7 in.

    a. What is the area of rectangle *A*?

    b. What is the area of rectangle *B*?

    c. What is the area of the whole polygon?

    d. Do the dashes show a line of symmetry for
    the figure?

*12. (**Analyze**) There were red checkers and black checkers on the
(94) checkerboard. There were 8 more red checkers than black checkers.
Altogether, there were 20 checkers. How many checkers were red, and
how many were black? Guess and check to solve.

*13. Find three fractions equivalent to $\frac{2}{3}$ by multiplying $\frac{2}{3}$ by $\frac{2}{2}$, $\frac{3}{3}$, and $\frac{10}{10}$.
(109)

*14. Since 63 equals 60 + 3, we may find 5 × 63 by finding 5(60 + 3).
(108) Use the Distributive Property to find 5(60 + 3).

*15. Find *ac* when *a* is 18 and *c* is 22.
(106)

16. To open the window, Natalie slides the rectangular pane
(73) of glass on the right to the position of the pane on the left.
Which transformation describes the movement of the pane
of glass?

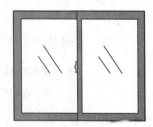

17. Find the median, mode, and range of this set of scores:
(97)

    100, 100, 95, 90, 90, 80, 80, 80, 60

*18. **Multiple Choice** If a quadrilateral has two pairs of parallel sides, then
(92) the quadrilateral is certain to be a _____.

    A rectangle   **B** parallelogram

    C trapezoid   **D** square

19. $v + 8.5 = 24.34$
(50)

20. $26.4 - 15.18$
(91)

21. $4 \times 3 \times 2 \times 1$
(62)

22. 26×30
(67)

23. $8)\overline{\$16.48}$
(76, 80)

*24. $10n = 250$
(41, 105)

*25. $\dfrac{5}{12} + \dfrac{6}{12}$
(107)

*26. $\dfrac{8}{12} - \dfrac{3}{12}$
(107)

27. How many square feet of paper are needed to cover a bulletin board
(Inv. 3) that is 3 feet tall and 6 feet wide?

*28. The bread recipe calls for $7\frac{1}{2}$ cups of flour to make 2 loaves of bread.
(107) The baker wants to make 4 loaves of bread. How many cups of flour does the baker need?

*29. The backpackers camped in a tent. Refer to the figure at right to
(98) answer parts **a–c.**

    a. The tent has the shape of what geometric solid?

    b. Including the bottom, how many faces does it have?

    c. How many edges does it have?

*30. The flag of the United States has thirteen stripes. Six of the stripes are
(11, 74) white, and the rest of the stripes are red.

    a. How many red stripes are on the flag?

    b. What fraction of the stripes on the flag are white?

    c. What fraction of the stripes on the flag are red?

*1. (Analyze) Eighty students were divided among three classrooms as
(88) equally as possible. Write three numbers to show how many students
were in each of the three classrooms.

*2. (Formulate) When the sum of three and four is subtracted from the
(94) product of three and four, what is the difference? Write an equation.

3. (Explain) Inma is twice as old as her sister and three years younger
(94) than her brother. Inma's sister is six years old. How old is Inma's
brother? What is the first step?

*4. Four ninths of 513 fans cheered when the touchdown was scored. How
(95) many fans cheered?

5. This sign has an error. Draw two different signs that show
(35) how to correct the error.

Cash for cans

.85¢
per
pound

*6. (Connect) These circles show fractions equivalent to $\frac{1}{2}$.
(109) Name the fractions shown.

*7. (Predict) The chance of winning the jackpot is 1%. Which is more
(Inv. 10) likely, winning or not winning?

*8. (Explain) In a sporting goods store, an aluminum baseball bat sells
(20, 22) for $38.49, a baseball sells for $4.99, and a baseball glove sells for
$24.95. What is a reasonable estimate of the cost to purchase a bat, a
glove, and two baseballs? Explain why your estimate is reasonable.

*9. Change the improper fraction $\frac{5}{2}$ to a mixed number.
(104)

10. Paul ran 7 miles in 42 minutes. What was the average number of minutes
(60, 96) it took Paul to run one mile?

*11. Kia bought 3 scarves priced at $2.75 each. Tax was 58¢. She paid with a
(83) $10 bill. How much change should Kia receive?

12. (Analyze) Two tickets for the play cost $26. At that rate, how much
(94)   would twenty tickets cost?

*13. Hikaru is $49\frac{1}{2}$ inches tall. Dawn is $47\frac{1}{2}$ inches tall. Hikaru is how many
(107)   inches taller than Dawn?

14. $7.43 + 6.25 + 12.7$
(50)

15. $q + 7.5 = 14.36$
(50)

16. 90×8000
(86)

17. 8×73¢
(48)

18. $7 \times 6 \times 5 \times 0$
(62)

19. 15^2
(Inv. 3, 62)

20. 60×5^2
(62, 67)

21. $\sqrt{49} \times \sqrt{49}$
(Inv. 3)

*22. $5\frac{1}{3} + 3\frac{1}{3}$
(107)

*23. $4\frac{4}{5} - 3\frac{3}{5}$
(107)

*24. $\frac{1240}{10}$
(105)

*25. $60\overline{)240}$
(110)

26. This square has a perimeter of 8 cm. Find the length of
(Inv. 2, Inv. 3)   each side. Then find the area of the square.

*27. Refer to the bus schedule below to answer parts **a–c.**
(27, 101)

Route 346

Terminal	6:43 a.m	7:25 a.m.	3:45 p.m.
5th & Western	6:50 a.m.	7:32 a.m.	3:50 p.m.
5th & Cypress	6:54 a.m.	7:36 a.m.	3:55 p.m.
Cypress & Hill	7:01 a.m.	7:43 a.m.	4:03 p.m.
Hill & Lincoln	7:08 a.m.	7:50 a.m.	4:12 p.m.
Lincoln & 5th	7:16 a.m.	7:58 a.m.	4:20 p.m.

Saxon Math Intermediate 4

Name _____

a. Ella catches the 6:50 a.m. bus at 5th and Western. When can she expect to arrive at Hill and Lincoln?

b. If the bus runs on schedule, how many minutes is her ride?

c. If Ella misses the 6:50 a.m. bus, then when can she catch the next Route 346 bus at that corner?

28. **Predict** When Xena says a number, Yihana doubles the number and
(94) adds 3. Xena and Yihana record their numbers in a table.

X	1	2	5	7
Y	5	7	13	17

What number does Yihana record in the table if Xena says 11?

*29. Workers are replacing a section of broken sidewalk. Before pouring the
(Inv. 3, concrete, the workers build a frame along the perimeter.
108)

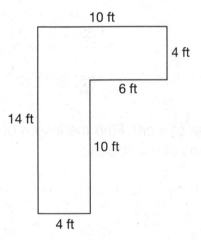

a. What is the perimeter of the replaced sidewalk?

b. What is the area of the replaced sidewalk?

***30.** <u>Represent</u> A variety of morning times and temperatures are
(Inv. 6) shown in the table below.

Morning Temperatures

Time	Temperature (°F)
12:00 a.m.	51
2:00 a.m.	48
4:00 a.m.	49
6:00 a.m.	50
8:00 a.m.	56
10:00 a.m.	62

Display the data in a line graph. Then write one statement that describes
the data.

Saxon Math Intermediate 4

*1. a. Three hundred seconds is how many minutes? (There are
(52, 110)   60 seconds in each minute.)

b. Sixty minutes is how many seconds?

*2. (Explain) Trevor, Ann, and Lee were playing marbles. Ann had twice
(94)   as many marbles as Trevor had, and Lee had 5 more marbles than Ann
had. Trevor had 9 marbles. How many marbles did Lee have? What is
the first step?

3. On each of 5 bookshelves there are 44 books. How many books are on
(49)   all 5 bookshelves?

*4. a. Nine tenths of the 30 students turned in their homework. How many
(Inv. 5,   students turned in their homework?
95)

b. What percent of the students did not turn in their homework?

5. For parts **a–c,** refer to this number line:
(37, 102)

a. The number for point *A* is what fraction?

b. The number for point *B* is what decimal number?

c. The number for point *C* is what fraction?

6. What fraction name for 1 has a denominator of 3?
(103)

*7. What equivalent fractions are shown?
(109)

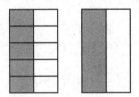

*8. (Represent) Draw a picture to show that $\frac{6}{8}$ and $\frac{3}{4}$ are equivalent
(109)   fractions.

9. Below is a golf scorecard for 9 holes of miniature golf. What was
(96) Michelle's average score per hole?

Putt 'N' Putt

Player	1	2	3	4	5	6	7	8	9	Total
Michelle	6	7	5	2	4	1	3	5	3	36
Mary	5	4	4	3	4	3	2	5	3	33

10. It was 11:00 a.m., and Sarah had to clean the laboratory by 4:20 p.m.
(27) How much time did she have to clean the lab?

*11. Draw a quadrilateral that has two sides that are parallel, a third side
(63) that is perpendicular to the parallel sides, and a fourth side that is
not perpendicular to the parallel sides. What type of quadrilateral did
you draw?

12. The factors of 10 are 1, 2, 5, 10. The factors of 15 are 1, 3, 5, 15. Which
(55) number is the largest factor of both 10 and 15?

13. List the factors of 8. List the factors of 12. Which number is the largest
(55) factor of both 8 and 12?

14. 4.3 + 12.6 + 3.75
(50)

15. 364.1 − 16.41
(91)

*16. $\dfrac{5}{8} + \dfrac{2}{8}$
(107)

*17. $\dfrac{3}{5} + \dfrac{1}{5}$
(107)

*18. $1\dfrac{9}{10} - 1\dfrac{2}{10}$
(107)

19. 60 × 800
(86)

20. 73 × 48
(90)

21. 9 × 78¢
(48)

22. 10^3
(62, 86)

23. 4x = 3500
(41, 76)

24. $\dfrac{4824}{8}$
(80)

*25. 60)‾540
(110)

*26. 10)‾463
(105)

*27. Estimate the perimeter and area of this figure. Each small
(111) square represents one square inch.

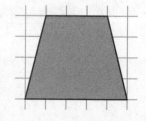

Saxon Math Intermediate 4

*28. (**Represent**) Draw a rectangle that is 4 cm long and 1 cm wide. Then
(21, Inv. 5) shade 25% of it.

29. Multiple Choice Which of the following is a cylinder?
(98)

A   B   C   D

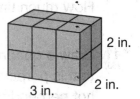

*30. (**Justify**) What is the volume of this rectangular solid?
(Inv. 11) Explain why your answer is reasonable.

2 in.

2 in.

3 in.

Early Finishers
Real-World Connection

a. Choose a box in your classroom, and estimate its perimeter, area, and volume. Then find the actual perimeter, area, and volume.

b. Explain how you found the perimeter, area, and volume of the box.

*1. Use the following information to answer parts **a** and **b**:
(94)

    One fence board costs 90¢. It takes 10 boards to build 5 feet of fence.

    a. How many boards are needed to build 50 feet of fence?

    b. How much will the boards cost altogether?

2. Find the perimeter and area of this rectangle:
(Inv. 2, Inv. 3)

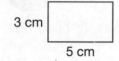

3 cm

5 cm

3. a. Find the length of this line segment in millimeters.
(69)

    b. Find the length of the segment in centimeters.

mm 10   20   30   40   50

cm 1   2   3   4   5

*4. Five ninths of the 36 horses were gray. How many of the horses were
(95) gray?

*5. Change each improper fraction to a whole number or a mixed number:
(104)

    a. $\frac{15}{2}$ **b.** $\frac{15}{3}$ **c.** $\frac{15}{4}$

*6. Angelina's mom is more than 32 years old but less than 40 years
(55) old, and her age in years is a prime number. How old is Angelina's
mom?

*7. a. What equivalent fractions are shown in the pictures at
(Inv. 5, 109) right?

    b. What percent of each large rectangle is
shaded?

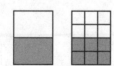

Saxon Math Intermediate 4

Name _____

*8. A regular polygon has all sides the same length and all angles the
(79, 92) same measure.

    a. Draw a regular quadrilateral. Show all the lines of symmetry.

    b. A regular quadrilateral has how many lines of symmetry?

    c. Does a regular quadrilateral have rotational symmetry?

*9. Write the reduced form of each fraction:
(112)
    a. $\dfrac{3}{6}$ **b.** $\dfrac{4}{6}$ **c.** $\dfrac{6}{12}$

10. In three tries, Rodney bounced the soccer ball on his foot 23 times,
(96) 36 times, and 34 times. What was the average number of bounces in
each try?

11. T-shirts were priced at $5 each. Yoshi had $27 and bought 5 T-shirts.
(83) Tax was $1.50. How much money did he have left?

*12. $3\dfrac{3}{9} + 4\dfrac{4}{9}$ ***13.** $\dfrac{1}{7} + \dfrac{2}{7} + \dfrac{3}{7}$ **14.**
(107)   (107)   (50)

$$\begin{array}{r} 37.2 \\ 135.7 \\ 10.62 \\ 2.47 \\ + \ 14.0 \\ \hline \end{array}$$

*15. $\dfrac{11}{12} - \dfrac{10}{12}$ ***16.** $\dfrac{8}{10} - \dfrac{5}{10}$
(107)   (107)

17.   48   **18.**   72   **19.** $4.08
(90) $\times\ 36$ (90) $\times\ 58$ (58) $\times\ \ \ \ 7$

20. $25.42 + 24.8$ **21.** $36.2 - 4.27$ ***22.** $90 \div 20$
(50)   (50)   (110)

23. $\dfrac{5}{8} - \dfrac{5}{8}$ **24.** $7\overline{)2549}$ ***25.** $19.40 \div 10$
(107)   (76)   (105)

26. What number is halfway between 400,000 and 500,000?
(Inv. 1)

27. (**Predict**) What is the probability that a tossed coin will land heads up?
(Inv. 10)

*28. **a.** What is the geometric name for the shape of this box?
(98, Inv. 11)

b. What is the volume of the box?

c. True or False: All of the opposite faces of the box are parallel.

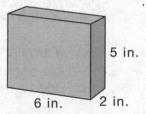

5 in.

6 in.   2 in.

29. Mallory opened her notebook and turned a page from the right side to the
(73) left. Turning the page is like which geometric transformation?

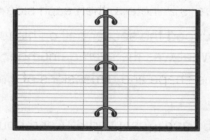

*30. (**Explain**) Estimate the perimeter and area of this shoe
(111) print. Each small square represents one square inch.
Describe the method you used.

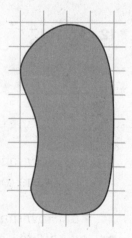

Saxon Math Intermediate 4

1. Carrie drove to visit her cousin who lives 3000 miles away. If Carrie
(11, 52) drove 638 miles the first day, 456 miles the second day, and 589 miles
the third day, how much farther does she need to drive to get to her
cousin's house?

2. Find the perimeter and area of this square:
(Inv. 2,
Inv. 3)

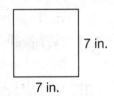

7 in.

7 in.

3. If the perimeter of a square is 2 meters, then each side is how many
(Inv. 2) centimeters long?

*4. The figure below shows the shape and dimensions of a room.
(Inv. 3,
108)

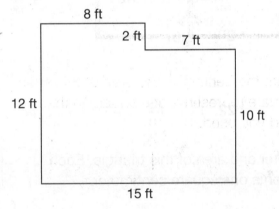

8 ft

2 ft   7 ft

12 ft

10 ft

15 ft

a. How many feet of molding are needed to go around the perimeter
of the room?

b. How many 1-foot square floor tiles are needed to cover the
floor?

5. (Estimate) Round 6843 to the nearest thousand.
(54)

*6. Write the reduced form of each fraction:
(112)

a. $\frac{4}{5}$ **b.** $\frac{5}{10}$ **c.** $\frac{4}{10}$

7. (Represent) Write 374.251 using words.
(84)

*8. (Represent) Draw a picture to show that $\frac{1}{2}$ and $\frac{4}{8}$ are equivalent
(109) fractions.

*9. **Connect** Write three fractions equivalent to $\frac{1}{4}$.
(109)

10. The concession stand at an elementary school basketball tournament
(96) earned a profit of $750 during a 3-day tournament. What is the average
profit earned during each day of the tournament?

*11. **Estimate** The explorer Zebulon Pike estimated that the mountain's
(12, 51) height was eight thousand, seven hundred forty-two feet. His estimate
was five thousand, three hundred sixty-eight feet less than the actual
height. Today we call this mountain Pikes Peak. What is the height of
Pikes Peak?

12. $6\overline{)4837}$ **13.** $\dfrac{1372}{\sqrt{16}}$ ***14.** $40\overline{)960}$ ***15.** $20\overline{)1360}$
(80)   (Inv. 3, 76)   (110)   (110)

16. $30.07 - 3.7$ **17.** $46.0 - 12.46$ **18.** $\begin{array}{r} 37.15 \\ 6.84 \\ 1.29 \\ 29.1 \\ + 3.6 \\ \hline \end{array}$
(50)   (91)   (50)

*19. $\begin{array}{r} \$3.20 \\ \times 46 \\ \hline \end{array}$ ***20.** $\begin{array}{r} 307 \\ \times 25 \\ \hline \end{array}$
(113)   (113)

*21. $\dfrac{8}{15} + \dfrac{6}{15}$ ***22.** $4\dfrac{4}{5} - 1\dfrac{3}{5}$
(107)   (107)

*23. Estimate the perimeter and area of this triangle. Each
(111) small square represents one square centimeter.

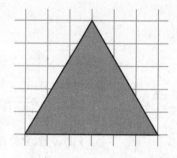

24. **Conclude** Write the next three numbers in this counting sequence:
(3)

$$\ldots, 10{,}000, 20{,}000, 30{,}000, \ldots$$

*25. **a. Multiple Choice** Which of these triangles appears to be an
(63, 78) equilateral triangle?

A   B   C   D

b. Describe the angles in triangle **B**.

c. Describe the segments in triangle **B**.

Saxon Math Intermediate 4

26. Multiple Choice To remove the lid from the pickle jar, J'Rhonda
(75) turned the lid counterclockwise two full turns. J'Rhonda turned the lid
about how many degrees?

A 360°   **B** 180°   **C** 720°   **D** 90°

*27. a. Which of the letters below has no lines of symmetry?
(79)

M I C K E Y

b. Which letter has rotational symmetry?

*28. Triangles *ABC* and *DEF* are congruent. Which
(73) transformations would move △*ABC* to the position
of △*DEF*?

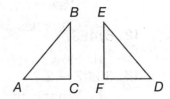

*29. If each side of an equilateral triangle is $2\frac{1}{4}$ inches long, what is the
(Inv. 2, 107) perimeter of the triangle?

*30. What is the volume of this stack of cubes?
(Inv. 11)

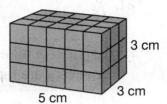

3 cm
3 cm
5 cm

*1. **Justify** Tessa made 70 photocopies. If she paid 6¢ per copy
(83) and the total tax was 25¢, how much change should she have gotten
back from a $5 bill? Is your answer reasonable? Why or why not?

2. **a.** What is the area of this square?
(Inv. 2,
Inv. 3) **b.** What is the perimeter of the square?

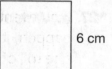

6 cm

*3. Use the information below to answer parts **a** and **b**.
(94, 96)
Walker has $9. Dembe has twice as much money as Walker.
Chris has $6 more than Dembe.

a. How much money does Chris have?

b. What is the average amount of money each boy has?

4. Use this table to answer the questions that follow:
(32)

Number of Bagels	12	24	36	48	60
Number of Dozens	1	2	3	4	5

a. **Generalize** Write a rule that describes the relationship of the data.

b. **Predict** How many bagels is 12 dozen bagels?

5. **Analyze** There are 40 quarters in a roll of quarters. What is the value
(94) of 2 rolls of quarters?

6. **Estimate** Lucio estimated that the exact quotient of 1754 divided
(76) by 9 was close to 20. Did Lucio make a reasonable estimate? Explain
why or why not.

*7. Write the reduced form of each fraction:
(112)
a. $\frac{2}{12}$ **b.** $\frac{6}{8}$ **c.** $\frac{3}{9}$

*8. **Analyze** Find a fraction equal to $\frac{1}{3}$ by multiplying $\frac{1}{3}$ by $\frac{2}{2}$. Write that
(107,
109) fraction, and then add it to $\frac{3}{6}$. What is the sum?

Saxon Math Intermediate 4

Name _____

*9. (Conclude) The three runners wore black, red, and green T-shirts. The
(72) runner wearing green finished one place ahead of the runner wearing
black, and the runner wearing red was not last. Who finished first?
Draw a diagram to solve this problem.

*10. If an event cannot happen, its probability is 0. If an event is certain to
(Inv. 10) happen, its probability is 1. What is the probability of rolling a 7 with
one roll of a standard number cube?

11. Dresses were on sale for 50% off. If the regular price of the dress
(Inv. 5, 70) was $40, then what was the sale price?

12. $4.62 + 16.7 + 9.8$
(50)

13. $14.62 - (6.3 - 2.37)$
(45, 91)

*14. $\frac{3}{5} + \frac{4}{5}$
(114)

*15. $16 + 3\frac{3}{4}$
(107)

*16. $1\frac{2}{3} + 3\frac{1}{3}$
(114)

*17. $\frac{2}{5} + \frac{3}{5}$
(114)

*18. $7\frac{4}{5} + 7\frac{1}{5}$
(114)

*19. $6\frac{2}{3} + 3\frac{2}{3}$
(114)

*20. 372×39
(113)

*21. 47×142
(113)

*22. $360 \times \sqrt{36}$
(Inv. 3, 58)

*23. Estimate the area of this circle. Each small square
(111) represents one square centimeter.

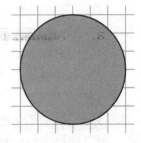

24. $8y = 4832$
(41, 80)

25. $\frac{2840}{2^3}$
(62, 76)

*26. $30\overline{)963}$
(110)

*27. (Represent) Which arrow could be pointing to 427,063?
(Inv. 1)

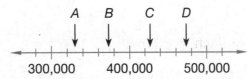

*28. If the length of each side of a square is $1\frac{1}{4}$ inches, then what is the
(Inv. 2, 114) perimeter of the square?

29. What is the geometric shape of a volleyball?
(98)

*30. Use the Distributive Property to multiply:
(108)

$$5(20 + 6)$$

Real-World Connection

Lun Lun is a giant panda at the Atlanta Zoo. Lun Lun eats about 210 pounds of bamboo a week.

a. If he eats $\frac{1}{7}$ of the bamboo on Monday and $\frac{2}{7}$ on Tuesday, what fractional part of his weekly serving did Lun Lun eat?

b. If Lun Lun eats $\frac{3}{7}$ of his bamboo Wednesday through Saturday, how much bamboo will he have left on Sunday? Write your answer as a fraction.

Saxon Math Intermediate 4

1. If a can of soup costs $1.50 and serves 3 people, how much would it
(94) cost to serve soup to 12 people?

*2. The polygon at right is divided into two rectangles.
(Inv. 3,
108)

    a. What is the perimeter of the figure?

    b. What is the area of the figure?

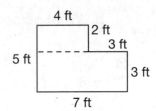

3. What number is eight less than the product of nine and ten? Write an
(94) expression.

4. Sanjay needs to learn 306 new words for the regional spelling bee.
(95) He has already memorized $\frac{2}{3}$ of the new words. How many words
does Sanjay still need to memorize? Draw a picture to illustrate the
problem.

*5. a. Find the length of this line segment in centimeters.
(69)

    b. Find the length of the segment in millimeters.

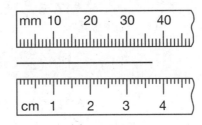

6. (Represent) Use words to write 356,420.
(33)

*7. (Represent) Which arrow could be pointing to 356,420?
(Inv. 1)

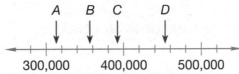

*8. Complete each equivalent fraction:
(115)

    a. $\frac{1}{2} = \frac{?}{6}$ **b.** $\frac{1}{3} = \frac{?}{6}$ **c.** $\frac{2}{3} = \frac{?}{6}$

*9. Write the reduced form of each fraction:
(112)

    a. $\frac{2}{6}$ **b.** $\frac{6}{9}$ **c.** $\frac{9}{16}$

*10. **a.** There were 40 workers on the job. Of those workers, 10 had worked
(Inv. 5, overtime. What fraction of the workers had worked overtime?
112) (Remember to reduce the fraction.)

   b. What percent of the workers had worked overtime?

11. How many different three-digit numbers can you write using the digits
(3) 6, 3, and 2? Each digit may be used only once in every number you
write.

12. (**Conclude**) Jamar received $10 for his tenth birthday. Each year after
(3, 94) that, he received $1 more than he did on his previous birthday. He
saved all his birthday money. In all, how much birthday money did
Jamar have on his fifteenth birthday?

*13. (**Analyze**) Every morning Marta walks $2\frac{1}{2}$ miles. How many miles does
(114) Marta walk in two mornings?

14. $9.36 - (4.37 - 3.8)$ **15.** $24.32 - (8.61 + 12.5)$
(45, 50)   (45, 50)

*16. $5\frac{5}{8} + 3\frac{3}{8}$ ***17.** $6\frac{3}{10} + 1\frac{2}{10}$
(114)   (114)

*18. $8\frac{2}{3} - 5\frac{1}{3}$ ***19.** $4\frac{3}{4} - 2\frac{1}{4}$
(107)   (114)

*20. 125×16 ***21.** $12 \times \$1.50$
(113)   (113)

22. $6m = 3642$ **23.** $\$125 \div 5$
(80)   (65, 76)

*24. $40\overline{)645}$ **25.** $3m = 6^2$
(110)   (61, 62)

26. (**Evaluate**) If n is 16, then what does $3n$ equal?
(106)

27. In three classrooms there were 18, 21, and 21 students. What was the
(96) average number of students per classroom?

28. Dion's temperature is 99.8°F. Normal body temperature is about
(31, 43) 98.6°F. Dion's temperature is how many degrees above normal body
temperature?

Saxon Math Intermediate 4

Name _____

*29. Estimate the perimeter and area of this piece of land. Each
(111) small square represents one square mile.

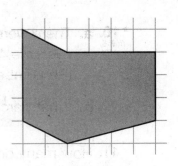

*30. **Predict** If the arrow is spun, what is the probability
(Inv. 10) that it will stop on a number greater than 5?

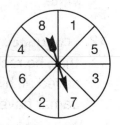

1. Evan found 24 seashells. If he gave one fourth of them to his brother,
(95) how many did he keep?

2. Rectangular Park is 2 miles long and 1 mile wide.
(Inv. 2) Gordon ran around the park twice. How many miles did
he run?

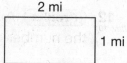

*3. If 2 oranges cost 42¢, how much would 8 oranges cost?
(94)

4. a. **Represent** Three fourths of the 64 baseball cards showed rookie
(Inv. 5, 95) players. How many of the baseball cards showed rookie players?
Draw a picture to illustrate the problem.

b. What percent of the baseball cards showed rookie players?

5. Write these numbers in order from greatest to least:
(Inv. 9)

$$7.2 \quad 7\frac{7}{10} \quad 7\frac{3}{10} \quad 7.5$$

*6. Multiple Choice Which of these fractions is *not* equivalent to $\frac{1}{2}$?
(103, 109)

A $\frac{3}{6}$ **B** $\frac{5}{10}$ **C** $\frac{10}{21}$ **D** $\frac{50}{100}$

*7. Complete each equivalent fraction:
(115)

a. $\frac{1}{2} = \frac{?}{12}$ **b.** $\frac{1}{3} = \frac{?}{12}$ **c.** $\frac{1}{4} = \frac{?}{12}$

*8. Write the reduced form of each fraction:
(112)

a. $\frac{5}{10}$ **b.** $\frac{8}{15}$ **c.** $\frac{6}{12}$

9. **Analyze** Darlene paid 42¢ for 6 clips and 64¢ for 8 erasers. What was
(94) the cost of each clip and each eraser? What would be the total cost of
10 clips and 20 erasers?

10. **Conclude** There were 14 volunteers the first year, 16 volunteers
(3, 72) the second year, and 18 volunteers the third year. If the number of
volunteers continued to increase by 2 each year, how many volunteers
would there be in the tenth year? Explain how you know.

Saxon Math Intermediate 4

Name _____

*11. **a.** Rename $\frac{1}{4}$ and $\frac{2}{3}$ by multiplying the denominators.
(116)

b. Rename $\frac{1}{3}$ and $\frac{3}{4}$ using their least common denominator.

12. **Predict** A standard dot cube is rolled. What is the probability that
(Inv. 10) the number of dots rolled will be less than seven?

13. $47.14 - (3.63 + 36.3)$ **14.** $50.1 + (6.4 - 1.46)$
(45, 50)   (45, 50)

*15. $\frac{3}{4} + \frac{3}{4} + \frac{3}{4}$ ***16.** $4\frac{1}{6} + 1\frac{1}{6}$ ***17.** $5\frac{3}{5} + 1\frac{2}{5}$
(114)   (114)   (114)

*18. $\frac{5}{6} + \frac{1}{6}$ ***19.** $12\frac{3}{4} - 3\frac{1}{4}$ ***20.** $6\frac{1}{5} - 1\frac{1}{5}$
(114)   (114)   (114)

*21. 340×15 ***22.** 26×307 ***23.** 70×250
(113)   (113)   (113)

24. $\frac{3550}{5}$ ***25.** $432 \div 30$ **26.** $9\overline{)5784}$
(80)   (110)   (76)

*27. Karen is planning a trip to Los Angeles from Chicago for her vacation.
(19, 101) She finds the following two round-trip flight schedules. Use the
information below to answer parts **a–c.**

Passengers: 1			Price: $246.00	
Flight number	Departure city	Date Time	Arrival city	Date Time
12A	ORD Chicago	7/21 06:11 p.m.	LAX Los Angeles	7/21 08:21 p.m.
46	LAX Los Angeles	7/28 06:39 p.m.	ORD Chicago	7/29 12:29 a.m.

Passengers: 1			Price: $412.00	
Flight number	Departure city	Date Time	Arrival city	Date Time
24	ORD Chicago	7/21 08:17 a.m.	LAX Los Angeles	7/21 10:28 a.m.
142	LAX Los Angeles	7/28 03:28 p.m.	ORD Chicago	7/28 09:18 p.m.

a. If Karen wants to arrive in Los Angeles in the morning, how much
will she pay for airfare?

Saxon Math Intermediate 4

b. If Karen chooses the more economical round-trip, when is her return flight scheduled to land?

c. Multiple Choice There is a 2-hour time difference between Chicago and Los Angeles. About how long does a flight between those cities last?

    A 2 hours   **B** 4 hours   **C** 6 hours   **D** 8 hours

For problems **28** and **29**, refer to the pentagon at right.

*28. Estimate the area of the pentagon. Each small square
(111) represents one square inch.

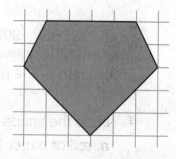

*29. a. Does the pentagon have reflective symmetry?
(79)

    b. Does the pentagon have rotational symmetry?

*30. Refer to the figure to answer parts **a** and **b**.
(73, 108)

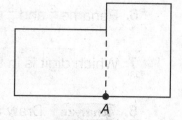

    a. The hexagon is formed by two joined rectangles. Which transformation would move one rectangle to the position of the other rectangle?

    b. If each rectangle is 5 inches by 7 inches, then what is the area of the hexagon?

Real-World Connection

A science fair was being held at Emmy's school. She wanted to design an experiment that tested giving bean plants liquids other than water. Emmy decided to test giving vinegar to a plant. Emmy had $\frac{9}{15}$ oz of vinegar. She gave the plant $\frac{2}{5}$ oz of vinegar. How much vinegar does Emmy have left after her experiment? Simplify your answer.

Saxon Math Intermediate 4

Name _____

1. ✏️ **Explain** Forty-five students are separated into four groups.
(88) The number of students in each group is as equal as possible.
How many students are in the largest group? Explain your
reasoning.

2. a. What is the area of this rectangle?
(Inv. 2, Inv. 3)
b. What is the perimeter of this rectangle?

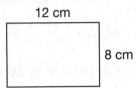

12 cm

8 cm

*3. **Represent** Iggy answered $\frac{5}{6}$ of the 90 questions correctly.
(95) How many questions did Iggy answer correctly? Draw a picture
to illustrate the problem.

4. Name the shape of each object:
(98)
a. roll of paper towels   **b.** baseball

*5. Write the reduced form of each fraction:
(112)
a. $\frac{3}{6}$ **b.** $\frac{5}{15}$ **c.** $\frac{8}{12}$

*6. Rename $\frac{3}{4}$ and $\frac{5}{6}$ using their least common denominator.
(116)

7. Which digit is in the ten-millions place in 328,496,175?
(33)

8. **Analyze** Draw a picture to help you solve this problem:
(25)

*The town of Winder is between Atlanta and Athens. It is 73 miles
from Athens to Atlanta. It is 23 miles from Winder to Athens. How
many miles is it from Winder to Atlanta?*

9. Caleb volunteers after school as a tutor. Each afternoon he
(27) begins a tutoring session at the time shown on the clock
and finishes three quarters of an hour later. What time
does each tutoring session end?

10. These thermometers show the average daily minimum and maximum
(18) temperatures in Helena, Montana, during the month of July. What are
those temperatures?

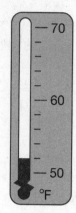 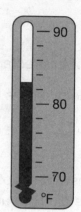

11. 4.36 + 12.7 + 10.72
(50)

12. 8.54 − (4.2 − 2.17)
(45, 91)

*13. $\frac{5}{9} + \frac{5}{9}$
(114)

*14. $3\frac{2}{3} + 1\frac{2}{3}$
(114)

15. $4\frac{5}{8} + 1$
(107)

*16. $7\frac{2}{3} + 1\frac{2}{3}$
(114)

*17. $4\frac{4}{9} + 1\frac{1}{9}$
(107)

*18. $\frac{11}{12} + \frac{1}{12}$
(114)

*19. 570 × 64
(113)

*20. 382 × 31
(113)

21. 54 × 18
(90)

22. $\frac{3731}{7}$
(76)

23. 9)5432
(80)

*24. 60)548
(110)

25. (**Predict**) The first five square numbers are 1, 4, 9, 16, and 25.
(Inv. 3)

What is the eighth term of this sequence? Write an equation to support
your answer.

*26. (**Estimate**) In the year 2000, the population of Texas was 20,851,820.
(117) Round that number to the nearest million.

*27. a. Multiple Choice Hasana built a square frame using
(92) pieces of wood, but when he leaned against it, the
frame shifted to this shape at right. What word does
not name this shape?

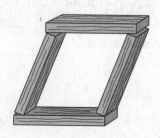

    A quadrilateral   **B** parallelogram

    C rhombus   **D** trapezoid

Saxon Math Intermediate 4

Name _____

b. Describe the angles.

c. Describe the sides.

28. If the perimeter of a square is 6 centimeters, then each side is how
(Inv. 2, 69) many millimeters long?

*29. a. This cube is made up of how many smaller cubes?
(98)

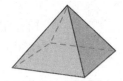

b. A cube has how many more vertices than this
pyramid?

*30. **Interpret** The graph shows the approximate elevations of four
(Inv. 6) cities in the United States.

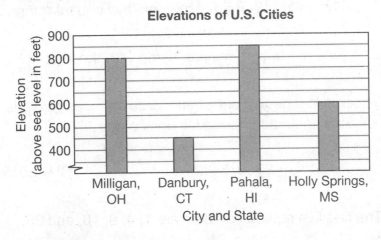

Use the graph to answer parts **a** and **b.**

a. Which cities have an elevation difference of 250 feet?

b. Which city is nearest sea level? Explain your answer.

Early Finishers

Real-World Connection

Earth is the third planet from the sun in our solar system. The average
distance from Earth to the sun is 92,750,000 miles. Mars is the fourth
planet from the sun in our solar system. The average distance from
Mars to the sun is 141,650,000 miles.

a. Round each distance to the nearest hundred thousand miles.

b. Round each distance to the nearest million miles.

Saxon Math Intermediate 4

*1. **Interpret** Use the information in the graph to answer parts **a–c**.
(Inv. 6)

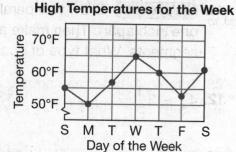

High Temperatures for the Week

a. On which day was the temperature the highest?

b. What was the high temperature on Tuesday?

c. From Monday to Wednesday, the high temperature went up how many degrees?

2. **a.** What is the perimeter of this rectangle?
(Inv. 2,
Inv. 3) **b.** What is the area of the rectangle?

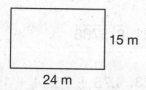

15 m

24 m

3. **Analyze** The first five square numbers are 1, 4, 9, 16, and 25, and their
(96) average is 11. What is the average of the next five square numbers?

4. What percent of the months of the year begin with the letter J?
(Inv. 5,
54)

5. There are 52 cards in a deck. Four of the cards are aces. What is the
(Inv. 10,
112) probability of drawing an ace from a full deck of cards?

6. **Classify** Name each shape:
(98)
a. **b.** **c.**

*7. Write the reduced form of each fraction:
(112)

a. $\frac{6}{8}$ **b.** $\frac{4}{9}$ **c.** $\frac{4}{16}$

*8. Rename $\frac{2}{3}$ and $\frac{3}{4}$ using their least common denominators.
(116)

*9. **Represent** Use words to write the number 27386415.
(34)

10. **Represent** Point W stands for what number on this number line?
(94)

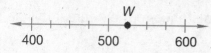

W

400   500   600

Saxon Math Intermediate 4

Name _____

*11. **Represent** Draw two parallel segments that are one inch long and
(23, 92) one inch apart. Then make a quadrilateral by drawing two more parallel
segments. What type of quadrilateral did you draw?

*12. $4\frac{4}{5} + 3\frac{3}{5}$ ***13.** $5\frac{1}{6} + 1\frac{2}{6}$ ***14.** $7\frac{3}{4} + \frac{1}{4}$
(114)   (114)   (114)

*15. $13\overline{)50}$ ***16.** $72\overline{)297}$ **17.** $5\frac{3}{8} + 5\frac{1}{8}$
(118)   (118)   (114)

18. $4\frac{1}{6} + 2\frac{1}{6}$ **19.** 720×36 **20.** 147×54
(114)   (113)   (113)

21. $8\overline{)5766}$ ***22.** $21\overline{)441}$
(80)   (118)

23. $4.75 + 16.14 + 10.9$ **24.** $18.4 - (4.32 - 2.6)$
(50)   (45, 91)

*25. **Estimate** In the year 2000, the population of the state of New York
(117) was 18,976,457. Round that number to the nearest million.

*26. **Estimate** Round 297,576,320 to the nearest hundred million.
(117)

*27. In Jahzara's first nine games she earned these scores:
(97)

$$90, 95, 80, 85, 100, 95, 75, 95, 90$$

Use this information to answer parts **a** and **b**.

   a. What is the median and range of Jahzara's scores?

   b. What is the mode of Jahzara's scores?

28. Write these numbers in order from least to greatest:
(Inv. 9)

$$5\frac{11}{100} \qquad 5.67 \qquad 5.02 \qquad 5\frac{83}{100}$$

29. Yasmine wanted to divide 57 buttons into groups of 13. How many
(118) groups will Yasmine have? Will there be any buttons left over?

30. Rename $\frac{2}{3}$ and $\frac{3}{5}$ so that they have a common denominator of 15.
(116)

Name _____

1. Zuna used 1-foot-square floor tiles to cover the floor of a room
(Inv. 3, 90) 15 feet long and 12 feet wide. How many floor tiles did she use?

2. a. What is the perimeter of this triangle?
(Inv. 2, 78)
   b. Is this triangle equilateral, isosceles, or scalene?

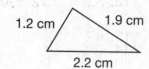
1.2 cm   1.9 cm
2.2 cm

*3. (**Represent**) Elsa found that $\frac{3}{8}$ of the 32 pencils in the room had no
(95) erasers. How many pencils had no erasers? Draw a picture to illustrate
the problem.   12 pencils

4. a. Seventy-two pencils is how many dozen pencils?
(41, Inv. 5)
   b. How many pencils is 50% of one dozen pencils?

*5. (**Estimate**) Using rounding or compatible numbers, which numbers
(42, 49) would you choose to estimate the exact product of 75 × 75? Explain
your reasoning.

6. This cube is constructed of smaller cubes that are each one cubic
(Inv. 11) centimeter in volume. What is the volume of the larger
cube?

7. Fausta bought 2 DVDs priced at $21.95 each and 2 CDs
(83) priced at $14.99 each. The tax was $4.62. What was the total cost of
the items? Explain how you found your answer.

8. T'Ron drove 285 miles in 5 hours. What was his average speed in
(96) miles per hour?

9. Multiple Choice Which of these fractions is *not* equivalent to $\frac{1}{2}$?
(103, 109)
   A $\frac{4}{8}$ **B** $\frac{11}{22}$ **C** $\frac{15}{30}$ **D** $\frac{12}{25}$

*10. Write the reduced form of each fraction:
(112)
   a. $\frac{8}{10}$ **b.** $\frac{6}{15}$ **c.** $\frac{8}{16}$

Saxon Math Intermediate 4

Name_____

*11. **Represent** Use words to write the number 123415720.
(33)

12. $8.3 + 4.72 + 0.6 + 12.1$
(50)

13. $17.42 - (6.7 - 1.23)$
(45, 91)

*14. $3\frac{3}{8} + 3\frac{3}{8}$
(114)

*15. $\frac{1}{4} + \frac{1}{8}$
(119)

*16. $\frac{1}{2} + \frac{1}{6}$
(119)

*17. $5\frac{5}{6} - 1\frac{1}{6}$
(114)

*18. $\frac{1}{4} - \frac{1}{8}$
(119)

*19. $\frac{1}{2} - \frac{1}{6}$
(119)

*20. 87×16
(90)

*21. 49×340
(86, 113)

*22. 504×30
(86, 113)

23. $\$35.40 \div 6$
(71, 80)

24. $\frac{5784}{4}$
(76)

25. $7\overline{)2385}$
(80)

26. $30\overline{)450}$
(110)

*27. $32\overline{)450}$
(118)

*28. $15\overline{)450}$
(118)

*29. **Predict** What is the probability of drawing a heart from a full deck of
(Inv. 10, 112) cards? (*Hint:* There are 13 hearts in a deck.)

*30. **Represent** Draw a rectangle that is 5 cm long and 2 cm wide, and
(21, Inv. 5) divide the rectangle into square centimeters. Then shade 30% of the
rectangle.

Real-World Connection

Vic wants to make a CD for his party. He bought a blank CD that holds 4 hours of music. One half of the space on Vic's CD is rock music, $\frac{1}{4}$ is hip-hop music, and $\frac{1}{8}$ is jazz. He wants to add a few country songs to the CD in the remaining space. The method Vic used to calculate the amount of space he has left to add country songs is shown below:

$\frac{1}{2} + \frac{1}{4} + \frac{1}{8} = \frac{2}{4} + \frac{1}{4} + \frac{1}{8} = \frac{3}{4} + \frac{1}{8} = \frac{6}{8} + \frac{1}{8} = \frac{7}{8}$ of music recorded.

$4 \text{ hours} - \frac{7}{8} = \frac{32}{8} - \frac{7}{8} = \frac{25}{8} = 3\frac{1}{8}$ hours left.

Is Vic's calculation correct? If not, where did he go wrong and what is the correct answer?

1. The Lorenzos drank 11 gallons of milk each month. How many quarts
(40) of milk did they drink each month?

2. Sixty people are in the marching band. If one fourth of them play trumpet,
(95) how many do not play trumpet? Draw a picture to illustrate the problem.

3. **a.** What is the area of this square?
(Inv. 2,
Inv. 3) **b.** What is the perimeter of the square?

10 mm

*4. **a.** (Analyze) Esteban is 8 inches taller than Trevin. Trevin is 5 inches taller
(94, 96) than Chelsea. Estaban is 61 inches tall. How many inches tall is Chelsea?

b. What is the average height of the three children?

5. Which line segments in figure *ABCD* appear to be parallel?
(23)

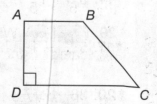

6. (Explain) Mayville is between Altoona and Watson. It is 47 miles from
(25) Mayville to Altoona. It is 24 miles from Mayville to Watson. How far is it
from Altoona to Watson? Explain why your answer is reasonable.

*7. (Predict) If the arrow is spun, what is the probability that it
(Inv. 10) will stop on a number greater than 4?

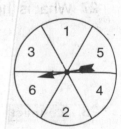

*8. (Estimate) The asking price for the new house was $298,900. Round
(117) that amount of money to the nearest hundred thousand dollars.

Name _____

*9. **Classify** Name each of the shapes below. Then list the number of
(98) vertices, edges, and faces that each shape has.

a.

b.

*10. Write the reduced form of each fraction:
(112)

a. $\frac{9}{15}$ b. $\frac{10}{12}$ c. $\frac{12}{16}$

11. **Represent** Use digits to write one hundred nineteen million, two
(34) hundred forty-seven thousand, nine hundred eighty-four.

12. $14.94 - (8.6 - 4.7)$ **13.** $6.8 - (1.37 + 2.2)$
(45, 50)   (45, 91)

*14. $3\frac{2}{5} + 1\frac{4}{5}$ ***15.** $\frac{5}{8} + \frac{1}{4}$ ***16.** $1\frac{1}{3} + 1\frac{1}{6}$
(114)   (119)   (120)

*17. $5\frac{9}{10} - 1\frac{1}{5}$ ***18.** $\frac{5}{8} - \frac{1}{4}$ ***19.** $\frac{1}{3} - \frac{1}{6}$
(120)   (119)   (119)

*20. 38×217 ***21.** 173×60 ***22.** 90×500
(113)   (113)   (86)

23. $7\overline{)2942}$ **24.** $10\overline{)453}$ ***25.** $11\overline{)453}$
(80)   (105)   (118)

*26. Evaluate $m + n$ when m is $3\frac{2}{5}$ and n is $2\frac{1}{10}$.
(106,
120)

27 What is the volume of this rectangular solid?
(Inv. 11)

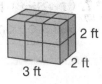

2 ft

2 ft

3 ft

*28. **Connect** Segment AC is $3\frac{1}{2}$ inches long. Segment AB is $1\frac{1}{2}$ inches
(114) long. How long is segment BC?

A   B   C

*29. **Estimate** Fewer people live in Wyoming than in any other state.
(117) According to the 2000 U.S. census, 493,782 people lived in
Wyoming. Round this number of people to the nearest hundred
thousand.

30. One half of a dollar plus $\frac{1}{4}$ of a dollar totals what percent of a dollar?
(36, Inv. 5)